WESTERN NEVADA COLLEGE

3 1439 00082 9575

S0-BHC-853

WITHDRAWN

LIBRARY & MEDIA SERVICES
WESTERN NEVADA COLLEGE
2201 WEST COLLEGE PARKWAY
CARSON CITY, NV 89703

CRITICAL INSIGHTS

Louisa May Alcott

WNC
PS
1018
.L685
2016
MR 15 '16

CRITICAL INSIGHTS

Louisa May Alcott

Editors

Anne K. Phillips and Gregory Eiselein
Kansas State University

SALEM PRESS
A Division of EBSCO Information Services, Inc.
Ipswich, Massachusetts

GREY HOUSE PUBLISHING

Copyright © 2016 by Grey House Publishing, Inc.

All rights reserved. No part of this work may be used or reproduced in any manner whatsoever or transmitted in any form or by any means, electronic or mechanical, including photocopy, recording, or any information storage and retrieval system, without written permission from the copyright owner. For information, contact Grey House Publishing/Salem Press, 4919 Route 22, PO Box 56, Amenia, NY 12501.

∞ The paper used in these volumes conforms to the American National Standard for Permanence of Paper for Printed Library Materials, Z39.48-1992 (R1997).

Publisher's Cataloging-In-Publication Data
(Prepared by The Donohue Group, Inc.)

Louisa May Alcott / editors, Anne K. Phillips and Gregory Eiselein,
  Kansas State University. -- [First edition].

   pages ; cm. -- (Critical insights)

   Edition statement supplied by publisher.
   Includes bibliographical references and index.
   ISBN: 978-1-61925-521-0 (hardcover)

   1. Alcott, Louisa May, 1832-1888--Criticism and interpretation. 2. American fiction--19th century--History and criticism. 3. American literature--Women authors--History and criticism. I. Eiselein, Gregory, 1965- II. Phillips, Anne K. III. Series: Critical insights.

PS1018 .L53 2016
813/.4

First Printing

PRINTED IN THE UNITED STATES OF AMERICA

Contents

About This Volume

Anne K. Phillips and Gregory Eiselein

In imagining and assembling *Critical Insights: Louisa May Alcott*, the editors have put students' interests first and foremost. The introductory essay, "On Louisa May Alcott," is inspired by actual questions asked by real students about Alcott and her works. The resources that conclude the volume also have been prepared with students in mind, including a chronology of her life, a list of her published works, and a forty-item bibliography that emphasizes the breadth of her work and the recent scholarly interest it is generating—as evidenced by the high number of entries published after 2000. As Beverly Lyon Clark has shown in connection with just one of Alcott's works, "scholarly respect for Alcott's work is accelerating: half of the pieces on *Little Women* currently indexed in the MLA online bibliography were published after 2000, twice the rate for the previous quarter century" (50).

Throughout the volume, readers will find top-notch scholarship on an impressive range of Alcott's works. Contributors include Alcott's Pulitzer Prize-winning biographer John Matteson, among several other leading figures in Alcott studies. The volume also benefits from the contributions of a number of up-and-coming Alcott scholars. All of the essays in this volume were crafted to be accessible, thought-provoking, and enjoyable. They should inspire readers to recognize the achievements of these critics, but also to draw on their concepts and approaches in creating original, additional scholarship. These essays should illuminate not only the specific Alcott texts addressed here but also her entire body of work.

A number of the essays in this volume position Alcott and her work in the context of nineteenth-century American literature. In "Lost in the Vortex: The Problem of Genius in the Fiction of Nathaniel Hawthorne and Louisa May Alcott," Christopher Fahy focuses on how Hawthorne's and Alcott's ideas and works overlap, particularly regarding the concept of genius. Fahy argues that Hawthorne and

Alcott both "tried to justify the pursuit of authorship and make it socially acceptable through strategies such as the domestication of literature, the use of an aestheticized notion of the fortunate fall, and (for Alcott), the adoption of Margaret Fuller's concept of celibate apprenticeship."

Katie Kornacki focuses in "'A Loving League of Sisters': The Legacy of Margaret Fuller's Boston Conversations in Alcott's *Work*" on the ways that protagonist Christie Devon and her associates embody the ideals of education, self-reliance, vocation, and sorority emphasized by Margaret Fuller in the Conversations series that she conducted in Boston and at Sing-Sing prison. These characters also bear "close resemblance to the real-life work of a group of women who had collaborated with and known Fuller, through her Conversations or otherwise, and who, in 1868, had formed the New England Woman's Club, of which Alcott herself had been an early member."

Monika Elbert positions Alcott's work within the context of authors from Nathaniel Hawthorne and Charlotte Brontë to Harriet Spofford and others whose works exemplify the Gothic. In "Divas, Drugs, and Desire on Alcott's Gothic Stage," Elbert acknowledges that "'bad' girls attracted [Alcott], whether they were governesses, adulteresses, or actresses." Elbert assesses the strategies of these heroines in thrillers that Alcott published from the late 1850s through the 1870s, with particular attention to relevant theatrical settings. Ultimately, Elbert concludes, the Gothic genre offers Alcott's female characters significant opportunities for liberation and emancipation.

Kristen B. Proehl argues in "Poverty and Social Critique in Postbellum America: *Little Women* and *Adventures of Huckleberry Finn*" that both Twain and Alcott depict scenes of poverty "in order to meditate upon cultural memory of the Civil War and examine the social issues of the Reconstruction era." Twain, according to Proehl, "implies that poverty contributes to other social problems, such as racism, illiteracy, and mob violence. By contrast, Alcott focuses on poverty itself as a social problem and insists that the poor themselves are in need of sympathy." Proehl's analysis shows us that Alcott sees a "parallel relationship between poverty and other forms of oppression, such as disability, sexism, and racial oppression."

No consideration of Alcott in the context of literary peers (and competitors?) would be complete without some attention to the work of Henry James. Although Henry was younger than Louisa and initially had less experience as a writer, he never let that inexperience constrain him from critiquing her work. In "American Girls and American Literature: Louisa May Alcott 'Talks Back' to Henry James," Christine Doyle traces the way that both authors famously focused on American girls in European as well as American settings, particularly in *Little Women* (1868–69) and *Daisy Miller* (1878). Doyle contends that "Alcott and James had radically different views of American womanhood—and, indeed, of American literature—and can be seen as being in dialogue with one another on both of those subjects for the last two decades of Alcott's life." Doyle demonstrates that Alcott continued throughout the final decade of her life to respond to and challenge James' theories about the art and purpose of literature.

A pair of essays in this collection examine the need for complex critical approaches to Alcott and her original critical and cultural contexts. In "Feminist Alcott?," Katherine Adams begins with her students' conversations about Alcott's support for women's rights. Yet rather than judging her by our own twenty-first-century understandings of feminism, Adams shows us how Alcott's novel *Work* (1873) encourages a kind of self-reflection about our feminist efforts that allows us to see that we are never able completely to escape the limitations of our own history and culture. Like *Work*'s protagonist Christie Devon, we are "not free *from* [our] culture," but we are "free *to* act meaningfully within it."

In "Looking for Louisa: Authors, Audiences, and Literatures in Alcott's Critical Reception," Amy M. Thomas provides us with another way of appreciating Alcott's complexity and the significance of her work within its original historical and critical context. Thomas emphasizes that Alcott was a professional writer who worked in a wide variety of genres. Additionally, attitudes about the kinds of texts she produced have been in flux for decades, resulting in her fluid status within the American literary canon. The most significant event in Alcott's reception, as Thomas explains, is the rediscovery and republication of Alcott's "thrillers" in the 1970s, which has prompted re-examination of all of her writings. "Which Alcott is 'real'?" Thomas asks, adding, "This is an exciting time to answer these questions because of the varied critical perspectives open to scholars and the increasing accessibility to all of Alcott's publications."

A third theme that runs throughout a number of the essays in this volume considers the American Civil War and its impact on Alcott and her career. In the volume's biographical essay, "'Happy Before I Die': The Strife and Success of Louisa May Alcott," which examines both the challenges that Alcott faced and the literary successes shaped by those challenges, Amy Harris-Aber touches on Alcott's service as a nurse during the war. Although her tour of duty was limited because she contracted typhoid fever after only a few weeks of nursing work, her experiences during the war led to significant and surprisingly immediate literary achievements.

John Matteson's essay, "'When Rude Hands Shake the Hive': Louisa May Alcott and the Transformation of America," aligns Alcott's life with America's history, suggesting that the two grew up together: "Just around the time when, as a young adult, Alcott felt as if her world were starting to fall apart, the country almost fell apart as well—and Alcott nearly sacrificed her life to keep it together." Like Harris-Aber, Matteson finds Alcott's war experience essential: "Though it nearly killed her, Alcott's nursing service also marked a decisive turning point in her career as a writer . . . [and] taught her to find excellent material for her writing within her lived experience."

Two additional essays attend to Alcott's war experience and the way that she represented that experience in subsequent writings. Emily Waples argues in "Alcott and the Work of Nursing" that on the one hand, nursing in the Civil War era was perceived to be "an exercise in feminine sentiment and sympathy." On the other hand, it was "prosaic and drudging labor: an extension of the often-taxing domestic duties typically assigned to nineteenth-century women." Unlike male writers such as Walt Whitman who depicted the work of caring for the injured and dying, Alcott "critiques the gendered associations of 'work' in the nineteenth century, while simultaneously exposing women's invisible labor in the domestic sphere."

A. Waller Hastings also takes on the Civil War as setting in *Little Women* in "Louisa's Civil War." While critics have generally suggested that the war is merely the backdrop to the March sisters' lives, Hastings wonders, "Is it possible that the presence of the Civil War in this novel in fact includes biography in a broader sense?" He concludes that it plays a far more prominent role, as evidenced by Alcott's infusion of war and battle references throughout the novel. Further, Hastings traces the diverse ways that Alcott processed and perpetuated in *Little Women* the tone and themes she included in earlier, more explicitly war-focused writings such as *Hospital Sketches* (1863).

A trio of essays in this volume addresses Alcott's lesser-studied novels for younger readers. In "Polly, Pygmalion, and the (Im)practicalities of an Independent Womanhood," Marilyn Bloss Koester turns to *An Old-Fashioned Girl* (1869), the novel Alcott published immediately after *Little Women*. Koester focuses on a single but significant chapter, "The Sunny Side," where musician and teacher Polly Milton introduces her socialite friend Fanny Shaw to friends who are, respectively, a sculptor, an engraver, and a writer. Koester characterizes this episode as encapsulating a "world of subversive and creative femininity," and she argues that Alcott is promoting progressive, alternative avenues for women, even though the novel as a whole might seem to espouse more conservative values. Assessing the significance of this vignette, Koester aligns Alcott's depiction of this female artistic community with the increasing visibility of female artists during the later decades of the nineteenth century.

Antoinette M. Tadolini responds to critics' assessments of Alcott's first March sequel in "Violence and Confinement in *Little Men*." Acknowledging the numerous depictions of violence, animal cruelty, destruction, and incarceration at the private school founded by Jo and her husband, Tadolini argues that "chaos and violence do exist, but they can be controlled and are survivable. Moreover, negotiating the violence of childhood, characters are better prepared to face the challenges offered by the world beyond the gates of Plumfield." Drawing on the theories of Bruno Bettelheim and Neil Gaiman, Tadolini suggests that the hardships encountered by Alcott's child characters actually prepare them to cope more effectively with the lives they will lead beyond Plumfield's borders.

Additionally, in "A Faith Truly Lived: Alcott's Use of Biblical Allusion in *Eight Cousins* and *Rose in Bloom*," Mo Li enters into the fray perpetuated by critics, students, and sometimes outraged Christian bloggers about Alcott's spirituality and its manifestations in her fiction. Li shows that Alcott has infused these two novels with numerous allusions to the Bible. The allusions in child-friendly *Eight Cousins* tend to be whimsical, but in the sequel, *Rose in Bloom*, intended for young adults, they have a more serious tenor. This essay contextualizes Alcott's use of the Bible within larger cultural trends, concluding that her approach is consistent with those trends but also distinctly unorthodox: "When incorporating the Bible in both texts, Alcott focuses less on its divine truth than on how it might guide readers' earthly lives."

In the volume's concluding essay, Gregory Eiselein places Alcott in dialogue with an equally unorthodox artist from a much later era, Patti Smith. Drawing from Smith's National Book Award-winning memoir *Just Kids* (2010) in addition to her legendary album *Horses* (1975) and other works, Eiselein demonstrates that Alcott's writings profoundly impacted Smith's world view. Further, consideration of Smith's life and works provides new perspective on Alcott's conceptions of gender, sexuality, and creativity. Both demonstrated "an intense and unabashed amateur energy" and a dedication to a passionate creative process. Considering these vanguard figures together, Eiselein builds a convincing, meaningful argument for Alcott's status as a significant influence on the "godmother of punk" and as a voice who remains relevant to twenty-first century audiences.

The essays collected here address a range of works by Louisa May Alcott. Some focus on indisputably famous books but offer fresh insights about them. Conversely, others offer fresh and tantalizing perspectives on lesser-known aspects of Alcott's career. Whatever readers' familiarity with Alcott's life and works, the essays commissioned for this volume offer diverse and original approaches to literary study, breadth and depth of literary and cultural history, and an invitation to take part in the ongoing critical conversation. The editors and contributors look forward to seeing how future generations of literary scholars build on the scholarship that comprises *Critical Insights: Louisa May Alcott*.

Works Cited

Clark, Beverly Lyon. "The Critical Reception of *Little Women*." *Critical Insights:* Little Women. Ed. Gregory Eiselein and Anne K. Phillips. Ipswich, MA: Salem Press, 2015. 41–53.

CAREER, LIFE, AND INFLUENCE

On Louisa May Alcott: Questions on Her Significance, Singularity, Sorority, and Staying Power_____

Anne K. Phillips and Gregory Eiselein

Who was Louisa May Alcott, and why should there be a volume dedicated to her in the Critical Insights Author Series?

Nineteenth-century American author Louisa May Alcott is best known for having written *Little Women* (1868–69), a bestselling and never-out-of-print novel detailing the lives of Meg, Jo, Beth, and Amy March and their next door neighbor Theodore (Laurie) Laurence. *Little Women* was originally inspired by an editor at a Boston publishing firm, Roberts Brothers, who noticed that "boy books" by authors such as Horatio Alger and "Oliver Optic" (William T. Adams) were highly successful. He suggested (more than once) to Louisa that she should write a book that might entertain and appeal to girls, and although she had protested—"I don't enjoy this sort of thing. Never liked girls or knew many, except my sisters" (Alcott, *Journals* 165–66)—and attempted for some time to dodge the whole project, she finally settled down to writing, especially after she realized that "lively, simple books are very much needed for girls, and perhaps I can supply the need" (*Journals* 166). After Niles tested the ensuing manuscript on his niece and some other girl readers, who "declared it wonderful" (qtd. in Meigs 206), he and Louisa began to realize that the novel might be a hit. It was published in early October 1868, and almost immediately, fans of the book began writing to the author to enthuse about her characters and cajole her to write a sequel. Alcott immediately set to work, finishing the second volume of *Little Women* in just a few months and publishing it in April of 1869 to great acclaim. As a reviewer for the *Boston Daily Evening Transcript* wrote,

[t]he volumes are good for girls, because they are free from cant and sham morality. They teach the religion of good works and teach wholesome truths. They are sunshiny and breezy and full of the abounding life which healthy young bodies and minds feel, and which breaks forth in the free speech and manner of the best type of our young men and women—pure, fresh, and fearless." (qtd. in Clark, *Louisa* 70)

Little Women didn't appeal solely to girls, however. Everyone read it: girls and boys, adolescents and adults. Frank Preston Stearns recalled, "it was the rage in '69" (85). Its widespread popularity has been documented throughout the ensuing century and a half. Teddy Roosevelt "worshiped" it (269). Immigrant Leo Lerman noted that it "was all so American, so full of a life I did not know but desperately hoped to be part of, an America full of promises, hopes, optimisms" (113). Even in its own era, *Little Women* already was acknowledged as a landmark text. A reviewer for the *American Literary Gazette* asserted in 1871, "[t]he success of this book is a matter of history," and furthermore, "[t]his success has few parallels, or none, all things considered, in American literature" (qtd. in Clark, *Louisa* 85).

Little Women has remained a success without parallel. It continues in print in dozens of editions today. Over the decades, it has continued to appeal to readers, remaining one of the most circulated library holdings and coming in at the top of a number of popular polls, including a 2014 Facebook poll of "10 books that have stayed with you," where it ranked twelfth across more than 130,000 submissions (Meyer). It has spawned countless adaptations, including radio, theatrical, operatic, film, television, and online productions. The March sisters have inspired dolls, stamps, jewelry, diaries, comic strips and graphic novels, and a wide range of other artifacts. As Beverly Lyon Clark masterfully demonstrates in her book-length study of the novel's continuing resonances, even in the twenty-first century, "*Little Women* has permeated American culture" (*Afterlife* 198). Scholars and fans continue to demonstrate a passion for and an attachment to Alcott's characters that is unique in American literary history.

Louisa May Alcott's reputation might rest solely on *Little Women*. However, a second reason she deserves to be the subject of a Critical Insights author volume is the breadth and diversity of her work and influence. *Little Women is* a masterpiece, but the whole range of her work deserves study and lends itself to critical analysis and scholarly examination. Her first book, *Flower Fables* (1854), for example, was a collection of fairy tales dedicated to Ellen Emerson, Ralph Waldo Emerson's daughter. Additionally, in the late 1850s and very early 1860s, Alcott placed stories in the prestigious, high-culture *Atlantic Monthly Magazine*. This "slice of life" work often was inspired by her family's experiences in Concord, Massachusetts. However, at the same time, she was publishing, often under a pseudonym such as "A. M. Barnard," a number of "sensation stories" or "blood-and-thunder tales" or "thrillers" in periodicals such as the *American Union, Frank Leslie's Illustrated Newspaper*, and *The Flag of Our Union*. In these wild creations, under titles such as "Marion Earle; or, Only an Actress," "The Skeleton in the Closet," and "Behind a Mask" (1866, perhaps her best known sensation story), characters commit evil deeds, take drugs, manipulate others, and indulge their most maniacal impulses. These works were inspired in part by Alcott's readings of the works of Johann Wolfgang von Goethe, Charlotte Brontë, Charles Dickens, and even Nathaniel Hawthorne (a neighbor in Concord), although they also emerged from her own inspired imagination. She once acknowledged, "I fancy 'lurid' things" (Alcott, *Journals* 63). In 1862, she won a $100 prize for "Pauline's Passion and Punishment." Many of these sensational stories, published in periodicals that subsequently lapsed into relative obscurity, were lost to Alcott scholars until Leona Rostenberg rediscovered them in the 1940s and Madeleine Stern republished them in the 1970s. They continue to offer significant insights into Alcott's attitudes toward gender, class, and sexuality, and they have inspired literary scholars to re-evaluate much of Alcott's work.

Additionally, during the Civil War in 1862, just after her thirtieth birthday, Alcott volunteered as a nurse, traveling to Washington, D.C., to serve at the Union Hotel Hospital. Arriving just before the casualties flowed in from the Battle of Fredericksburg, Alcott initially was shocked by her proximity to so many injured and desperate patients and to the pestilence and confusion that surrounded them. Nonetheless, she found a satisfaction in her work, writing, "Though often home sick, heart sick & worn out, I like it—find real pleasure in comforting tending & cheering these poor souls" (*Journals* 113). Although her service abruptly ended when she contracted typhoid, requiring her father Bronson Alcott to retrieve her and take her home to Concord to convalesce, she soon depicted her experiences in autobiographical fiction that was initially serialized in 1863 in *The Commonwealth* and then published as *Hospital Sketches*. Writing during the war, Alcott made it real for many Americans who never set foot on a battlefield, and for readers of later eras, she offered a perspective on the conflict that rounds out the work of other Civil War-era writers, such as Walt Whitman.

An additional reason Alcott is deserving of an "author" volume in the Critical Insights series is that she knew and corresponded with and wrote about some of the most significant figures in mid-nineteenth-century American literature. Emerson loaned her books from his library and occasionally funded the Alcotts' continued subsistence. Thoreau tutored the Alcott sisters in natural history. They played with the Hawthorne children and put on plays with members of the James family. Later, as a professional author, Alcott wrote letters to a wide range of editors, writers, artists, and professors, including William Warland Clapp, Jr.; James Redpath; Thomas Wentworth Higginson; James T. Fields; James R. Osgood; Lucy Larcom; Elizabeth B. Greene; Moses Coit Tyler; John Seely Hart; and numerous others. Her writings, including her journals and letters, provide insight into the literary milieu of nineteenth-century America that is distinctive and significant. And her life, career, and work link us to so many others aspects of American culture and life, past and present—from the Pilgrims in Massachusetts and the American Revolution (which started in Concord!) to our contemporary culture's on-going fascination with coming-of-age stories that feature four distinct and distinctive young women (the HBO television series *Girls* [2012–], for instance).

How might we distinguish Louisa May Alcott's works from those written by other nineteenth-century authors? Alcott's innovations and contributions to the development of U.S. literary history and children's literature come in the form of important and original but usually well-defined and specific modifications or alterations within a larger literary field.

For example, literary Transcendentalism clearly precedes and gives shape to Alcott's own career. All of the movement's defining authors—Emerson, Thoreau, Margaret Fuller, and Alcott's father, Bronson Alcott, among others—wrote before and influenced Louisa May Alcott's own ideas, style, and writing. Nevertheless, Louisa Alcott did pioneer, in novels like *Moods* and *Work*, the attempt to create the Transcendentalist novel of ideas. Before Alcott, most attempts to incorporate Transcendentalist ideas into fictional forms appear in the form of critical satire or parody—as in the 35th chapter of *Moby-Dick* (1851), where Ishmael warns "ye Pantheists" about the dangers of their perspectives that may cause them to "drop through that transparent air into the summer sea, no more to rise for ever" (Melville 136). And Alcott herself did use thinly veiled autobiographical fiction, in "Transcendental Wild Oats" (1873), to satirize Transcendentalist communal efforts, their sexism, and even their naïve idealism. On the other hand, in novels like *Moods* (1864) and *Work* (1873), she explores in direct and concrete ways how Transcendentalist ideas about love, marriage, family, labor, purpose, and reform might be used in practical ways to improve the lives of individual female agents. For example, inspired very directly by the Transcendentalist reformer and minister Theodore Parker's 1853 lecture about women's right to economic independence and equality in the worlds of education and work (see Tomasek 254), Alcott's novel *Work* examines Christie Devon's attempt to "travel away into the world and seek my fortune" (5) but also the many challenges she faces and the various successes she achieves along the way. Parker also appears as the figure of Mr. Power in the novel. In *Moods*, however, Alcott tries to study and critically evaluate what freedom (that much-prized value among the Transcendentalists) might look like for a woman in terms of her romantic relationships, choices, and marriage. What should determine a young woman's romantic and marital decisions: traditional social expectations for women, love, passion, intellectual fulfillment, or something else? Moreover, as in *Work*, Alcott uses her Transcendentalist heroes, in this case Emerson and Thoreau, as the models in this novel for the characters Geoffrey Moor and Adam Warwick, who constitute the other two points in the romantic/erotic triangle in which the protagonist Sylvia Yule finds herself immersed.

While her contribution to Transcendentalism might be best characterized as an adaptation of the movement and its ideas to the novel form, Alcott's contribution to realism is similarly definite and specific, if limited. Alcott is certainly not an inventor of realism by any means or the originator of American literary realism. Instead, as one of the earliest U.S. authors writing in a realist mode, she helped define the style and the period with a few specific, noteworthy contributions. For instance, by incorporating everyday language and slang, she made her characters more lifelike and her fiction livelier and more relevant to readers. In many of her more famous works, she focuses on delightful, but still ordinary, young women and men, whose struggles, cares, and woes—not wanting to pursue the business career expected by a grandfather (Laurie in *Little Women*), recovering from a sunstroke (Mac in *Eight Cousins* [1875]), worrying what others of a higher social class might think of you and how you dress (Polly in *An Old-Fashioned Girl* [1870])—are not less vivid and interesting just because they are common. Significantly, Alcott helps expand the scope of realism by including in her fictional worlds rich, complex, and naturalistic representations of the lives, emotions, and psyches of young women. Even though Alcott is not typically considered a practitioner of "local color"—a movement embodied by late nineteenth-century realist writers known for the ways they vividly brought to life the customs, dialects, landscapes, and cultures of a particular area or region— she did significantly contribute to the development of New England local color by using the region's dialect and slang to distinguish her characters; by making identifiably New England villages and small towns (in addition to Boston) the setting of many of her fictions; and by celebrating the region's customs, traditions, games, and play. For instance, as Anne K. Phillips has carefully documented in her essay "'Fun Forever'? Toys, Games, and Play in *Little Women*," Alcott fills her children's fictions with detailed, very specific accounts of "nineteenth-century American child culture," such as games (for example, croquet) and toys and various forms of play ("Rigmarole" or "Authors," among others) in order to show that "play is not only desirable but a necessary component of a well-rounded life" (402).

Perhaps most importantly, while Alcott did not invent children's literature as a genre, she did contribute to its evolution in landmark ways. For example, *Little Women* eschews overtly didactic morals and lessons. Instead, it blends minor moments of didacticism with extended scenes of play and fun. Written within a year of Martha Finley's *Elsie Dinsmore* (1867), *Little Women* depicts lively young women who stage theatricals (on Christmas!), scatter hairpins while racing down the street, write a family newspaper, participate in a "Busy Bee Society," and support each other's artistic and vocational hopes and dreams. Unlike Elsie, who piously refused to play the piano on Sunday and wept copious tears on almost every occasion, Alcott's March sisters occasionally behave very badly. Amy burns her sister's manuscript of fairy tales, and Jo subsequently allows Amy to skate on thin ice. Ears are boxed. Names are called. Faux-love letters purportedly from an earnest suitor are written and unwittingly responded to. Although these misdemeanors are eventually acknowledged, apologized for, and forgiven, it is the realistic mischief and the memorable detail that linger, rather than the moral eventually associated with the badness, the allure of the pickled limes that we remember, rather than the lesson directed to Amy on the importance of modesty and humility. Yet within this lively, realistic, and fresh (in all senses) fiction, there are still meaningful and memorable conversations about growing up, finding meaningful work, balancing love and family commitments, and finding and maintaining confidence, despite societal judgments and pressures.

Alcott often is heralded as a feminist author. Why is it, then, that most of her female characters appear to settle for conventional lives as wives and mothers?

Some of Alcott's most beloved characters are loving mothers: Marmee March in *Little Women* is most famous of all, but there are some others, such as Christie Devon in *Work* or Aunt Jessie in *Eight Cousins*. Alcott's female figures are also sometimes good wives: three of the four March girls marry in the second volume of *Little Women* (known as "Good Wives" in the version published in England in 1869), and Rose Campbell happily chooses to wed her cousin Mac, a book-loving physician and poet, instead of another cousin, the hard-drinking Charlie in *Rose in Bloom* (1876).

Alcott does also at times romanticize motherhood, when, for example, at the end of *Little Women*, Marmee hugs her daughters and grandchildren and exclaims: "Oh, my girls, however long you may live, I never can wish you a greater happiness than this!" (380). Within a nineteenth-century U.S. culture that idealized women in domestic roles and often figured women primarily as mothers or future mothers, Alcott's identification of the apex of human happiness, from Marmee's perspective, as successful mothering and grandmothering, can certainly seem conventional. Moreover, even a brief look at Alcott's life story or her writings quickly reveals a writer who felt deeply, intensely attached to the members of her immediate family—father, sisters, and mother.

One might note that Alcott is primarily a comic writer, and following a long tradition of comedy in Western literature, she conventionally ends several of her fictions with heterosexual marriages. *An Old-Fashioned Girl,* for example, ends with Polly wedding Tom and Fanny marrying Mr. Sydney. In other words, it concludes in a deeply conventional way: as the narrator explains, "in the words of the dear old fairy tales, 'And so they were married, and all lived happily till they died'" (345).

Nevertheless, a survey of Alcott's body of work, especially with attention to her own explicit views about women's rights and her deep interest in "literary paradoxy" (see Eiselein 25), could not support the general claim that Alcott usually creates women characters who settle for conventional lives as wives and mothers. Such a claim ignores the diverse range of female characters Alcott created, her explicit criticism of marriage and patriarchy, and her tendency to subvert in comic ways or make more complex her representation of women in relationship to marriage and family.

Many of her female characters, it is important to remember, choose not to marry or have children. In *An Old-Fashioned Girl*, for instance, the sculptor Becky and the writer Kate are single, as is the novel's moral center, Miss Mills, who spreads an "old-fashioned" feminist gospel that says "women can do a great deal for each other" (194). As the novel concludes amid weddings, the narrator also wants us to know that Maud Shaw, Fanny's younger sister, chose a different path and "did *not* marry Will but remained a busy, lively spinster all her days" (345). The protagonist of *Hospital Sketches* (1863), the resolute Tribulation Periwinkle, is pursuing an independent, unmarried life, with joy and meaning and purpose. Nan Harding, from *Little Men* and its sequel, *Jo's Boys*, emphatically rejects marriage and pursues a career as a doctor. While the list of admirable single women, both major and minor characters, in Alcott's writings is long, it is perhaps equally important to note the places where Alcott explicitly celebrates unmarried women, their freedoms, and their contributions to culture and society. In "Happy Women" (1868), for instance, she sketches the rich, accomplished, and happy lives of four very different women who decided to "remain single, and devote themselves to some earnest work" (203). In the chapter set "Among the Maids" in *Jo's Boys*, Alcott develops this theme but shifts her focus from happy and accomplished adult women to girls and young adults when Jo asks the female students at Laurence College to consider alternatives to marriage by starting up "a brisk discussion...concerning careers for women" (245).

Yet even when Alcott has her women characters marry and bear and raise children, it is usually difficult to see those figures as unambiguous homage to conventional marriage or domesticity. Her feminist perspective makes her alert to the ways that marriage and child-bearing can limit women's freedoms within patriarchy. For instance, although Meg may seem to be a candidate for the most conventional wife and mother in Alcott's writings, the representation of her marriage to John Brooke in the "Domestic Experiences" chapter of *Little Women* is nearly devastating in its realism. Although Meg has long dreamed of being "a model housekeeper" and pursues her domestic tasks with "love, energy, and cheerfulness" (Alcott, *Little Women* 217), she descends into depression, her ego much bruised, and John grows angry, as a series of seemingly trivial events and the relationship conflicts they create transform Meg's hoped-for "paradise" (217, 223) into a less idealized, somewhat claustrophobic, and difficult domestic world. She soon realizes that "married life is very trying" (222). Although John and Meg weather their storms and Meg adopts a more realistic perspective on marriage and housekeeping, Alcott's portrayal of married life and its emphasis on its sorrows, limitations, and conflicts is far from idealized. Though more philosophical in some respects than *Little Women*, *Moods* is another novel that represents, in a sometimes stark and depressing fashion, the constraints and the discontent that can exemplify women's experience of conventional marriage and romance.

While realism is certainly a powerful feminist tool for representing the confining nature of married life within a heteronormative, patriarchal society, Alcott also deploys humor, irony, and literary contradiction to illustrate the limitations of conventional wife and mother roles as well as their alternatives. In *Behind a Mask*, Jean Muir marries Sir John to become "Lady Coventry." However, this story, with its multiple deceptions and Jean's brilliant manipulation of the whole Coventry family, does not end *happily ever after* in a conventional way. Instead, Jean is left smiling at the end because "the game was won" (Alcott, *Behind* 202). Despite her disreputable background and humble origins, she manages to use her acting skills to control a domestic scene and manipulate heterosexual courtship conventions for her own social and economic advantage. In a much different way, readers should be alert to the humor and irony in Alcott's decision to have Jo marry Friedrich Bhaer. As Alcott's correspondence makes clear (as does the opening chapter of *Jo's Boys*, in which Jo says "I sometimes feel as if I'd missed my vocation and ought to have remained single" [15]), Alcott seems to have felt that "'Jo' should have remained a literary spinster" (*Selected Letters* 125). And so rather than bow to fan pressure "clamorously demanding that she should marry Laurie," Alcott decided instead to make "a funny match for her" (125). Whether we focus on Jo's own admission that perhaps she should have stayed single or on the fact that Friedrich Bhaer is both a hilarious and perfect match for Jo, their marriage is not exactly or purely conventional or stultifying, as Jo enjoys two successful careers in the March family trilogy—one as the head of a boys' school (that also admits girls) and the other as an author who eventually, but unexpectedly, becomes famous.

Finally, we might add, Alcott doesn't necessarily accept the premise that love of one's family or the cultivation of domestic skills is opposed to feminist reform efforts. It is quite true that in texts like *Little Women* or, say, "Psyche's Art," she explores the very real tension felt by nineteenth-century women like herself (and perhaps also even some women today) between wanting the freedom to pursue a career and a life unencumbered by narrow gender or domestic expectations and feeling the yearning or obligation to fulfill with humility and love one's domestic duties. Though the tensions may be real, according to Alcott, they should not force young women into thinking of life as perpetually filled with mutually exclusive choices. Jo March marries and has two sons, but she also successfully embraces two careers. Rose Campbell prioritizes her career as a philanthropist in *Rose in Bloom*, but she also, eventually, finds a way to make marriage a part of her life by choosing a husband who will "work together [with her] to try to make the world better" (Alcott, *Rose* 374–75), someone who respects her and her agency and supports her commitment to her philanthropic vocation. Christie Devon pursues several careers, then marries, bears and raises a child, and finds fulfillment at age forty as a women's rights activist.

What makes Alcott's work relevant to twenty-first-century American readers?

A number of signs clearly indicate that Alcott's literary works continue to remain relevant for a whole range of readers. Since 2000, for example, several new editions of *Little Women* have been published by companies such as Broadview, W. W. Norton, the Library of America, and Harvard University Press, among others. The Library of America has also issued a second volume of Alcott's works, including her adult novel *Work* and her novels of adolescence and young adulthood, *Eight Cousins* and *Rose in Bloom*. These editions range from the scholarly to the collectible— see, for example, Daniel Shealy's *Little Women: An Annotated Edition* (2013), which is both an impressive work of scholarship and a beautifully illustrated and very collectible coffee table volume. As Clark notes, "since 1960 scholarship addressing *Little Women* has exploded—by one measure more than a hundredfold" (*Afterlife* 198), and along with that scholarship come new waves of popular attention. In children's literature, the first volume of Heather Vogel Frederick's popular *The Mother-Daughter Book Club* series (2007) features four contemporary girls and their mothers reading and discussing (and to some extent paralleling) the events of Alcott's novel. According to the front flap of its dust jacket, "what begins as a mom-imposed ritual of reading *Little Women* soon helps four unlikely friends navigate the drama of middle school.... They can't help but wonder: What would Jo March do?" The 2005 National Book Award-winning novel, *The Penderwicks: A Summer Tale of Four Sisters, Two Rabbits, and a Very Interesting Boy*, is an homage to Alcott's work. As *Penderwicks* author Jeanne Birdsall has acknowledged on her website, "I also borrow from other books, especially the ones I loved best when I was young. The idea of four sisters came from *Little Women*." New television and film adaptations are in the works, and an innovative and comical online rendering, *The March Family Letters*, combines live-action footage of Meg, Jo, Beth, and Amy with representations of their presence on social media.

Moreover, the experiences and feelings of Alcott's characters continue to resonate with twenty-first century audiences. Young people still are stung by peer and sibling interactions. They still struggle to delineate friendship from love. They still find it challenging to balance their artistic and vocational ambitions with their familial obligations, or to find the vocation for which they are best suited. *Little Women* and Alcott's other works continue to speak to these feelings and experiences. In 2014, critic Ivy Schweitzer admitted that upon rereading *Little Women*, "I was abashed at what I found in the novel this time around that I had forgotten or overlooked in my unmemorable reading years before: Marmee's cleansing anger; Jo's radical expression of sexuality—not the by-now-familiar and somewhat generalized 'queerness' but a surprising articulation of transgender desire; and an overarching religious piety that comfortably embraces both of them" (14). In 2015, actress Julianne Moore identified *Little Women* as "the novel I've read over and over," explaining,

> I read my copy until it was in tatters. I couldn't believe that I was experiencing the lives of these four very different sisters in such a different time and found it so relatable. I would reread the passages that made me cry, because I loved that a book could elicit such an emotional response in me. Of course, when I grew older I was struck by how much the book was about personal responsibility, morality, and self-determinism, all ideas that young people are in the throes of trying to understand. (66)

Alcott's works continue to move readers emotionally and to stimulate them intellectually as they ponder issue of personal ethics and obligation to others, freedom, and self-determination. And while *Little Women* remains most vivid in the popular imagination, this volume hopes to reveal, in various ways, how Alcott's whole diverse body of work has the power to move, to teach, and to inspire its readers from the nineteenth through the twentieth and into the twenty-first centuries.

Works Cited

Alcott, Louisa May. "Behind a Mask." 1866. *Alternative Alcott.* Ed. Elaine Showalter. New Brunswick: Rutgers UP, 1988. 95–202.

_____. *Eight Cousins; or, The Aunt-Hill.* 1875. Boston: Little, Brown, 1927.

_____. "Happy Women." 1868. *Alternative Alcott.* Ed. Elaine Showalter. New Brunswick: Rutgers UP, 1988. 203–06.

_____. *Jo's Boys, and How They Turned Out*. 1886. Boston: Little, Brown, 1994.

_____. *The Journals of Louisa May Alcott*. Ed. Joel Myerson, Daniel Shealy, and Madeleine B. Stern. Boston: Little, Brown, 1989.

_____. *An Old-Fashioned Girl*. 1870. New York: Puffin, 1996.

_____. *Rose in Bloom*. 1876. New York: Puffin, 1989.

_____. *The Selected Letters of Louisa May Alcott*. Ed. Joel Myerson, Daniel Shealy, and Madeleine B. Stern. Boston: Little, Brown, 1987.

_____. *Work: A Story of Experience*. 1873. Ed. Joy S. Kasson. New York: Penguin, 1994.

Birdsall, Jeanne. "Frequently Asked Questions." *JeanneBirdsall.com*. Jeanne Birdsall, 2013. Web. 15 April 2013.

Clark, Beverly Lyon. *The Afterlife of* Little Women. Baltimore: Johns Hopkins UP, 2014.

_____, ed. *Louisa May Alcott: The Contemporary Reviews*. Cambridge: Cambridge UP, 2004.

Eiselein, Gregory. "Contradiction in Louisa May Alcott's *Little Men*." *New England Quarterly* 78.1 (2005): 3–25.

Frederick, Heather Vogel. *The Mother-Daughter Book Club*. New York: Simon & Schuster Books for Young Readers, 2007.

Girls. Created by Lena Dunham. HBO. Apatow Productions. 2012.

Lerman, Leo. "*Little Women*: Who's in Love with Miss Louisa May Alcott? I Am." *Mademoiselle* (Dec. 1973). Reprinted in *Critical Essays on Louisa May Alcott*. Ed. Madeleine B. Stern. Boston: G.K. Hall, 1984. 113.

Meigs, Cornelia. *Invincible Louisa*. Boston: Little, Brown, 1934.

Melville, Herman. *Moby-Dick*. 2nd ed. Ed. Hershel Parker and Harrison Hayford. New York: Norton, 2002.

Meyer, Robinson. "The 100 Books Facebook Users Love." *The Atlantic*. The Atlantic Monthly Group, 8 Sept. 2014. Web. 24 October 2014.

Moore, Julianne. "Books of My Life." *Entertainment Weekly* (11 Sept. 2015): 66.

Phillips, Anne K. "'Fun Forever'? Toys, Games, and Play in *Little Women*." *American Journal of Play* 2.4 (2010): 401–418.

Roosevelt, Theodore. *The Rough Riders; An Autobiography*. 1899, 1913. Ed. Louis Auchincloss. New York: Library of America, 2004.

Schweitzer, Ivy. "Most Pleasurable Reading We're Not Doing: Louisa May Alcott's *Little Women.*" *J19 [The Journal of Nineteenth-Century Americanists]* 2.1 (2014): 13–24.

Showalter, Elaine, ed. *Alternative Alcott.* New Brunswick: Rutgers UP, 1988.

Shealy, Daniel, ed. *Little Women: An Annotated Edition.* Cambridge, MA: Belknap-Harvard UP, 2013.

Stearns, Frank Preston. "From *Sketches from Concord and Appledore.*" 1895. *Alcott in Her Own Time.* Ed. Daniel Shealy. Iowa City: U of Iowa P, 2005. 78–88.

Tomasek, Kathryn. "Parker, Theodore." *The Louisa May Alcott Encyclopedia.* Ed. Gregory Eiselein and Anne K. Phillips. Westport, CT: Greenwood, 2001. 254.

"Happy Before I Die": The Strife and Success of Louisa May Alcott

Amy Harris-Aber

Though a prolific writer, Louisa May Alcott did not always garner accolades. In *The Portable Louisa May Alcott*, Elizabeth Lennox Keyser explains that for literary critics, "although her name had been a household word since the publication of *Little Women* in 1868 ... Alcott had never been considered even a minor figure" (vii). Thankfully, Alcott's critical renown has grown even as popular audiences continue to pay tribute to her work. Multiple theatrical, literary, musical, and other adaptations of *Little Women* have appeared throughout the years. Recently, for example, Pemberley Digital, a production company invested in recreating classics, debuted a popular web series entitled *The March Family Letters*. Through a sequence of digital "entries," Jo, Amy, Meg, and Beth are given updated storylines that correspond with companion social media feeds—including Facebook and Tumblr pages (Shelson). This multimodal experience creates an accessible entry point for new fans as well as longtime enthusiasts.

It is no wonder that people are still drawn to Alcott's body of work. There is something compelling about her material that will likely appeal to countless future generations. Several elements of her writings are based on real events and individuals in the Alcott family, and perhaps it is this authenticity that continues to create strong connections to Alcott's work. Though much of Alcott's most familiar work, including *Little Women*, feels warm and idyllic, events in Louisa's early life were far from perfect. These experiences had an understandable impact on the writer and provided her with the motivation to succeed.

Louisa May Alcott was born November 29, 1832—her father Bronson Alcott's birthday. From the beginning, Bronson discerned that she had a willful disposition, which he theorized she had inherited from her mother Abigail: "They are more alike: the elements of their beings are similar: the will is the predominating power" (qtd. in Matteson 63). At the same time, Louisa's mother rejoiced in a letter to her brother that Louisa was "a sprightly merry little puss, quirking up her mouth and cooing at every sound" (qtd. in LaPlante 48). Louisa, the second-oldest, and her three sisters were test-subjects for their father, a student of progressive pedagogy who "wanted to observe his daughters with the eyes of both a parent and a scientist" (Matteson 62). His Transcendental leanings caused him to encourage his children to strive for perfection. His parenting regimen included a vegetarian diet and an "incessant need to instruct and enlighten" throughout his children's day-to-day activities (Matteson 178). Bronson's methods may have been unusual, but he was heavily invested in the work of raising his daughters.

Though he would attribute to himself the highest motives, Bronson's dedication to the life of the mind detracted from earthly duties such as caring for the material needs of his family. Ralph Waldo Emerson, a close friend of Bronson's, once wrote that Louisa's father was "quite ready at any moment to abandon his wife and children … to put any new dream into practice which has bubbled in the effervescence of discourse" (qtd. in Porte 281), and scholars have often castigated Bronson's failures as husband and parent. For example, critic Deborah Weisgall regards Bronson, the son of Connecticut subsistence farmers, as "self-educated, charismatic, and manipulative" (72). Certainly, Bronson led his family into their most desolate experience, an idealistic and ultimately doomed attempt at communal living in Harvard, Massachusetts. With Bronson's English friend Charles Lane, the Alcotts set out in June 1843 to live sustainably at an old farm that Bronson idealistically dubbed "Fruitlands." Once there, Bronson did his best to create a commune that provided "escape from the world's depravity" (Matteson 138), but they nearly starved, and the family faced despair and potential dissolution. Ultimately, hardships such as sickness and the severe New England climate caused them to leave the farm in January of 1844. In "Transcendental Wild Oats," fiction inspired by their commune experiences, Louisa highlights the irony of this name:

"Poor Fruitlands! The name was as great a failure as the rest!" (qtd. in Keyser 552).

Despite the family's failures, her parents' participation within the Transcendental movement was a great advantage to the young writer. She was surrounded by some of the most notable figures of the nineteenth century, such as Margaret Fuller, Nathanial Hawthorne, Henry David Thoreau, and the James family. Elizabeth Peabody co-taught with Bronson at his Temple school. These connections would serve as an invaluable advantage to the young writer who had no shortage of role models. Ralph Waldo Emerson himself acted as a literary mentor to Louisa, recommending "high-minded books" by writers such as "Carlyle, Goethe, Plutarch, Schiller, Madame de Staël, Charlotte Brontë, and Harriet Beecher Stowe" (Reisen 118).

Although wealthy relatives on her mother's side of the family (Reisen 111) occasionally provided assistance, as did Emerson, the Alcotts struggled to avoid destitution. Louisa, her mother, and her sisters did what they could to supplement the family's income. Despite feeling helpless amidst her family's troubles, Louisa determined to "do something by-and-by. Don't care what, teach, sew, act, write, anything to help the family; and I'll be rich and famous and happy before I die, see if I won't!" (qtd. in Matteson 194). When Louisa was eighteen, she served as a companion for the sister of James Richardson. This difficult experience provided material for Louisa's short piece "How I Went Out to Service." The memory of working in such strenuous circumstances made an impression that continued to drive her ambition and instinct for self-preservation. She continued to draw from these memories for the rest of her career, as is evident in works such as *An Old-Fashioned Girl* (1869), whose protagonist, Polly, travels from the country to the city for an extended visit with affluent relatives. Her challenge, as scholar Harriet Reisen notes, is "to find her way to maturity while holding on to her own family's simpler habits and stronger values in the face of condescension and rejection" (223). The dichotomous relationship between survival and integrity is a motif that persists in much of Alcott's work.

Wishing to support the Union cause in the Civil War, Louisa applied for a position as a nurse as soon as she turned thirty, the minimum required age. Arriving in Washington, she served at the Union Hotel Hospital in Georgetown, where she encountered the human cost of war at every turn. In a journal entry, Louisa wrote that she "never began the year in a stranger place than this, five hundred miles from home, alone among strangers, doing painful duties all day long ... Though often home sick, heart sick & worn out, I like it" (113). Unfortunately, she contracted typhoid, and it became necessary for Bronson to bring her home. Even though she had not been able to serve her full three-month appointment, Louisa faithfully recorded her experiences, and she drew from them to write *Hospital Sketches*, which was serialized in May and June of 1863 in *The Commonwealth* and then "published to acclaim" (Keyser xxv).

Even after this success, Louisa faced challenges in her writing career. Her 1864 novel *Moods* was greeted with mixed reviews. A review in *The Commonwealth* compliments the prose of the novel, calling Alcott "a writer of quick fancy, lively wit, and clear observation," but also notes that there is "far too much moralizing" (qtd. in Clark 28). During the next few years, Alcott anonymously published a number of sensational or Gothic stories, dramatic narratives that showcased themes of revenge, tragedy, and dangerous power dynamics between casts of vivid characters. In 1868, Louisa's ambitions came to greater fruition. For financial purposes, she assumed editorship of the children's periodical *Merry's Museum*, though, years later, she acknowledged distaste for this work (Matteson 331). She also was charged with the task of writing a "girls book" (Alcott 158) by Thomas Niles of the Boston-based Roberts Brothers publishing company. Ironically, Bronson had some hand in initiating the relationship between Niles and his daughter that would eventually culminate in Louisa's most recognized work, though she initially resisted the idea, writing "I don't enjoy this sort of thing. Never liked girls or knew many, except my sisters" (Alcott 165–66). By the time she finished *Little Women*, Louisa was mentally and physically exhausted, stating later that she believed writing the novel had been "too much work for one young woman" (qtd. in Matteson 336). She did not have to wait long for a positive reaction: *The Independent* immediately hailed her as "unquestionably one of the best writers for the young that New England has produced for many years" (qtd. in Clark 61), and fans immediately besieged her. Years later, she wrote that the success she had been afforded was contingent upon "[a]n honest publisher and a lucky author…the 'dull book' was the first golden egg of the ugly duckling" (qtd. in Stern 31). By January 1869, she had finished an eagerly awaited sequel. The legacy that Louisa had fought for was cemented, and her financial future secure. Nonetheless, critic Sarah T. Lahey has recognized that Alcott's financial struggles continued to affect her: "[a]s someone who labored almost incessantly in order to support her family, Alcott well understood the complex joys and unavoidable hardships of employment, not to mention the conflicting goals of financial need and personal fulfillment" (134).

Louisa never forgot her formative years of toil and strife, and she was a life-long champion of social justice. Her family identified with the abolitionist cause to the degree that when the controversial antislavery advocate John Brown, "an Alcott family hero" (Reisen 152), spoke in Concord, both Bronson and Abigail were in attendance. Louisa also was an ardent supporter of women's suffrage, once penning an article for *The New York Ledger* in which she claimed that "liberty is a better husband than love to many of us" and advised her readers against poorly considered marriages (qtd. in Reisen 263). Louisa also claimed in 1879 to have been "*the first woman to register my name as a voter*" in Concord (Alcott 216, italics in the original source) following passage of an act that gave women the right to vote for members of the school board.

For the rest of her life, she fought on behalf of those less fortunate, including members of her own family. Louisa had always provided financial support, but after her sister May's death in 1879, she adopted her niece and namesake Louise Marie "Lulu" Nieriker, who came to live with Louisa in 1880. Mothering her niece distracted Louisa from her writing. Young Lulu seemed to be just as spirited as her aunt had been when she was a baby and, years later, would confirm this by stating, "I don't think I was afraid of the devil. I was a little devil myself" (qtd. in Reisen 281). The adoption of Lulu also coincided with Louisa's ever-increasing ill health, which made it difficult for her to write with the same determined ferocity that had once characterized her work habits.

Even though Louisa finally had monetary security, she could not ignore the cruel irony that her body was declining. She wrote, "[w]hen I had the youth I had no money; now I have the money I have no time; and when I get the time, if I ever do, I shall have no health to enjoy life" (191). Louisa died in 1888 of what researchers are now saying may have been systemic lupus erythematosus (Hirschhorn and Greaves), departing the earth only two days after her father's death. By the end of her life, however, she had achieved enduring success, and her legacy lives on in the works her readers still enjoy.

Works Cited

Alcott, Louisa May. *The Journals of Louisa May Alcott.* Ed. Joel Myerson, Daniel Shealy, and Madeleine B. Stern. Boston: Little, Brown, 1989.

Clark, Beverly Lyon, ed. *Louisa May Alcott: The Contemporary Reviews.* Cambridge: Cambridge UP, 2004.

Hirschhorn, Norbert and Ian Greaves. "Louisa May Alcott: her mysterious illness." *Perspectives in Biology and Medicine* 50.2 (Spring 2007): 243–259. *Pub Med.* Web. 14 Aug. 2015.

Keyser, Elizabeth Lennox, ed. *The Portable Louisa May Alcott.* New York: Penguin, 2000.

Lahey, Sarah T. "Honeybees and Discontented Workers: A Critique of Labor in Louisa May Alcott." *American Literary Realism* 44.2 (Winter 2012): 133–156. *JSTOR.* Web. 24 Apr. 2015.

LaPlante, Eve, ed. *My Heart Is Boundless: Writings of Abigail May Alcott.* New York: Free Press, 2012.

Matteson, John. *Eden's Outcasts: The Story of Louisa May Alcott and Her Father.* New York: Norton, 2007.

Porte, Joel, ed. *Emerson in His Journals.* Cambridge, MA: Belknap, 1982.

Reisen, Harriet. *Louisa May Alcott: The Woman Behind* Little Women. New York: Henry Holt, 2009.

Shelson, Sarah. *The March Family Letters.* Cherrydale Productions, 25 Dec. 2014. Web. 27 Jul. 2015.

Stern, Madeleine B. "Introduction." *The Journals of Louisa May Alcott.* Ed. Joel Myerson, Daniel Shealy and Madeleine B. Stern. Boston: Little, Brown, 1989. 3–39.

Weisgall, Deborah. "Dangerous Happiness: Louisa May Alcott and the mother of all girls' books." *The American Prospect.* The American Prospect, 11 Jun. 2012. Web. 5 Apr. 2015.

CRITICAL CONTEXTS

"When Rude Hands Shake the Hive": Louisa May Alcott and the Transformation of America

John Matteson

The years that formed Louisa May Alcott also transformed her country. It grew as she grew. Just around the time when, as a young adult, Alcott felt as if her world were starting to fall apart, the country almost fell apart as well—and Alcott nearly sacrificed her life to help keep it together. Alcott learned much from her own extraordinary trials, and when, scarred and shattered, America struggled to pull itself back together, she was ready to supply a vision of how people could find strength in themselves and their families and discover ways to move forward.

When Louisa May Alcott was born, the American Union contained only twenty-four states, only two of which, Louisiana and Missouri, were wholly or partly west of the Mississippi River. The land that was later to comprise Texas, California, and a number of other states belonged to Mexico. The Pacific Northwest was claimed by Great Britain. The first regular passenger rail service in the United States had begun just two years earlier. And slavery was such an accepted part of the structure of wealth and power that every American president thus far had either owned slaves or had the last name of Adams. By the time Alcott published the first part of *Little Women* in 1868, the landscape of her nation had dramatically changed. Secession had broken the Union in two, and the Civil War had restored it. Not only had slavery been abolished, but the Fourteenth Amendment to the Constitution had extended the rights of citizenship to all native-born persons, regardless of color. The republic spanned the continent, and the following year would see the completion of the first transcontinental railroad. During Alcott's first thirty-six years, the country transformed itself. And, at the end of that period, Alcott wrote a book that helped to transform American literature.

Understanding Alcott and comprehending American life in the nineteenth century can go hand in hand, but the relation between the two subjects should be approached with some caution. Thanks to the enduring popularity of *Little Women*, the March family, whom Alcott brought to life in that novel, may still be the best-known family, real or fictitious, of nineteenth-century America. Because the Marches are so well known, one may feel tempted to presume that they— as well as the real-life Alcotts who inspired them—were a more or less typical family for their period. But the Alcotts were almost as far from typicality as one can imagine. Few girls in Louisa May Alcott's time grew up with great writers like Ralph Waldo Emerson, Henry David Thoreau, and Nathaniel Hawthorne as family friends, but Louisa did. It was far from the rule for a mother of four children to work outside the home, but, from time to time, Louisa's mother did. It was also uncommon for a father of that time to take a strong interest in educating his daughters, but Bronson Alcott's desire to give his girls the perfect education was, for him, a consuming obsession. And it is rare indeed for a family of any era to involve itself in almost every conceivable movement of social reform: from vegetarianism to communal living and from abolition to women's rights, the Alcotts got involved. In their activism as well as their personal circumstances, the Alcotts were anything *but* ordinary.

Because the Alcotts were so deeply engaged in all the major issues of their times, it is impossible to get to know them without learning a great deal about the nation in which they lived. To know Louisa May Alcott is also to understand the America that she knew so well. A place of both tremendous problems and amazing possibilities, it resembled Alcott herself.

When Alcott was born in 1832, America was changing its ideas about children and education, and her father was soon to be at the center of the transformation. In earlier generations, people regarded children as miniature adults. It seldom occurred to them that a child's mind was different from that of an adult, or that it needed to undergo various stages of development before it reached maturity. Many people also believed as a matter of religious faith that children were born wicked and required harsh discipline to be shaped into proper citizens. Schools, therefore, tended to be unpleasant and even frightening places. Children sat on uncomfortable benches. They were expected to learn their lessons by heart, and questions and interpretations were discouraged. Furthermore, it was thought that a schoolmaster who did not beat his pupils for misbehavior or poor performance could not possibly be a good teacher. Bronson Alcott, himself a schoolteacher, openly rejected all of these notions. In 1834, when Louisa was a toddler, Bronson opened a school in Boston called the Temple School, so named because it occupied an upper floor in a Masonic temple. In place of stiff benches, Bronson brought in comfortable seats, and he decorated the room with maps, pictures, and busts of great thinkers. He taught, not through forced memorization, but by asking questions. He thought that children were innately good and that the true meaning of education was its literal one: the word comes from a Latin verb, *educare,* which means to draw out. Bronson Alcott wanted to bring the best nature of a pupil to the surface and to instill strong ethics as well as knowledge. He would not punish a student until he and the child agreed that punishment was reasonable. Once, when a pair of boys misbehaved, he told them that it was worse to inflict harm than to receive it and demanded that they strike *him.* Horrified, the boys dissolved into tears and, it is said, never misbehaved again (Peabody 24).

Bronson Alcott's progressive theories of teaching emerged indirectly from the theories of the French philosopher Jean-Jacques Rousseau, who also believed that people were naturally good but were corrupted by society. Rousseau had observed, "Everything is good as it leaves the hands of the Author of things; everything degenerates in the hands of man" (37). But Bronson did Rousseau one better. He believed that when children were born, they were not merely good; they were very nearly divine. Deciding to raise his three eldest daughters in a way that would preserve that divinity, he tried to create the perfect environment for their nurture and kept detailed notebooks on their mental and moral development. Before he finally gave up his project, he had compiled more than 1,500 handwritten pages. He was, in a sense, America's first child psychologist, and he treated his observation of his daughters like a science of the soul.

Though never published, Bronson's notebooks on childhood behavior were among the first major works of American Transcendentalism, a philosophy that meant different things to different people, but which had at its core a handful of assumptions on which all the Transcendentalists more or less agreed: first, that there is a holiness in nature and that nature is a teacher of profound spiritual truths; second, that the physical world is secondary in importance to an invisible world of soul and spirit, of which the physical world is both the symbol and the mask; and, third, that one could and should strive for a kind of mystical union with a higher spirit. Bronson Alcott stressed the primacy of inner vision when he wrote, "Erudition is not insight. It is not what I take upon my memory that sheds light into my soul, but what I see by self-intuition, that makes me wise" (*Journals* 106). Transcendentalism appealed deeply to spiritually-minded people who found organized religion overly restrictive and formalistic. Its emphasis on the inner life also offered a refuge to Americans who were repelled by the industrializing, increasingly materialistic world they saw around them. Bronson Alcott sought to retreat from this world, and he found both sanctuary and sanctity in the spirit of family. In one of his journals on child development, after describing how, in a moment of panic, his daughter Lizzie had been calmed and comforted by her parents and siblings, Bronson wrote, "Thus doth infancy find relief in love; and, in a world of doubts and fears, of images of loneliness and danger, feels itself protected and at ease, if but the presence of familiar and loved ones are around it. And thus, too, is it…with the good and innocent" ("Psyche"). For his own part, Bronson wrote, "Childhood hath saved me" (*Journals* 55). Both Bronson and Louisa's mother, Abigail May Alcott, strongly insisted upon the virtues of family. A similar emphasis was, of course, essential to Louisa May Alcott's fiction.

Among the Transcendentalists, two strains emerged. One, which included Emerson and Thoreau, emphasized an individual quest for truth. The other, represented by thinkers such as George Ripley and Bronson Alcott, hoped to bring together communities of believers, who would find enlightenment by living and working together, apart from the larger society. They weren't alone; from 1820 to 1850, Americans created hundreds of utopian societies. Ripley founded an agricultural commune called Brook Farm. When Louisa was ten, Alcott cofounded a model society called Fruitlands on a farm near Harvard, Massachusetts.

The Alcotts and their fellow Fruitlanders were ambitiously moral. They abolished money, foreswore coffee and tea, and made minimal use of the labor and products of animals, which they felt they had no right to appropriate. That meant no meat or dairy products on the table and no leather for shoes. Cotton was banned as a product of slave labor; silk was excluded as having been stolen from worms. Perhaps even more radically, the Fruitlanders proclaimed themselves a single "consociate" family and forbade showing preference for one's own blood relatives. Paralyzed by its good intentions, Fruitlands never attracted more than a dozen members and collapsed after seven months. In the story she later wrote about the experience, "Transcendental Wild Oats," Louisa portrayed Fruitlands' moral excesses comically, as in this scene where the commune's only adult female recruit (apart from Mrs. Alcott) is excommunicated for indulging in animal protein:

> Unfortunately, the poor lady hankered after the fleshpots, and endeavored to stay herself with private sips of milk, crackers, and cheese, and on one dire occasion she partook of fish at a neighbor's table.
>
> One of the children reported this sad lapse from virtue, and poor Jane was publicly reprimanded...
>
> "I only took a little bit of the tail," sobbed the penitent poetess.
>
> "Yes, but the whole fish had to be tortured and slain that you might tempt your carnal appetite with that one taste of the tail. Know ye not, consumers of flesh meat, that ye are nourishing the wolf and tiger in your bosoms?"
>
> At this awful question and the peal of laughter which arose from some of the younger brethren, tickled by the ludicrous contrast between the stout sinner, the stern judge, and the naughty satisfaction of the young detective, poor Jane fled from the room to pack her trunk, and return to a world where fishes' tails were not forbidden fruit. ("Transcendental Wild Oats" 96–7)

Even as she poked fun at Fruitlands, however, Alcott also lamented that such an experiment could find no place in an all-too-practical world. She adapted some of Fruitlands' principles to create the fictitious progressive school, Plumfield, which supplies the backdrop for her novels *Little Men* and *Jo's Boys*.

Beyond doubt, America's pivotal reform movement during the first half of Alcott's life was the struggle to end slavery. Slavery's opponents spanned a broad spectrum of opinion, encompassing some who supported gradual emancipation; others who wanted to repatriate the slaves to Africa; and those who urged immediate liberty for the slaves—the abolitionists. The Alcotts belonged to this latter, most radical category. They were, in their time, remarkable for their lack of racial prejudice. Although Bronson did not believe wholeheartedly in racial equality, he admitted a black girl to study at the Temple School, a move that resulted in the school's closing after the white parents revolted (Matteson 84). The antislavery movement acquired an unprecedented intensity in 1850 when Congress adopted a new Fugitive Slave Law, which criminalized the rendering of aid to fugitives and stripped suspected runaways of almost all their procedural protections. Emerson, the Alcotts' friend, called the law a "filthy enactment" and swore, "I will not obey it, by God" (560). In 1853, Bronson Alcott risked his life in a failed attempt to rescue a captured fugitive, Anthony Burns, from a Boston jail. The Alcotts harbored runaway slaves on their way to Canada. Louisa, whom a black man had saved from drowning when she was a toddler, claimed to have been "an abolitionist [from] the age of three" ("Recollections" 33). In a letter to her sister Anna about an antislavery rally in 1856, Louisa enthused, "I was so excited I pitched about like a mad woman, shouted, waved...& swarmed about in a state [of] rapterous insanity till it was all over" (*Selected Letters* 22). In her writings, Louisa expressed contempt for slaveholders, and she was proud when her parents took in as boarders members of the family of John Brown, who had been hanged after leading a violent antislavery raid on Harpers Ferry, Virginia, in October 1859.

Louisa May Alcott's participation in the Civil War transformed her in ways both good and bad. When the conflict began in 1861,

Alcott wished she were male so that she could enlist in the Union army. Along with other supporters of the Union cause, she "began to stir with the ominous hum of bees when rude hands shake the hive" (*Work* 258). She sewed uniforms for the volunteers and bided her time until November 1862 when, upon turning thirty, she reached the minimum age for the army's nursing service. She arrived at the Union Hotel Hospital in Georgetown just as the Battle of Fredericksburg was unfolding fifty miles to the southwest. After the casualties poured in a few days later, Alcott worked fifteen-hour days, cleaning wounds, changing dressings, giving out rations and medicine, and fighting her own daily battle with "disorder, discomfort, [and] bad management" (*Hospital Sketches* 97). Alcott was deeply affected by the suffering she had come to help ease. She wrote, "the courage, loyalty, fortitude & self-sacrifice I saw & learned to love & admire in both Northern & Southern soldiers can never be forgotten" (*Selected Letters* 339). Alcott was at the hospital on January 1, 1863, when, at midnight, the Emancipation Proclamation took effect. When the city's bells rang in the New Year, she danced to her window and waved a handkerchief at some black men who were celebrating in the street below (Matteson 279).

Alcott conceived a special sympathy for one of her charges, a gravely wounded private from the 133rd Pennsylvania Infantry named John Suhre. With his quiet courage and gentle demeanor, Suhre inspired Alcott. However, she soon learned he was beyond saving and was given the dreadful task of telling him he could not survive. Her news still undelivered, she saw tears falling from the wounded man's eyes. Alcott described the scene:

> [S]traightway my fear vanished, my heart opened wide and took him in, as, gathering the bent head in my arms, as freely as if he had been a little child, I said, "Let me help you bear it, John."
>
> Never, on any human countenance, have I seen so swift and beautiful a look of gratitude, surprise and comfort, as that which answered me more eloquently than the whispered—
>
> "Thank you, ma'am, this is right good! This is what I wanted!" (*Hospital Sketches* 88)

Alcott's fiction often features a pivotal scene in which one character offers to share the burdens of another. These moments of compassion find an origin in Alcott's time with Private Suhre.

Two days after Alcott cradled his head in her arms, Private Suhre was dead. Alcott nearly followed him. Less than two months into her military service, the lamentable sanitary conditions in the hospital combined with overwork to undermine Alcott's health, and she came down with typhoid. Rescued by her father and brought back to Concord, she lay delirious for several weeks, hovering between life and death. Though she recovered from the illness, her doctors treated the illness with a mercury compound called calomel, which proved worse than the disease; the mercury settled in her system, and she was never completely well for the rest of her life.

Though it nearly killed her, Alcott's nursing service also marked a decisive turning point in her career as a writer. Up to this point, Alcott had had some small success writing sensationalist fiction for magazines. Though entertaining, these tales were melodramatic and not terribly realistic, and they lacked a mature, independent voice. She wrote a slightly fictionalized memoir of her nursing experience, called *Hospital Sketches,* which brought her first important commercial success. More importantly, though, *Hospital Sketches* taught her to find excellent material for her writing within her lived experience—better, in fact, than her imagination could supply. Moreover, as Alcott herself observed, writing *Hospital Sketches* "showed me '*my style*'": a direct, engaging voice, seasoned with both humor and personal empathy (*Journals* 124, n. 24, emphasis in the original). Through suffering, Alcott had acquired a deeper consciousness of truth. Had it not been for *Hospital Sketches* and the episodes it describes, Alcott could never have written *Little Women.*

Alcott's lifetime coincided with the first stirrings of an organized movement for women's rights in America. Alcott was twelve when the noted journalist and intellectual Margaret Fuller published the first great work of American feminism, *Woman in the Nineteenth Century.* Alcott was fifteen when the country's first women's rights convention convened at Seneca Falls, New York, in 1848. Both her parents supported giving women an equal role in government; they believed that a female influence would help restore compassion and decency to politics. In 1853, Alcott's mother, Abigail May Alcott, started a petition demanding that Massachusetts women be given the right to vote on amendments to the state constitution. She wrote, "I say to all the dear girls keep up, be something in yourself. Let the world feel at some stage of its diurnal revolution that you are on its surface alive, not in its bowels a dead, decaying thing" (qtd. in Barton 156). Alcott took her mother's counsel to heart. Just a few months before writing *Little Women*, she published an essay called "Happy Women," in which she passionately argued that the goal of a woman's life need not be marriage and that young women eager to find husbands should pause to consider "that the loss of liberty, happiness, and self-respect" was not always worth "the barren honor of being called 'Mrs.' instead of 'Miss'" (146). Alcott's essay told of four women in her acquaintance who had chosen careers instead of marriage and had found greater fulfillment thereby. She wrote: "the world is full of work, needing all the heads, hearts, and hands we can bring to do it. ...Be true to yourselves; cherish whatever talent you possess, and in using it faithfully for the good of others you will most assuredly find happiness for yourself, and make of life no failure, but a beautiful success" (L. Alcott, "Happy" 149).

On the subject of women's suffrage, Alcott wrote, "I earnestly desire to go forward on that line as far and as fast as the prejudices, selfishness and blindness of the world will let us" ("Louisa May Alcott" 220). The times moved neither as far nor as fast as Alcott would have wished. She did not live to see the Nineteenth Amendment to the Constitution, which, in 1920, some thirty-two years after her death, conferred upon women the right to vote. Nevertheless, in 1879, Alcott became the first woman in the history of Concord, Massachusetts, to legally register to vote, after a state law authorized women to vote in school board elections. Even so, the town officials observed every formality: Alcott, who was by then an internationally famous author, was required to read aloud from the Constitution, to prove that she was literate, and to sign her name, to prove that she could write (*Selected Letters* 238). Like the great majority of first-wave feminists, Alcott focused her attention

---

on trying to achieve political and economic equality for women; issues that would later have pivotal significance in the women's rights movement, like birth control and reproductive rights, do not surface in her writings..

Alcott is typically regarded more as a children's novelist than as a political commentator. Nevertheless, her fiction returns continually to the subjects of reform that engaged the public conversation of her time. Her first published novel, *Moods*, makes a case for liberalized divorce laws. In *Little Women*, the March sisters raise money for the support of freed slaves and persuade Laurie to give up alcohol. In *An Old-Fashioned Girl*, Alcott speaks out against a consumerist culture that reduces women to ornamental commodities. *Eight Cousins* urges girls to pursue healthful diets and extols the merits of "spring sunshine and healthy exercise" (288), reminding them that "Nature knows how to mould a woman better than any corset-maker" (209). In *Jo's Boys*, the girls anticipate Billie Jean King by besting the boys on the tennis court, and Laurence College, the institution of higher learning that has been appended to Plumfield, practices race- and need-blind admissions, believing so heartily in "the right of all sexes, colors, creeds, and ranks to education that there was room for everyone who knocked" (*Jo's Boys* 1004). The world that her father tried and failed to create in real life, Louisa May Alcott brought to public awareness in her novels, proudly acknowledging her indebtedness to "the wise and beautiful truths of the father" (qtd. in Matteson 370). But Alcott did not simply follow her father. In both the boldness of her social visions and in her eventual influence, she far surpassed him. For every person who has heard of Fruitlands, there are countless more for whom the March sisters were indispensable friends, adding both humor and guidance to the serious task of growing up.

Chronologically, Alcott stands almost at the founding moment of modern children's fiction. Lewis Carroll's Alice is Jo March's senior by three years. Otherwise, virtually all the classic figures of the genre—Huck and Tom; Jim Hawkins; Sara Crewe; Pinocchio; Peter and Wendy; and Dorothy and the Wizard, to name just a few— came after. Since the publication of *Little Women,* books have had so many forthright, courageous girl heroines—from Anne Shirley and Mary Lennox to Katniss Everdeen and Hermione Granger—that it is sometimes hard to realize what a surprise it was to the literary world when Meg, Jo, Beth, and Amy March made their first appearances in 1868. The impact, however, was tremendous. Alcott was virtually without precedent in informing the reading world that girls could be heroic without being perfect angels, that they had deep and serious inner struggles, and that they could have interests and ambitions apart from marrying the handsome boy next door. (Indeed, Alcott initially did not want for Jo to marry at all. Annoyed at the presumption that girl characters should be "married off in a wholesale manner," she wanted Jo to end up as "a literary spinster" [*Selected Letters* 125]. Told by her publisher that Jo ought to marry Laurie, Alcott flatly refused, only to finally compromise by pairing her with Professor Bhaer [125].) It is at least arguable that, in creating Jo March, Alcott did more than evolve a new character type; through the tremendous popularity of *Little Women*, she created a new kind of girl: one who dared to dream big, to speak her mind, and to choose an authentic path through life instead of a conventional, expected one. Almost 150 years after *Little Women* was published, some of the most prominent women in the world, including Annie Leibovitz, J. K. Rowling, and Hillary Clinton, claim it as an early inspiration. The transformations continue.

Works Cited

Alcott, Amos Bronson. *The Journals of Bronson Alcott*. Ed. Odell Shepard. Boston: Little, Brown, 1938.

_____. "Psyche, or The Breath of Childhood." *BMS Am* 1130.10 (9). Houghton Library, Harvard University.

Alcott, Louisa May. *Eight Cousins; or, The Aunt-Hill*. Boston: Little, Brown, 1911.

_____. "Happy Women." *L. M. Alcott, Signature of Reform*. Ed. Madeleine B. Stern. Boston: Northeastern UP, 2002. 146–149.

_____. *Hospital Sketches*. Ed. Alice Fahs. Boston: Bedford/St. Martin's Press, 2004.

_____. *Jo's Boys, And How They Turned Out. Little Women; Little Men; Jo's Boys.* Ed. Elaine Showalter. New York: Library of America, 2005. 801–1064.

_____. *The Journals of Louisa May Alcott.* Ed. Joel Myerson, Daniel Shealy, and Madeleine B. Stern. Athens, GA: U of Georgia P, 1997.

_____. "Louisa May Alcott to the American Woman Suffrage Association." *L. M. Alcott, Signature of Reform.* Ed. Madeleine B. Stern. Boston: Northeastern UP, 2002. 220.

_____. "Recollections of My Childhood." *Alcott in Her Own Time.* Ed. Daniel Shealy. Iowa City: U of Iowa P, 2005. 32–39.

_____. *The Selected Letters of Louisa May Alcott.* Eds. Joel Myerson, Daniel Shealy, and Madeleine B. Stern. Athens, GA: U of Georgia P, 1995.

_____. "Transcendental Wild Oats." *L. M. Alcott, Signature of Reform* Ed. Madeleine B. Stern. Boston: Northeastern UP, 2002. 87–102.

_____. *Work: A Story of Experience.* Work; Eight Cousins; Rose in Bloom; *Stories & Other Writings.* Ed. Susan Cheever. New York: Library of America, 2014. 1-318.

Barton, Cynthia H. *Transcendental Wife: The Life of Abigail May Alcott.* Lanham, Maryland: UP of America, 1996.

Emerson, Ralph Waldo. *Selected Journals, 1841–1877.* Ed. Lawrence Rosenwald. New York: Library of America, 2010.

Matteson, John. *Eden's Outcasts: The Story of Louisa May Alcott and Her Father.* New York: Norton, 2007.

Peabody, Elizabeth Palmer. *Record of a School, Exemplifying The General Principles of Spiritual Culture.* 2nd ed. Boston: Russell, Shattuck and Co., 1836.

Rousseau, Jean-Jacques. Émile, *or, On Education.* Trans. Allan Bloom. New York: Basic Books, 1979.

Critical Insights

Looking for Louisa: Authors, Audiences, and Literatures in Alcott's Critical Reception_____

Amy M. Thomas

Alcott's critical reception has been extensively addressed by Beverly Lyon Clark in *Kiddie Lit: The Construction of Children's Literature in America* (2003), *Louisa May Alcott: The Contemporary Reviews* (2004), and *The Afterlife of* Little Women (2014). Drawing on Clark's insights in these works as well as other critics' observations, this article explores patterns in Alcott's critical reception. During her lifetime, Alcott wrote in a variety of literary genres that were read by equally varied audiences. Book reviews, fan writings, and the original publications themselves provide windows into the different ways these works were received. In the twentieth century, while Alcott's works continued to attract popular audiences, literary scholars began to focus on Alcott's writings, partly because of the rediscovery and republication of "lost" literary works that transformed all audiences' views of Alcott as an author. For a multifaceted author such as Alcott, "critical reception" is best thought of as continually in flux, with multiple views of authors, audiences, and literatures existing at the same time.

Alcott's Reception in the Literary Marketplace of Her Time

Beginning a study of Alcott's critical reception by examining how she built her career as a writer before the success of *Little Women* enables us to see that she was an author who wrote many different types of literature and sought to reach many different audiences. Alcott was just shy of her nineteenth birthday when her poem "Sunlight" appeared in *Peterson's Magazine* in September 1851 under the pseudonym "Flora Fairfield." Between "Sunlight" and the first volume of *Little Women* in 1868, Alcott published almost eighty-five literary works, and from *Little Women* until her death in 1888, as detailed by Madeleine B. Stern, Alcott published nearly two hundred more pieces (*LMA: A Biography* 342–359). While such numbers can be read as a sign of a talented and hardworking author, they also represent a flourishing and diverse literary marketplace that provided authors with multiple venues for presenting their works to a growing number of audiences (Zboray 65–82). The timing was also perfect for Alcott for a second reason: women authors' position in the literary marketplace had been solidified by the success of Harriet Beecher Stowe's *Uncle Tom's Cabin* in 1851–1852.

This inclusive literary marketplace was matched by an expansive view of literature, which seems to have been a perfect fit for an author like Alcott. The language and categories that are now used to classify and evaluate literary works were not yet developed, particularly classifications of genres. For example, during the 1850s, Alcott published twelve stories in the *Saturday Evening Gazette*. Each story was presented on the page with its title and without any kind of genre designation, such as "romance," "mystery," "thriller," or even "tale" or "short story." Perhaps this lack of categorization is one reason why the subjects of Alcott's *Gazette* stories vary so widely, from a jealous ballerina who brings about her rival's death to a young man's journey to learn what "success" means for him. The same variety of subjects is seen in Alcott's early book publications. *Flower Fables* (1854) collects fairy tales Alcott created for Ellen Emerson; *Hospital Sketches* (1863) grew out of Alcott's experience as a Civil War nurse; and the novel *Moods* (1864) explores a young woman's uncertainty about relationships and marriage.

Publishing her varied works in a variety of formats and venues, Alcott reached multiple audiences, often within one publication. Newspapers and magazines were an important medium for literature in the 1800s, and Alcott published her writings in approximately forty different periodicals (Stern, *LMA: From* 130–131). Each publication distinguished itself through its particular mix of news and/or literature along with a special focus. For example, the *Saturday Evening Gazette* was known for its emphasis on music and theater, while the cutting-edge illustration of current events was the hallmark of *Frank Leslie's Illustrated Newspaper*. Many of the newspapers and magazines Alcott contributed to included special features for young children or tailored their contents to appeal to all members of a family. For example, *The Flag of Our Union* described itself as "An Elegant, Moral, and Refined Miscellaneous Family Journal." There were also publications targeted to younger readers, including *The Youth's Companion*, but even here, its masthead emphasized that it purposefully appealed to a very broad audience: "A family paper, devoted to piety, morality, brotherly love—no sectarians, no controversy." The various publications also distinguished themselves through fancy typefaces and ornamental mastheads, and their low cost made them accessible to a wide range of readers. It is no accident that they often emphasized their "moral" nature through their titles and appearance. These publications extended the reach of reading material to new audiences, which in turn triggered concerns about the dangerous effects of fictions, a concern as old as fiction itself (Sicherman, "Ideologies" 291). Richard Brodhead has argued that literary periodicals were "stratifying" at this time along class lines (77–79), but an examination of the actual publications that published Alcott's writings suggests that the opposite was true, that many of the publications were tailored to appeal to a range of readers. Alcott took full advantage of the opportunity provided by these diverse venues.

In 1860, Alcott published two short works in Boston-based periodicals that had significant national readerships: *The Liberator* and *The Atlantic Monthly*. Alcott's national reputation was furthered by the publication in 1863 of stories about her experience as a Civil War nurse. Her *Hospital Sketches* were first serialized in the Boston literary newspaper *The Commonwealth*, under the pseudonym Tribulation Periwinkle, and would have been reprinted nationally through the newspaper "exchange" practice common at the time. As she would do throughout her career, Alcott was "paid twice" for her work by serializing it first then publishing it in book form, a common publishing practice of the time (Shealy, "Author" 72–73). Alcott also reached national audiences through works she published anonymously and pseudonymously in *The Flag of Our Union* (Boston) and *Frank Leslie's Illustrated Newspaper* (New York). Alcott published poems under her name in both venues; additionally, in 1862, under the pseudonym "A. M. Barnard," she won $100 in a competition for the "American Prize Story" with a "sensation" piece, "Pauline's Passion and Punishment."

Perhaps it was her success in all of these venues that led Thomas Niles, editor at the Boston publishing firm Roberts Brothers, to ask Alcott to write the "girls story," which would become *Little Women*. This was actually Niles's second attempt to secure Alcott as an author— he had earlier offered to publish the book version of *Hospital Sketches*—but Alcott had decided to work with another publisher (Shealy, "Author" 67). Now the time was right for Alcott and Niles to collaborate, a pairing of an author and editor who were both skilled readers of the literary marketplace. Roberts Brothers, while not the largest firm in Boston, had a reputation for publishing quality authors in beautifully crafted books, and they were expert advertisers (Kilgour vii). The stage was set for *Little Women* to be a blockbuster novel.

After the success of *Little Women*, Alcott wrote a number of *Little Women*-like books. Although she could have finished her career solely writing such works, she continued to show many of the authorship patterns of her early career. She published novels on more mature topics, such as *Work* (1873) and, later, a revised version of *Moods* (1882). She continued to write short works for publication in a variety of magazines and newspapers, even though, as Daniel Shealy has noted, her editor discouraged such work, fearing it would tax her resources ("Author" 72). Earning money was always a goal for Alcott, but perhaps she also liked reaching the widest possible reading public. New audiences that Alcott reached out to near the end of her career were supporters of woman's suffrage. Between 1874 and 1887, Alcott published almost twenty pieces in the *Woman's Journal*, which Stern notes was "the only woman's suffrage paper published in Massachusetts" (*LMA: From* 147). While Alcott primarily published fictional works throughout her career, most of her *Woman's Journal* contributions were letters about her suffrage work in Concord, and her status as a beloved American author enabled her to write boldly about the cause she fervently supported.

Alcott's Reception by Nineteenth-Century Readers and Reviewers

Since literary scholarship as we know it today is a phenomenon of the twentieth century, the book reviews published in newspapers and magazines of Alcott's time record the views of "professional" literary critics. Discussing reviewers' reception makes it necessary to discuss readers' reception as well because, throughout Alcott's lifetime, the two were often one and the same. In her study of nineteenth-century American reviews, Nina Baym found that reviewers wrote from a position of respect for readers and their preferences:

> During the second quarter of the century reviewers and serious novelists introduced the concept of the 'better novel.' But no matter how vigorously reviewers strove to create public esteem for what they considered superior examples of this form, they could not forget—indeed, as Americans they did not want to forget—that the popular reader who had made the form had to be its final judge. (44)

While the outlines of distinctions between types of literature and their value can be seen during Alcott's lifetime, in general, the hierarchies of literature familiar to us today did not yet exist.

The broad language used by reviewers, or the categories they used to evaluate literary works, reflects the "openness" of the literary marketplace. The reviewers Baym studied valued literary works that depicted "real" characters whose "real" lives reflected important "moral" beliefs, told in engaging stories that captured readers' "interest" (152–195). These traits are noted by reviewers even in reviews of Alcott's earliest books. *Flower Fables* was praised for offering "truths" to children in an entertaining way (qtd. in Clark, *Louisa* 3). Reviewers highlighted Alcott's "eye-witness" experience as the author of *Hospital Sketches*, along with her ability to capture emotions in her writing (qtd. in Clark, *Louisa* 11). The reviews for *Moods* praised Alcott's writing abilities even as they questioned if her story was "real" in its treatment of "moral" questions about marriage (qtd. in Clark, *Louisa* 35).

Clark notes that Alcott was held in high esteem as an author during her lifetime, and the language of *Little Women* reviews captures why. A review in *Putnam's Magazine* is representative: "This is a thoroughly natural and charming book, fresh and full of life, and we heartily recommend it to all young people, big or little" (qtd. in Clark, *Louisa* 67). This quotation also demonstrates a key finding made by Clark about Alcott's reception in the 1800s: that categories for readers and literary works were more "fluid" than today, that children and adults often read the same literary works (*Louisa* xv). In part, this fluidity might be the result of differences between nineteenth- and twentieth-century views of childhood. Anne Scott MacLeod notes, "Alcott, like many of her contemporaries, saw childhood primarily as a period of preparation; children were properly engaged in learning, becoming, forming a worthy character for the future" (23).

The national and international respect Alcott gained as the author of *Little Women* continued throughout the rest of her career. In fact, many reviews of her post-*Little Women* books assume that her works will be good. For example, the review of *Rose in Bloom* in *The Providence Daily Journal* opens,

> Miss Alcott's name on the cover of a book is a talisman for the little men and women she loves so well, and whatever is found upon the pages turns to gold in their eyes. We need not therefore say a single word to commend "Rose in Bloom" to their tender care, for she has already become "the rose that all are praising." (qtd. in Clark, *Louisa* 279)

This confidence in Alcott's gifts as an author also extended to her other novels. For example, *The Commonwealth*'s reviewer describes *Work* as "another of the volumes which attest the large observation, wholesome teachings, elevating purpose, and generous nature of the popular author" (qtd. in Clark, *Louisa* 193) and was "glad to see a new edition of *Moods*, by Miss Louisa M. Alcott. It was her first novel, but it did not get fair treatment" (qtd. in Clark, *Louisa* 39). Though reviewers occasionally criticized Alcott for allowing her characters to use slang and dispense with the rules of standard grammar, she was also praised for the realism and humor of her works. Summarizing the response of nineteenth-century readers to Alcott's works, critic Janet Zehr writes, "[t]hough Alcott was frequently criticized by her demanding audiences, she was praised far more often. Clearly, she knew … what nineteenth-century readers did want" (339).

Although *Little Women* appealed to readers of both genders, Barbara Sicherman's study of women readers found that *Little Women* held special appeal for young women who had dreams of being authors and intellectuals. The Marches' genteel poverty spoke to Charlotte Perkins Gilman, who came from a similar background (Sicherman, "Reading" 25). M. Carey Thomas, who later would become the president of Bryn Mawr, opened the journal she began writing at age thirteen by naming herself "Jo," finding in this character what Sicherman calls "a portrait of female creativity" ("Reading" 26). Simone De Beauvoir "found in Jo a model of authentic selfhood, someone she could not only emulate in the present but through whom she could read—and invent—her own destiny" (Sicherman, "Reading" 28). In *The Afterlife of* Little Women, Clark documents the ways in which Alcott's powerful story has lived on into the twentieth century, reimagined for new audiences through changing media.

Alcott's Reception in the Academy
Scholars have devoted less copious attention to how Alcott's literary works have been included in classrooms. Alcott's works were included in textbooks used in secondary schools and early college courses in American literature. For example, *McGuffey's Fifth Eclectic Reader* (1879) includes an excerpt from *An Old-Fashioned Girl*, and Alcott is also discussed in *A Manual of American Literature: A Text-Book for Schools and Colleges* (1872), edited by John Hart. The conceptions of literature in these textbooks mirror those of the literary marketplace and periodical reviews. The *McGuffey's* editor uses language about literature that echoes nineteenth-century book reviews: "It has been the object to obtain as wide a range of leading authors as possible, to present the best specimens of style, to insure

interest in the subjects, to impart valuable information, and to exert a decided and healthful moral influence" (iii). Hart's textbook includes literature published in a wide variety of formats, including periodicals, and is divided by loosely defined genres: Alcott is included in a section on "Novels and Tales."

Dramatic changes in views of Alcott as an author take place in the academy over the next twenty years. Simply stated, the "fluid" categories of the 1800s are gradually replaced by classifications that create divisions between types of authors, audiences, and genres. Clark's research on Alcott's reception in the academy and the construction of the category of "children's literature" documents the effects of these changes in depth. Combining her findings with information about the history of education leads to provocative questions about the larger cultural changes that took place soon after Alcott's death in 1888.

Clark examined the *Cambridge Literary History of America* (1917–1921) to identify the place of children's literature in the academy during the World War I period. She found Alcott, along with other women authors, such as Harriet Beecher Stowe and Susan Warner, in the chapter titled "Books for Children," although Mark Twain is discussed as the author of "world classics" (*Kiddie* 63–64). Elsewhere in the *Cambridge Literary History of America* (*CLHA*), gender seems less consequential, with Lydia Maria Child appearing in the sections on "Magazinists" and "Annuals" and Catharine Maria Sedgwick in the latter. Differing views of the "value" of literary works are found in these chapters as well. The author of "Books for Children" praises the high quality of this literature, especially for what it records about American culture, while the authors of the chapters on "Annuals" and "Magazinists" note the historical importance of this literature at the same time that they describe its lower "quality" compared to current standards (Trent 167, 173).

The mixed views of authors and literature in the *CLHA* are like a blurry snapshot of American culture in motion. Are changing views of childhood reflected in "Books for Children"? Has the intensified debate about woman's suffrage during the WWI period affected attitudes toward women authors (the Nineteenth Amendment was

---

ratified in 1920s, while the *CLHA* was being published)? Why have some genres (and genders) been marked and others not, since many annuals (fancy books published for the Christmas market) and magazines also appealed to young readers? Were there any women professors at research universities at this time? Do the statements about differing "tastes" suggest that the relationship between the critics and their subject shifted when the scholar-expert-Ph.D. model was introduced to universities during the turn of the century (Renker 13–14)? While much more work needs to be done to answer these questions, it is clear that the *CLHA* captures multiple views of authors, audiences, and literatures rather than a monolithic one.

Clark's examination of the 1948 *Literary History of the United States* shows a further growth of categories and divisions that separate types of authors, readers, and literatures. Children's literature no longer merited its own chapter. Longfellow is discussed as if he were read only by adults. Hawthorne's writing for children is dismissed in a sentence about his need to write for money. Clark found a few references to children's literature in a chapter about the reception of American literature in Europe—along with the comment that the "popular" literature of the time would not be discussed—and linked such writing with "sentimental romances" (*Kiddie* 65–66). These growing divisions and distinctions reflect the rise of New Criticism in the mid-1900s. Jane Tompkins and Nina Baym, among others, have examined the impact of New Criticism, its narrowing of "literature" to poetry and fiction, with a focus on a small cadre of authors, mostly male, and their "masterpieces."

But in a plot twist reminiscent of "Behind a Mask," Madeleine Stern, without whom Alcott studies would not exist, was the product of this training, earning her M.A. in English literature from Columbia University in 1934. Stern published five articles on Alcott between 1943 and 1945 as she worked on her biography of the author, which was published in 1950 and remains an indispensable source for Alcott scholars. The slow but steady increase in Alcott-related citations in the *MLA International Bibliography* for the 1950s and 1960s shows that Stern was not the only woman scholar being trained in research universities. It is also important to note that Stern accomplished her work outside of the academy—working as an independent scholar while she earned a living as a rare book dealer—because many of the changes that take place in the academy between the 1960s and 1970s come from the outside, particularly as a result of the women's movement.

As Alcott is reinstated within the academy, her reputation is reconstructed. Different aspects of her writing are revalued, including the very aspects that were dismissed earlier in the century. The growth of children's literature as a field, both within English and other disciplines, also leads to a large and diverse body of scholarship about *Little Women*. The publication of a selection of Alcott's "sensation" fiction in *Behind a Mask* in 1975 further transforms Alcott scholarship. Leona Rostenberg, Stern's business partner, is credited with "discovering" Alcott's "sensation" writings while she assisted Stern with her research. Though Rostenberg published her findings in 1943, the climate wasn't right for Stern to pursue reprinting Alcott's thrillers until 1975.

As Daniel Shealy notes, the publication of Alcott's sensation writings transformed Alcott studies and the public's perception of Alcott as well ("Louisa" 108). Stern described its impact in the introduction to the new edition of her biography:

> The Alcott persona was revised to reflect the darker aspects of the woman who had come to be revered as the "Children's Friend" but was now becoming a character in her own sensation fiction. At the same time, all of the Alcott oeuvre was reevaluated in light of her thrillers. Even *Little Women* and its successors, *Little Men* and *Jo's Boys*, were not immune from critics in hot pursuit of gender relations, power struggles, and sexual politics. (*LMA: A Biography* xx)

Indeed, it could be said that "gender relations, power struggles, and sexual politics" have been at the heart of Alcott scholarship since the 1960s. Janice M. Alberghene and Beverly Lyon Clark acknowledged this in the title for their 1999 edited collection of essays on Alcott's most famous work, Little Women *and the Feminist Imagination: Criticism, Controversy, Personal Essays*, which brings together a number of previously published and significant essays by scholars such as Nina Auerbach, Judith Fetterley, Catharine R. Stimpson, and Elizabeth Lennox Keyser, as well as original essays by other established and emerging scholars. This collection captures many different views of gender issues in Alcott's novel and her life and autobiographical readings of Alcott's "sensation" writings are prevalent as well. As Sheryl Englund observes, "Recent scholarly publications maintain an unquestioned focus on Alcott's historical identity and its relationship to her writing" (202).

If Alcott's reception in the 1800s was marked by unanimity, the opposite is true today, perhaps because of our complex views of gender and sexual identities. The relationship between Alcott's "sensation" writing and the rest of her works is, in many ways, the great puzzle of Alcott criticism. Which Alcott is "real"? Or are both? This is an exciting time to pursue answers to these questions because of the varied critical perspectives open to scholars and the increasing accessibility to all of Alcott's publications. Alcott's "adult" novels have received increasing attention in the past few years, and the digitization of periodicals where her works originally appeared is enabling reconsideration of her works as well. Perhaps new perspectives on these materials will inspire an understanding of Alcott as an author of many literatures, mirroring her initial position in the expansive literary marketplace of the 1800s, where she originally made her name.

Works Cited

Alberghene, Janice M., and Beverly Lyon Clark, eds. Little Women *and the Feminist Imagination: Criticism, Controversy, Personal Essays.* New York: Garland, 1999.

Baym, Nina. *Novels, Readers, and Reviewers: Responses to Fiction in Antebellum America.* Ithaca, NY: Cornell UP, 1987.

Brodhead, Richard. *Cultures of Letters: Scenes of Reading and Writing in Nineteenth-Century America.* Chicago: U of Chicago P, 1993.

Clark, Beverly Lyon. *The Afterlife of* Little Women. Baltimore, MD: Johns Hopkins UP, 2014.

_____. *Kiddie Lit: The Construction of Children's Literature in America.* Baltimore, MD: Johns Hopkins UP, 2003.

_____, ed. *Louisa May Alcott: The Contemporary Reviews*. Cambridge: Cambridge UP, 2004.

Englund, Sheryl A. "Reading the Author of *Little Women*: A Biography of a Book." *ATQ*, ns 12.3 (Sept. 1998): 199–219.

The Flag of Our Union (7 Jan. 1854): 8. *American Periodicals Series Online, 1741–1900*. 15 Aug. 2015.

Frank Leslie's Illustrated Newspaper, "Our American Prize Story," January 3, 1863, 266.

Hart, John. *A Manual of American Literature: A Text-Book for Schools and Colleges*. Philadelphia: Eldredge and Brother, 1872.

Kilgour, Raymond. *Messrs. Roberts Brothers, Publishers*. Ann Arbor: U of Michigan P, 1952.

MacLeod, Anne Scott. "American Girlhood in the Nineteenth Century: Caddie Woodlawn's Sisters." *American Childhood: Essays on Children's Literature of the Nineteenth and Twentieth Centuries*. U of Georgia P, 1994. 3–29.

McGuffey's Fifth Eclectic Reader. 1879. Rev. ed. New York: American Book Company, 1920.

Renker, Elizabeth. "The Birth of the Ph.D.: The Johns Hopkins Research Model." *The Origins of American Literature Studies: An Institutional History*. Baltimore, MD: Johns Hopkins UP, 2007. 13–39.

Roberts Brothers. "Louisa M. Alcott's Writings." *An Old-Fashioned Girl*. Roberts: Boston, 1896. Web. 15 August 2015.

Rostenberg, Leona. "Some Anonymous and Pseudonymous Thrillers of Louisa May Alcott." *Papers of the Bibliographical Society of America* 37 (1943): 131–140. *JSTOR*. 15 Aug. 2015.

Shealy, Daniel. "The Author-Publisher Relationships of Louisa May Alcott." *Book Research Quarterly* (Spring 1987): 63–74.

_____. "Louisa May Alcott." *Prospects for the Study of American Literature II*. Ed. Richard Kopely and Barbara Cantalupo. New York: AMS, 2009. 97–118.

Sicherman, Barbara. "Ideologies and Practices of Reading." *A History of the Book in America. Volume 3. The Industrial Book, 1840–1880*. Ed. Scott E. Casper, et al. Chapel Hill, NC: U of North Carolina P, 2007. 279–302.

_____. "Reading *Little Women.*" *Well-Read Lives: How Books Inspired a Generation of American Women*. Chapel Hill: U of North Carolina P, 2010. 13-36.

Stern, Madeleine. *Louisa May Alcott: A Biography*. Boston: Northeastern UP, 1950.

_____. *Louisa May Alcott: From Blood & Thunder to Hearth & Home*. Boston: Northeastern UP, 1998.

Tompkins, Jane. *Sensational Designs: The Cultural Work of Antebellum Fiction*. New York: Oxford UP, 1986. 186–202.

Trent, William Peterfield, et al., eds. *The Cambridge History of American Literature*. New York: Macmillan, 1917–21. *Internet Archive*. 15 August 2015.

The Youth's Companion (19 Apr. 1855). *American Periodicals Series Online, 1741–1900*. Web. 15 August 2015.

Zboray, Ronald J. "Antebellum Reading and the Ironies of Technological Innovation." *American Quarterly* 40.1 (Mar. 1988): 65–82. *JSTOR*. 15 Aug. 2015.

Zehr, Janet S. "The Response of Nineteenth-Century Audiences to Louisa May Alcott's Fiction." *ATQ*, ns 1.4 (Dec. 1987): 323–42.

Feminist Alcott?

Katherine Adams

Was Louisa May Alcott a feminist? When I teach her 1873 novel, *Work*, this question usually comes up. For many students the answer is obvious. How could Alcott *not* be a feminist when the novel's protagonist, Christie Devon, announces in its very first line, "there's going to be a new Declaration of Independence," then spurns her uncle's patriarchal authority and the confines of marriage and domesticity in favor of self-reliance? (5). Students familiar with early U.S. history might compare Christie's "Declaration" to Elizabeth Cady Stanton's "Declaration of Sentiments" from the 1848 Women's Rights Convention at Seneca Falls. Like Stanton, they argue, Alcott revised Thomas Jefferson's founding document for nineteenth-century feminists. Other students are less certain. They object to the stereotyped portraits of poor and non-white women that appear later in *Work* and claim the novel ultimately betrays its radical premise by presenting marriage and domesticity as solutions to the hardship of working life. At this point, a third group usually speaks up. They insist it is inappropriate to judge Alcott by today's standards. We should, they advise, recognize how progressive she was for her time and value her works as a step in the right direction.

None of these responses is wrong. In fact, together they epitomize a larger scholarly conversation about Alcott's writing. Introduced into the academic literary canon by feminist critics during the 1970s, after decades of being dismissed as a mere children's author, she has been celebrated and censured by feminist criteria ever since. The question of whether Alcott was a feminist writer is, perhaps, unresolvable. Yet asking it can be useful for what it reveals about Alcott and our own critical approaches. Here I begin by reviewing some of the ways Alcott does and does not answer to contemporary feminist views and the problems with asking her to do so. I then turn to *Work* to consider how the novel can help us reframe the feminism question in more productive terms. I show that by repeatedly stepping back to contemplate positions it seems to espouse, the novel invites us to do the same. It encourages us to recognize that even "feminist" Declarations of Independence arise from and must be enacted within the same contexts they seek to transform. Thus, rather than reading Alcott's narrative *for* feminism (asking it to affirm our views by echoing them, betraying them, or pointing toward them from the past), we can read it *as* feminists, committed to questioning and reflecting on the origins, implications, and limits of our own beliefs.

Reading for Feminism

Reading Alcott through the lens of contemporary feminist values produces mixed results. In many ways, that lens seems to fit. Raised within a community of reformers, Alcott participated in the anti-slavery and women's movements as an adult through activism and writing. The extraordinary success of her literary career, which supported her family and made her one of the nineteenth-century's most popular authors, evinces the sort of ambition and talent we look for in feminist icons. And she created strong heroines, like Christie, *Little Women*'s Jo March, and *Hospital Sketches*' Tribulation Periwinkle, who exhibit similar qualities in narratives where strong men are often conspicuously absent. Many of Alcott's works portray intense relationships among women that emphasize the necessity of female solidarity and, in several cases, seem to carry romantic and homoerotic overtones. Alcott's writing demonstrates skill in both materialist and ideological gender critique. That is, she exposes women's vulnerability to economic injustice and physical hardship, *and* she skewers sexist belief systems and social codes. Frequently, she does both together, showing how material relations and ideology intersect. In "Transcendental Wild Oats," for example, gender prescriptions make women beasts of burden; and the (anti) heroine of "Behind a Mask," actress Jean Muir, literally performs femininity as a disguise to gain financial security. Jean's story also interests feminist critics for its surprisingly modern treatment of femininity as a social script acted out with others. Indeed, Alcott appears to have recognized all gender identities as fluid—as evinced by tomboy characters like Jo March, another actor-protagonist who strongly prefers cross-dressing roles.

Still, Alcott's writing disappoints some feminist readers. Her works frequently idealize female selflessness, service, and submission to duty—even "punishing" rebellious heroines, such as *Little Men*'s "wild girl," Nan Harding, who learns self-control by being tied to a chair. Elsewhere, Alcott seems to endorse the suppression of women's creativity. Many readers have lamented Jo March's decision to burn her "immoral" story manuscripts and, as critic Veronica Bassil shows, Alcott forces other artist-protagonists to choose domesticity and service to others over aesthetic self-expression. Her treatment of class, ethnic, and racial differences among women also merits critique. While Christie and Jean Muir's stories expose class injustice, showing how it intersects with and intensifies gender oppression, other working-class characters are caricatured. Alcott's sentimentalized, often condescending, representations of black women—including *Work*'s Hepsey—strike a discordant note, even when they appear in radically anti-slavery works.

Some scholars have coped with these problems by identifying two distinct Alcotts. One is the author of domestic fiction and children's literature who enshrined middle-class values and conventional femininity to sell books in a conservative age. The other wrote what we call sensation fiction—tales of criminality, suspense, and violence that were marketed primarily to working-class readers and published anonymously or pseudonymously. It is easy to see why these latter works, discovered by Leona Rostenberg in 1943, have been republished in collections with titles like *Alternative Alcott* and *Feminist Alcott*. Featuring women characters who manipulate, deceive, and take revenge upon male oppressors, they diverge from Alcott's other writing in tone and content. But, as Gail Smith notes, the two-Alcott solution cannot really allow for multiple viewpoints. Rather, it assumes *one* Alcott who sometimes wrote in her "real" voice and sometimes suppressed that voice to avoid condemnation. It suggests we can detect Alcott's "true" beliefs (which, of course, resemble ours) beneath the surface of works that only *seem* conservative.

The trouble with this approach is that it reflects what literary critics and historians call "presentism"—a tendency to read the past through the lens of the present, imposing political judgments and conceptual frameworks that would not be available, or even recognizable, to nineteenth-century writers. This is an easy trap to fall into, since many of the causes addressed by early women's rights activists resonate closely with contemporary politics. They also fought for economic and educational opportunity, laws protecting women's property and wages, and entitlements to vote and hold political office. But how those demands were framed and pursued can differ sharply from what we expect. Nineteenth-century women's advocates typically participated in a range of reforms. These included the anti-slavery movement, but also campaigns for temperance, religious perfectionism, and the salvation of fallen women that may seem less "feminist" from today's perspective. Early arguments for women's rights emphasized the sanctity of motherhood and marriage and the conviction that feminine authority naturally operated in indirect ways, through moral example and influence rather than direct action. Some who supported causes like married women's property rights also felt that women would be "unsexed" by voting. Even suffragists rooted their arguments in the idea of essential differences between the sexes, promising that women voters would bring much-needed morality and civility to the political sphere. It is a mistake to interpret such claims as strategies for softening or disguising radicalism, or as being beside the point. For many nineteenth-century reformers, these claims *were* the point: women's rights were pathways to womanly duty, even self-sacrifice, not self-actualization.

Some scholars point out that the word "feminist" did not even exist until 1882, just a few years before Alcott's death in 1888. Does terminology matter? Sometimes it does. For example, using the twentieth-century term "lesbian" to describe nineteenth-century writers is problematic because it ignores a seismic shift in ideas about sexuality and human difference. Before 1868, when the term "homosexuality" first appeared, homosexual practices and desires were recognized but not viewed as evidence of a categorically different kind of person. The emergence of these new terms marked the invention of "the homosexual" and "the heterosexual" as fixed identities, which transformed how we think about sexuality so profoundly that many scholars believe we—people born after the shift—cannot grasp the mentality that precedes it. This is important: it reminds us to consider not only that *Alcott* was the product of a different time, but that we are *likewise* products of a particular historical moment that shapes our interpretation of the past *and* present. As scholar Lora Romero points out, nobody stands outside of their era's ideology—meaning the assumptions and belief systems that inform its world view. Feminist analysis helps us recognize and criticize aspects of our culture's problematic beliefs. But it cannot remove us from their influence entirely. Romero shows that literary critics often seem to assume writers like Alcott *can* transcend their historical context to judge it from above. She argues that when critics project this state of "high authorial consciousness" onto writers, it is a way of pretending we can occupy such a vantage point ourselves (2).

Reading as a Feminist

Luckily, Alcott's novel *Work* demonstrates a more self-reflective approach, and Christie's "Declaration" provides an excellent starting point for exploring it (5). As noted above, our protagonist seeks freedom from dependence on her Uncle Enos, from marrying "in sheer desperation" (13), from domestic "drudgery," and from an existence driven by profit motive: "I can't help feeling," she explains, "that there is a better sort of life than this dull one made up of everlasting work, with no object but money. I can't starve my soul for the sake of my body" (Alcott 10–11). In just a few pages, Christie invokes the Greatest Hits of feminist philosophy: she champions self-determination, individualism, and authenticity; she disavows patriarchy, marriage, gender-conformity, and capitalism. But how tenable is such a plan? What does it mean to define independence as freedom *from* so many things—even, it would seem, from her own body, as though she could become purely "soul," unconstrained by material needs? Christie claims she wants to "travel away into the world" (5). But she also seems to imagine traveling *out* of the world, liberating herself from its traditions and institutions.

Uncle Enos is correct (if callous) when he responds "you need breakin' in, my girl, and you are goin' where you'll get it" (Alcott 11). In the chapters that follow, Christie discovers there is no freedom outside the systems of power and social belief that organize nineteenth-century America and her own selfhood—body *and* soul—within it. Alcott's decision to revise her title from *Success*, her original choice, to *Work: A Story of Experience* may suggest that she agrees with Enos. The former title refers literally to having "risen above" something. The latter implies immersion. And yet *Work* repeatedly implies that loneliness is more injurious than poverty—as with its portrait of Rachel, an outcast who loses her job but survives thanks to knowledge of Christie's love. Thus, Alcott seems rather attached herself to this nineteenth-century fantasy of transcending the body's confines, even as she criticizes it.

That said, this treatment of Christie's "Declaration" reflects a larger pattern within *Work* of convictions coming under review. Anyone who has read much Alcott knows she loves declarative sentences. Her writing is peppered with pronouncements (often punctuated with exclamation points), self-affirming assertions of moral truth and home-spun wisdom. Just as typical, however, are the places where Alcott satirizes trite or hyper-conventional sentiment. Some of these expose hypocrisy; others offer pleasure in the absurdity of human certainty. For example, before Christie meets her future husband, David Sterling, she "settles[s his] character" as "[m]elancholy, learned, and sentimental," based on the contents of his room. Then she discovers "[n]ot the faintest trace of the melancholy" in the actual man, "nothing interesting, romantic, pensive, or even stern... What a blow it was to be sure! Christie actually felt vexed with him for disappointing her so" (Alcott 174–75). It is this tendency to assert and then investigate "settled" belief that makes *Work* a useful model for feminist self-reflection—especially since it applies not just to judgments about the world and other people, but also to the self (our most basic belief). In *Work*, Christie conducts a series of "experiments," trying on different roles available to nineteenth-century U.S. women and examining them from within. The process reveals the limits of each gendered identity script in turn, but also confirms their inevitability. No amount of insight enables Christie to disavow the modes of being and belief her culture offers. She can, however, cultivate critical awareness and live more effectively within them.

Christie's "experiments" with female selfhood drive *Work*'s plot, as our heroine takes up a series of jobs (all of which Alcott tried herself). Each chapter in Book I is titled for the employment it depicts—"Servant," "Actress," "Governess," "Companion," "Seamstress"—except the first, which is titled "Christie," as though to imply job titles are equivalent to names. As our protagonist moves in this explicit way from one feminized "situation" to the next, she also experiments with styles of femininity she encounters in other women. She scrutinizes her first employer, Mrs. Stuart: "and practice[s] certain little elegancies that [strike] her fancy" (Alcott 24). She emulates a friend, Lucy, in the ensuing chapter, "Actress," and reads *Jane Eyre* when working as a governess. Throughout Book I, *Work* emphasizes Christie's self-conscious identification with differing cultural modes of femininity.

The full implications of this experimentation emerge when Christie wins her first theatrical role as an "Amazon Queen" in *The Demon's Daughter.* Costumed for opening night, she is led to a mirror and instructed, "look at yourself" (Alcott 35). The narrator reports:

> She liked the picture, for there was much of the heroic spirit in the girl, and even this poor counterfeit pleased her eye and filled her fancy with martial memories of Joan of Arc, Zenobia, and Britomarte. (35)

Here Christie explicitly tries on a female role. But, as the mirror and Lucy's command ("look at yourself") signal, the scene also takes that motif to a deeper, more internalized level. As Christie contemplates this new role, she contemplates *herself*. The lines emphasize the strange self-division effected by self-examination: one self looks at

---

a reflected self, experiencing her in the third person as "the picture" and "this counterfeit"; yet the line between them is blurred: which self does "the girl" refer to? We might think of this moment as a freeze-frame that pauses the plot of Alcott's *bildungsroman* (novel of development) to examine the tangled relationship between its protagonist and the experiences through which she develops—between experimenter and experiment.

Freezing this particular frame enables us to investigate Christie's relationship to the experiments of femininity and "feminism." Referring to an all-female tribe of warriors who serve the mythological goddess Diana, the term Amazon was used in the nineteenth century to describe physically assertive women and, later, to deride suffrage advocates. Here it also recalls Christie's desire for freedom *from* oppressive male authority, since Amazons were a separatist community who shunned contact with men, and Christie decides to play the role partly because she knows Uncle Enos would object: "a delicious sense of freedom pervaded her soul, and the old defiant spirit seemed to rise up within her at the memory of her Uncle's grim prophecies and narrow views" (Alcott 32). More, the "martial memories" that "[fill] her fancy" as she gazes in the mirror all concern heroines who appropriate and defy male authority—the last of whom had starred in a serialized novel by another woman writer, E.D.E.N. Southworth, titled *Britomarte, The Man-Hater* (1865–66). In a sense, what Christie confronts in the mirror are her own political ideals, her "Declaration of Independence" *and* the self it has engendered. The reflection casts her ideals in an ironic light: Alcott plays up the absurd costume and script for comic effect, and we cannot miss the irony that by spurning Enos's control, she subjects herself to the tyranny and objectifying gaze of the theatrical manager, "Mr. Sharp," who orders her to march about while assessing her figure (33). Playing the "feminist" freedom fighter is not very freeing.

But this insight does not lead Christie to shed the character as a mere costume or digression from her "real" self. In fact, Lucy has to call her away from the mirror: "Don't admire yourself any longer, but tie up your sandals and come on" (Alcott 35–36); and she continues to perform the Amazon and other preposterous female roles until a piece of falling equipment nearly kills her. Christie is attached to role-playing. She enjoys it, *and* role-playing is her only option: there is no "real" self outside of roles. Even when Christie finally leaves the stage, the line between experiment and experimenter remains blurred:

> The very ardor and insight which gave power to the actress made that mimic life unsatisfactory to the woman, for hers was an earnest nature that took fast hold of whatever task she gave herself to do, and lived in it heartily while duty made it right, or novelty lent it charms. But when she saw the error of a step, the emptiness of a belief, with a like earnestness she tried to retrieve the one and to replace the other with a better substitute. (Alcott 47–48)

Initially, this passage seems to present Christie's decision to give up acting as a return to authenticity from artifice—to being "the woman" vs. "the actress." But the term "substitute" implies something different. Christie's next experiment will be another substitute rather than an original, another female role to "live in" rather than a return to unscripted selfhood. Like Alcott herself, Christie is a product of her cultural setting. There is no freedom *from* the gendered roles available in her historic moment, no transcendent or authentic self to actualize. Another illustration comes from the "Governess" chapter, where she decides to stop flirting with a wealthy admirer. Addressing herself in another mirror, she scolds, "Don't be foolish, Christie! ... for you are only a woman, and in things of this sort we are so blind and silly," then changes her pretty outfit for an "old brown [hat]" and "rusty boots," and "trudge[s] away...bent on being very quiet and reserved, as became a meek and lowly governess" (Alcott 61). Even where she means to correct an "error" or "emptiness" and to remember she's "only a woman," Christie only dons another role.

From a feminist perspective, the insight that one never achieves freedom from cultural roles may seem depressing, even disabling. But it does not represent a failure on Christie's part (or Alcott's, or ours). In *Work*, it is simply the nature of things. As one character puts it, again playing on the costume metaphor, "folks is very like clothes, and a sight has to be done ... before any of us is fit for wear a Sunday morning'" (Alcott 157–8). For the speaker, a laundress, being like clothes does not make people false or superficial. It's just how we are. Nor does it preclude meaningful action. Late in the novel, Christie reprises some of her former theatrical roles for David and other friends, and as she moves from one character to another, "she soon forg[ets] St. Clair in poor Juliet" and performs the latter "with all the power and passion she possessed" (210). Far from implying inauthenticity, Christie's immersion in role-playing becomes a medium for "power and passion" and even "earnestness" that makes it "most effective" for others (210).

Moreover, Christie only rarely and temporarily "forgets" in this way. Although she is never free to transcend her culture's scripts for and beliefs about female being, she is also never fully consumed by them. We recall that fact whenever she addresses herself in a mirror. Another reminder is the narrator's habit of using similes to describe Christie's relationship to womanhood: preparing for an outing with David, she "would have been more than woman" if she hadn't smoothed her hair and changed her apron (Alcott 177); later, she helps him make bouquets "with a woman's interest" (179); and when she announces her plan to enlist in the Union army, it is "with the look of a woman bent on doing her part" (281). Repeatedly, Alcott's protagonist is *like* a woman—identified with, but not identical to the category—a pattern that seems less about casting doubt on these generalities regarding "woman" than opening a space between them and Christie. Other women also exhibit this quality of suspended and incomplete identification, especially Helen Carrol, the mentally ill woman for whom Christie serves as a paid companion: "what a comfort it is to see her like herself again," remarks Helen's brother during a good spell—a wonderfully ambiguous phrase (81). In *Work*, women are never free from the cultural options for being "woman," but they are able to confront "womanhood" in the mirror. It is unavoidably *how* they are, but not entirely *who* they are.

Feminist (Dis)Identification

What does any of this have to do with reading as a feminist? I propose that we think of Christie as an allegory for the impossibility of what Romero calls "high authorial consciousness"—that is, for Alcott's immersion in and attachment to the very belief systems she wants to analyze, and for our *own* culturally-immersed feminisms. What can the novel teach us about how to proceed? First, that feminist self-reflection can be painful. *Work* is never glib about the difficult path it exemplifies. It acknowledges that movement forward—from a self that feels like "error" or "emptiness" into something new—can be traumatic. Many of Christie's transitions are prompted by near-death encounters with fire, injury, illness, and despair. Is this what it takes to make us question the beliefs we "live in" (47)? Is this the price of change?

There is also danger when self-division becomes too pronounced. Christie's darkest hour results from excessive self-reflection: "her mind preyed on itself," warns the narrator, "slowly and surely" (Alcott 117). Paradoxically, this leads to a near-fatal inability to *sustain* self-reflection. Looking into yet another mirror, Christie recites a misogynist gendered script, forcing it upon herself: "Yes, I'm growing old; my youth is nearly over, and at thirty I shall be a faded, dreary woman, like so many I see and pity" (119). This self-encounter displays no playful confusion of first- and third-person address, no space for pleasure, insight, or change. A few pages later, as Christie stands on a riverbank, again studying her reflection, she confronts the same image, now in the guise of a bloated corpse, and loses herself to it even further:

> She seemed to see the phantom she had conjured up, and it wore the likeness of herself... So plainly did she see it, so peaceful was the white face, so full of rest the folded hands, so strangely like, and yet unlike, herself, that she seemed to lose her identity, and wondered which was the real and which the imaginary Christie. (Alcott 124)

Like Christie, Helen Carrol suffers from too much self-reflection. Rather than "faded, dreary womanhood," it is her own congenital madness she contemplates, and the fact that she cannot marry lest she reproduce it. We might view her plight as a metaphor for feminist despair, as we recognize our own inheritance of misogynist and racist ideologies and the prospect of passing it on. But, perhaps even more than Christie, Helen reminds us there is no alternative to the struggle. It is only after her death that the doctor pronounces her "sane and safe at last, thank God!" (Alcott 97).

Given that we—like Christie and Alcott—are immersed in the gender ideologies of our time and that the work of feminist critical awareness can be challenging, it is fortunate that *Work* presents opportunities for practice. Unlike Jean Muir from Alcott's "Behind a Mask," whose performance of femininity often fools readers along with fellow characters, Christie allows us to experience gendered roles and beliefs along with her, enabling us to cultivate critical distance within them and experiment with their possibilities and limits. We have already seen how the novel invites us to identify, alongside Christie, with the radical ideals of self-determination and independence, then compels us to examine them more critically. Less radical positions receive similar treatment. Self-sacrifice and sympathy for the needy, values that shaped nineteenth-century women's reforms, also come under review in *Work*. They inform Christie's actions at many points: she shares her wages with Hepsey, a fugitive saving to purchase her mother from slavery; saves Lucy from injury by throwing herself in its path; and supports the outcast Rachel by leaving their employer in solidarity. All these acts ennoble Christie, and we enjoy vicariously identifying with her as she performs them. We abandon this co-identification, however, when she considers marrying the wrong man because it would make him happy and enable her "to comfort many poor souls":

> This idea attracted her, as it does all generous natures; she became enamored of self-sacrifice, and almost persuaded herself that it was her duty to marry ... in order that she might dedicate her life to the service of poorer sadder creatures than herself. (Alcott 250)

Alcott takes the ideal that we have happily embraced and hyperbolizes it, spelling out its less appealing logic. Once again, this reconsideration does not wholly discredit self-sacrifice. Although we are glad when Christie rejects her suitor, we never regret her earlier generosity. But it does establish a more informed perspective on such feminized virtue. When Christie herself becomes a "poor and sad" creature, contemplating suicide at the river, her rescuer is Rachel, the former recipient of her sympathy. Now we discover how it is to be the pathetic object of another's sympathetic gaze ("when I saw you...I knew why I was sent" [Alcott 127]), to feel ashamed and beholden ("I am afraid you think me something better than I am ... you should know whom you are helping" [134]). Like self-sacrifice, sympathy is not wrong. But experiencing its power dynamics from both ends may prevent us from admiring our angelic self-image too long.

Christie's experiments with roles and beliefs that shaped femininity in the nineteenth-century U.S. do not enable her to rise above them. They do make her wiser and more effective. She becomes, in the novel's final chapter, a kind of translator, who facilitates understanding between upper-class lady reformers and the working-class women they wish to help. As someone who has both experienced and contemplated those positions, Christie is empowered to mediate among them. She is not free *from* her culture, but free *to* act meaningfully within it.

Is Christie a feminist? Was Alcott? We may never agree. We can, however, make *Work* an opportunity for stepping back to investigate our own feminisms and the ways they can and cannot set us free.

Works Cited

Alcott, Louisa May. *Work: A Story of Experience.* 1873. New York: Penguin Books, 1994.

Bassil, Veronica. "The Artist at Home: The Domestication of Louisa May Alcott." *Studies in American Fiction* 15.2 (Autumn 1987): 187–97.

Romero, Lora. *Home Fronts: Domesticity and Its Critics in the Antebellum United States.* Durham, NC: Duke UP, 1997.

Rostenberg, Leona. "Some Anonymous and Pseudonymous Thrillers of Louisa May Alcott." *Papers of the Bibliographical Society of America* 37 (1943): 131–40.

Smith, Gail K. "Who Was That Masked Woman? Gender and Form in Louisa May Alcott's Confidence Stories." *American Women Short Story Writers: A Collection of Critical Essays*. Ed. Julie Brown. New York: Psychology Press, 2000. 45–59.

Yellin, Jean Fagan. "From Success to Experience: Louisa May Alcott's Work." *The Massachusetts Review* 21.3 (Fall 1980): 527–39.

Poverty and Social Critique in Postbellum America: *Little Women* and *Adventures of Huckleberry Finn*

Kristen B. Proehl

In a famous scene in Chapter XV of Mark Twain's *Adventures of Huckleberry Finn* (1885), Huck and Jim are separated from one another when their raft collides with a steamboat on the Mississippi River. They are forced to retreat to the shore, and Huck finds himself in the company of the Grangerfords, an aristocratic clan of Kentuckians who are embroiled in a violent feud with the Shepherdson family. As Huck examines the lavish, if rather gaudy, décor of their home, he discovers the maudlin poetry and art of Emmeline Grangerford, a young woman who was not only preoccupied with death but also died prematurely at the age of fifteen. She left behind elegiac portraits, such as "I Shall Never Hear Thy Sweet Chirrup More Alas," which mourns the death of a pet bird, and poems, such as "Ode To Stephen Dowling Bots, Dec'd." As she writes in her overly sentimental style, "O no. Then list with tearful eye, / Whilst I his fate do tell. / His soul did from this cold world fly, / By falling down a well" (Twain 113). Twain's satirical portrayal of Emmeline's poetry and art transforms what scholars often refer to as the nineteenth-century "cult of mourning" (Halttunen 124), as well as the era's predilections for highly emotional death scenes, into a source of humor. He not only critiques the pervasive sentimentality of women's literature in the mid-nineteenth century, but also the privileged white, middle-class readership that fueled its popularity.[1] Twain's humor strikes at the unprecedented popularity of women writers in this era, including perhaps that of his postbellum literary contemporary, Louisa May Alcott.

Twain and Alcott arguably produced the two most iconic works of nineteenth-century American children's literature, *Adventures of Huckleberry Finn* and *Little Women*, respectively, which have each had a remarkable cultural afterlife. Beyond this, however, the two authors may appear to have little in common. Indeed, readers and literary critics have long tended to categorize Twain's and Alcott's literary contributions in ways that emphasize their differences rather than their commonalities.[2] To cite just a few examples, Alcott is often geographically associated with the Northeastern United States and, more precisely, the literary community of Concord, Massachusetts, whereas Twain is associated with the Deep South and his childhood home of Hannibal, Missouri. *Adventures of Huckleberry Finn* nostalgically invokes the myth of the open American landscape; *Little Women*, by contrast, is typically remembered for its intimate, sentimental portrayals of the domestic sphere. Alcott and Twain have, moreover, been categorized quite differently in American literary history: Alcott is remembered primarily as a sentimental novelist, who penned "domestic stories" for girls, whereas Twain is celebrated for his "adventure stories" about boyhood and satirical representations of American life (Trites x).

That said, the differences between Twain and Alcott, particularly in terms of theme and literary style, have often been overstated. For example, while Alcott's writing about girlhood undoubtedly contributed to her fame, she wrote *Little Women* only at the insistence of her publisher and claimed that boys were in fact her preferred subject matter (Cheney 189). Indeed, her later additions to the March family trilogy, *Little Men* (1871) and *Jo's Boys* (1886), focus largely upon the experiences of young, male students at the Plumfield Estate School. Alcott's iconic status as a female writer, combined with the remarkable success of *Little Women*, may have contributed to the American reading public's failure to recognize her as a writer who was, in many ways, as invested in writing about boyhood as Twain. The categorization of Twain and Alcott as realist and sentimental writers, respectively, is likewise rather reductionist. As Gregg Camfield argues in *Sentimental Twain*, although Twain is recognized primarily as a realist writer, his writing bears the imprint of nineteenth-century sentimental culture and its ideologies. Likewise, scholars often refer to *Little Women* as a sentimental text, but in many ways, it disrupts and transcends the conventions of sentimentalism. Gregory Eiselein, for instance, has called attention to Alcott's investment in modernity: "sometimes satirizing its complexities, sometimes turning away from it and toward a simpler times, and sometimes embracing it" (84). Although Twain is more often associated with the mythos of the American landscape, both Twain and Alcott were also deeply influenced by romantic and Transcendentalist understandings of the child's relationship to the natural world.[3]

As writers of the Civil War era, Twain and Alcott not only witnessed tremendous historical change during their lifetimes, but also shared a deep commitment to issues of social justice and equality. As Trites has argued, they transform young protagonists, such as Huck Finn and Jo March, the tomboy protagonist of *Little Women*, into vehicles of social critique and, in so doing, contribute to the rise of the adolescent reform novel. While *Adventures of Huckleberry Finn* and *Little Women* both critique class hierarchies, Twain's novel does so primarily in order to deconstruct nineteenth-century racist ideologies, whereas Alcott explores the ties between classism and gender expectations and norms for women. *Little Women* and *Adventures of Huckleberry Finn* were both written in the post-Civil War years; even though Twain's novel is set during the antebellum era, the Civil War is simultaneously present and absent in both of these texts. The memory of the war and its immediate historical effects, such as the rise of the Ku Klux Klan and racial violence as well as shifts in class structures, hover over both texts and influenced their social criticism. Synthesizing close readings of several key passages from *Little Women* and *Adventures of Huckleberry Finn*, as well as related literary and historical scholarship, this essay addresses the different ways in which Twain and Alcott explore the intersections of poverty and other forms of oppression. Both authors, I suggest, turn to poverty in order to meditate upon cultural memory of the Civil War and examine the social issues of the Reconstruction era.

In their childhood and adolescence, both Twain and Alcott experienced the threat of poverty, so it is, perhaps, unsurprising that it became a major thematic focus of their work. Twain's family lived on the verge of poverty throughout the 1840s and 50s and, when his father died, he was forced to rely on the charity of others (Coulombe

15). Alcott's family struggled in "genteel poverty" (Elbert 20), in large part because her father's dedication to philanthropy often left her family in debt. As young adults, Alcott and Twain found themselves in the paradoxical position of desiring and coveting wealth and the stability it might provide even though they remained skeptical of class privilege.[4] Throughout *Adventures of Huckleberry Finn*, Twain implies that poverty contributes to other social problems, such as racism, illiteracy, and mob violence. By contrast, Alcott focuses on poverty itself as a social problem and insists that the poor themselves are in need of sympathy. She suggests a parallel relationship between poverty and other forms of oppression, such as disability, sexism, and racial oppression. Twain examines poverty in the context of rural communities, whereas Alcott focuses more on immigrants as well as neglected and disabled youth. Twain suggests that classism and poverty, combined with a lack of education, contributes to racism. In both *Little Women* and *Adventures of Huckleberry Finn*, children and adolescents serve as ideal social critics because they raise questions about the individual's capacity to transcend his or her social position. Twain and Alcott are both deeply interested in the extent to which children and adolescents may be able to overcome the effects of poverty.

The opening paragraphs of *Little Women* and *Adventures of Huckleberry Finn*, for instance, each signal the varying roles that social class will play in each of these texts. *Little Women* begins with the March girls lamenting their poverty: as Meg exclaims, "it's so dreadful to be poor" (11). The March daughters are clearly frustrated by their lack of material wealth, but their poverty is also, to an extent, circumstantial and self-imposed, given that Mr. March lost his fortune while trying to help an impoverished friend. Although their situation seems dire to them, they remain deeply entrenched in the middle class. *Adventures of Huckleberry Finn*, by contrast, opens with a reference to the fact that Tom and Huck have found "money that the robbers hid in a cave"—a sum total that amounts to "6,000 dollars apiece, all gold" (33). With this rather improbable rags-to-riches backstory, Twain establishes *Adventures of Huckleberry Finn* as a boys' adventure narrative. By contrast, Alcott's exploration of class issues in relation to childhood is more explicitly instructional: Jo March and her sisters learn a great deal about poverty throughout the novel, and this is crucial to their growth and development as adolescents.

After complaining about their Spartan Christmas celebration, the March daughters, with their mother's encouragement, resolve to donate their dinner to their impoverished, German immigrant neighbors, the Hummels. "A poor, bare miserable room it was," Alcott writes of the Hummel family's household, "How the big eyes stared, and the blue lips smiled, as the girls went in" (*Little Women* 21). The Hummel children proceed to devour the March family's food offerings like "so many hungry birds" (22). While Alcott describes the Hummel children in ravenous, animalistic terms, she refers to the March daughters, by contrast, as "angels in hoods and mittens" (21). This act of philanthropy not only spiritually elevates Jo and her sisters but also teaches them to appreciate their own material wealth. "Oftentimes," Monika Elbert explains, "the well-meaning young benefactors of the stories are rewarded far more amply than the impoverished child whom they help out of a sense of duty, but not exactly out of love" (21). Although close neighbors to the March family, the Hummel children largely disappear from the narrative after the March daughters complete their acts of charity. By contrast, Laurie Laurence, the March family's wealthy, semi-orphaned neighbor, plays an increasingly key role in the girls' lives and eventually even marries into the family.

Alcott may not present the March daughters' generosity toward the Hummels in explicitly negative terms, but she nevertheless reveals the limitations of this gesture of philanthropy. As Martha Saxton has noted, Louisa's mother, Abba Alcott, was critical of philanthropists who wished merely to alleviate the symptoms of poverty rather than address its origins (176). The March daughters enter into the Hummel family's domestic space to administer aid, but this boundary-crossing is generally one-sided: the Hummel children neither enter the March household nor develop friendships with Jo and her sisters. Laurie is welcomed into the household as a friend, although he quickly develops a sibling-like relationship with the

March daughters. The girls also benefit materially and emotionally from their generosity to him: Laurie's grandfather, for instance, gives Beth a piano as a present. The March family's generosity to the Hummels, however, has fewer rewards and functions as a kind of warning. As Elbert notes, the March family's relationship with the Hummels suggests that there are certain dangers inherent in being a bit too sympathetic (32). Immigrant poverty, even that of the Germans, whom the Alcotts and their fellow Northeasterners often considered to be more cultured than other national groups, such as the Irish (Doyle 150), becomes a source of contagion in the novel: Beth contracts scarlet fever when she overextends herself in terms of her responsibilities to the Hummel family, and this leads to her eventual death in Part II.

Twain was even more skeptical than Alcott about the potential for philanthropy to help ameliorate the effects of poverty. As biographers Ryan and McCullough note, Twain presents "poverty as inexorable and the charity it inspires as hollow" (52). Huck's visit to a small town in rural Arkansas plays a key role in developing the novel's class critique and presents a revealing juxtaposition to Alcott's portrayal of the Hummels. The town is clearly in a state of physical disarray: the stores and houses "most all old, shackly, dried up frame concerns that hadn't ever been painted … The fences was made of different kinds of boards, nailed on at different times" (Twain 141). Twain's representation of this town is, of course, part satire, but it nevertheless clearly associates the Southern poor with dirt and disorder. "All the streets and lanes was just mud," Huck describes, "mud as black as tar, and nigh about a foot deep in some places" (142). He continues on to describe a "muddy sow" with her litter "lazying along the street" (142) and townspeople who derive pleasure from watching their dogs attack the town's free-roaming pigs.

Twain uses this small-town setting to suggest a close relationship between mob violence and poverty. In one of the novel's most classic scenes, Huck witnesses a violent conflict between Boggs, the town's belligerent but harmless drunk, and Colonel Sherburn, his affluent neighbor. When Sherburn grows weary of Boggs's relentless threats and abuse, he simply shoots him. The local townspeople are so enraged by Sherburn's casual violence that they threaten, rather ironically, to lynch him. As Huck explains, "well, by-and-by somebody said Sherburn ought to be lynched. In about a minute everybody was saying it; so away they went, mad and yelling, and snatching down every clothes-line they come to, to do the hanging with" (Twain 146). Twain thus suggests that emotion and a desire for conformity easily sway the behavior of the citizens of this economically underprivileged small town.

Twain's portrayal of Sherburn also speaks to the inequities of the Southern judicial system:

> Why don't your juries hang murderers? Because they're afraid the man's friends will shoot them in the back, in the dark—and it's just what they *would* do.
>
> So they always acquit; and then a *man* goes in the night, with a hundred masked cowards at his back, and lynches the rascal" (147).

Through Sherburn's reference to "masked cowards," Twain gestures to the rise of the Ku Klux Klan and racial violence of the Reconstruction era and suggests a constitutive relationship between class inequality, mob violence, and racial oppression. With that said, it is important to note that poverty is far from the only instigator of violence and racism in *Adventures of Huckleberry Finn*. Twain repeatedly highlights the racism of affluent, white Southerners, such as the Widow Douglass and Miss Watson, two wealthy sisters who adopt Huck. Moreover, his portrayal of the feud between the Grangerford and Shepherdson clans suggests that affluent whites are as inclined to violence as the poor. In all of these instances, class inequality is closely tied to other forms of oppression.

In many ways, Huck's foray into small-town Arkansas serves as a meditation upon his own familial origins and, in particular, his relationship with his wayward, abusive father. Pap's alcoholism, along with his educational and class insecurities, fuels his racist tirades. He seems particularly disturbed by his encounter with a black man who is also a college professor. "They said he could *vote*, when he was at home. Well, that let me out. Thinks I, what is the country a-coming to? ... And to see the cool way of that nigger ... I says to the people, why ain't this nigger put up at auction and sold?" (Twain 52–3). Like many other classic *bildungsromans*, *Adventures of Huckleberry Finn* explores whether or not Huck will have the capacity to transcend the racism associated with his class status.

Rather than suggesting a causal relationship between poverty and racism, Alcott instead emphasizes how the poor are themselves a disadvantaged group and considers them in relation to those who are marginalized due to race or disability. She is especially concerned, however, with the ways in which class intersects with gender and affects the experience of coming-of-age for young women. Chapter 9, "Meg Goes to Vanity Fair," devotes special attention to how the March daughters' place in the social hierarchy is connected to their marital prospects. Meg allows Belle Moffat, a girl from a wealthier family, to dress her up for a party; she borrows a fancy gown and jewelry, which allow her to pass as a member of a more privileged social group than her family in fact occupies. She overhears gossip about her family's relationship with Laurie that includes speculation that the March girls simply wish to marry him for his wealth. Meg, who feels guilty about having been wooed by upper-class privilege, eventually confesses this episode to Marmee. Her response is an important one, as it links the novel's representation of poverty to gender expectations. "Money is a needful and precious thing," Marmee explains, "and, when well used, a noble thing, but I never want you to think it is the first or only prize to strive for. I'd rather see you poor men's wives, if you were happy, beloved, contented, than queens on thrones, without self-respect and peace" (Alcott 84). As Sarah Sherman notes in *Sacramental Shopping*, Marmee intervenes at a crucial moment here—one in which Meg feels an acute sense of disillusionment about the promises of materialism (38). Part I of the novel portrays Marmee's attempts to establish an anti-materialist philosophy, which is in part a response to the rise of industrial capitalism in the nineteenth century, and Part II examines the repercussions of the March daughters' attempts to follow her advice.

Through her portrayal of Jo's romantic relationship with Professor Friedrich Bhaer, Alcott brings the novel back full circle to the March daughters' treatment of the Hummel children. To the dismay of many of her adolescent readers, Jo opts to marry Bhaer instead of Laurie. Jo, who claims to have only platonic feelings for Laurie, rejects his marital offer and, with it, his money and class status. By marrying Bhaer instead, she commits to a particular philosophy of philanthropy that includes a self-selected poverty. As Alcott writes: "He was neither rich nor great, young nor handsome,— in no respect what is called fascinating … He was poor, yet always appeared to be giving something away…" (276). Indeed, Jo falls in love with Bhaer precisely *because* he presents her with a model of sympathetic masculinity that includes a commitment to others.

With land inherited from her wealthy, cantankerous Aunt March—a character who, ironically, aggressively polices class norms throughout the novel—Jo and her husband establish the Plumfield Estate School. They develop the school primarily to serve the needs of impoverished and disabled children. Education becomes one of the primary means through which Alcott envisions social change and, in particular, the eradication of the effects of poverty. In contrast to the opening scenes of *Little Women*, in which the March daughters endeavor to alleviate the symptoms of poverty, Plumfield works to transform the social order. In the final chapter of *Little Women*, Alcott mentions the enrollment of an African American child at Plumfield: "a merry little quadroon, who could not be taken in elsewhere" (377). While the focus of the school's philanthropy remains primarily upon white boys who are orphaned, impoverished, and/or disabled, Alcott nevertheless establishes a parallel relationship between poverty and other forms of social inequality.

In some ways, Alcott's vision of philanthropy in *Little Women* seems to have evolved considerably since its opening chapters, but in other ways, little appears to have changed. Just as Jo and her sister are elevated by their interactions with the Hummels, so, too, does Jo appear to derive a sense of pleasure from her philanthropic plans for Plumfield. As she tells Laurie, "I shall have rich pupils, also,—

perhaps begin with such altogether; then, when I've got a start, I can take a ragamuffin or two, just for a relish" (Alcott 375). Throughout the remainder of the trilogy, Jo and Bhaer's predominately white, impoverished pupils raise questions about the power of education to transform the individual.[5] As Elbert notes, Alcott's relationship to the poor in her public and private life might be characterized as "ambivalent" or at least inconsistent, as she alternately aestheticizes, romanticizes, and patronizes them (21). In *Little Women*, the poverty of Irish immigrants, in particular, is treated with a degree of ambivalence.[6] In an oft-remembered scene in Chapter 7, Amy March's overly pedantic teacher, Mr. Davis, tosses her contraband pickled limes out of a classroom window. The "little Irish children" on the street outside the school, whom Alcott describes as "sworn foes" to Amy and her classmates, hungrily devour them (Alcott 59). This does not, however, prove to be a moment that instructs Amy about the virtues of generosity; rather than appreciating the fact that her limes are, at the very least, going to disadvantaged children, Amy is so distressed by what she perceives as the inequity of the situation that she bursts into tears.

Twain and Alcott, in their different ways, demonstrate the extent to which class issues play a central role in the adolescent reform novel. In contrast to *Adventures of Huckleberry Finn*, *Little Women* turns to poverty as a vehicle for the growth and development of her young protagonists. In particular, Alcott celebrates the virtues of self-selected or chosen poverty, whether it's through the March daughters' decision to give up their Christmas breakfast, or Professor Bhaer, who "always appeared to be giving something away" (276). Alcott suggests that when we forgo wealth in order to help others, we are ourselves improved through the experience. As child protagonists grow and develop, they raise questions about their relationship to the social hierarchy and, in so doing, often unmask its paradoxes and inequalities. In Twain's world, however, poverty and the philanthropic responses to it often lack the transformative and redemptive qualities portrayed in *Little Women*.

Literary scholars have long accused both Twain and Alcott of retreating from their radical social critiques as their novels draw to rather conventional conclusions. This criticism emerges in part from the sense that Huck and Jim do not fully demonstrate the growth, development, and self-awareness that one might hope for in an adolescent protagonist of the *bildungsroman*. Jo appears to abandon her tomboy traits and, in certain ways, conforms to normative femininity when she marries Professor Bhaer. Huck retreats from racist ideologies throughout most of the novel, but he appears to return to them when he and Tom Sawyer concoct a rather elaborate, dehumanizing plot to "set Jim free," even though they know that Jim has already been legally emancipated through Miss Watson's will. Many critics would argue that in the final chapters of *Little Women* and *Adventures of Huckleberry Finn*, Alcott's and Twain's radical social critiques fade into the backdrop. And yet, despite these arguably regressive conclusions, Huck and Jo persist in their resistance to class expectations until the final pages of the novel: Huck through his famous decision to "light out" into the western territories and flee normative, middle-class domesticity, and Jo through her choice to marry a poor, but generous, schoolteacher and devote her own life to helping underprivileged students. While Twain and Alcott offer substantially different critiques of class inequality, it is certainly an issue that connects their adolescent protagonists. Considered together, their novels demonstrate the extent to which poverty remained a persistent topic of interest and concern in postbellum America.[7]

Notes

1. For a book-length study of the intersections of class and mourning in nineteenth-century America, see Kete.

2. For a more extensive comparative analysis of Twain's and Alcott's biographies and place in American literary history, see Trites.

3. For more on Alcott and romanticism, see Proehl.

4. For a more detailed analysis of Alcott's conflicted feelings about wealth, poverty and class privilege, see Elbert 24. For more on Twain, see Coulombe 32.

5. See Proehl.

6. For more on Alcott's attitudes about the Irish, see Doyle.

7. As Stephanie Foote has argued, Alcott also shows us that "class was an already fractured and multiply determined idea, encompassing ideas of status, family name and honor, intellectual and community repute, as well as more conventional economic markers" (81).

Works Cited

Alcott, Louisa May. *Little Women*. 1868–69. Ed. Anne K. Phillips and Gregory Eiselein. New York: Norton, 2004.

Camfield, Gregg. *Sentimental Twain: Samuel Clemens in the Maze of Moral Philosophy*. Philadelphia: U of Pennsylvania P, 1994.

Cheney, Ednah D., ed. *Louisa May Alcott: Her Life, Letters, and Journals*. 1889. Carlisle, MA: Applewood Books, 2010.

Coulombe, Joseph L. *Mark Twain and the American West*. Columbia, MO: U of Missouri P, 2003.

Doyle, Christine. "Irish, Attitudes Toward." *The Louisa May Alcott Encyclopedia*. Ed. Gregory Eiselein and Anne K. Phillips. Westport, CT: Greenwood, 2001. 150–151.

Eiselein, Gregory. "Modernity and Louisa May Alcott's *Jo's Boys*." *Children's Literature* 34.1 (2006): 83–108.

Elbert, Monika. "Charitable (Mis)givings and the Aesthetics of Poverty in Louisa May Alcott's Christmas Stories." *Enterprising Youth: Social Values and Acculturation in Nineteenth-Century American Children's Literature*. Ed. Monika Elbert. New York: Routledge, 2008. 19–38.

Foote, Stephanie. "Resentful *Little Women*: Gender and Class Feeling in Louisa May Alcott." *College Literature* 32.1 (2005): 63–85.

Halttunen, Karen. *Confidence Men and Painted Women: A Study of Middle-Class Culture in America, 1830–1870*. New Haven: Yale UP, 1992.

Kete, Mary Louise. *Sentimental Collaborations: Mourning and Middle-Class Identity in Nineteenth-Century America*. Durham, NC: Duke UP, 2000.

Proehl, Kristen. "Educating Jo March: Sympathy, Plumfield, and the Tomboy Trajectory in the Alcott Trilogy." *Romantic Education in Nineteenth-Century American Literature*. Ed. Monika Elbert and Lesley Ginsberg. New York: Routledge, 2014. 42–56.

Ryan, Ann M., and Joseph McCullough. *Cosmopolitan Twain*. Columbia: U of Missouri P, 2008.

Trites, Roberta Seelinger. *Twain, Alcott, and the Birth of the Adolescent Reform Novel*. Iowa City: U of Iowa P, 2007.

Twain, Mark, Gerald Graff, and James Phelan. Adventures of Huckleberry Finn: *A Case Study in Critical Controversy*. 2nd ed. Boston: Bedford St. Martins, 2004.

Saxton, Martha. *Louisa May Alcott: A Modern Biography*. New York: Farrar, Straus and Giroux, 1995.

Sherman, Sarah Way. *Sacramental Shopping: Louisa May Alcott, Edith Wharton, and the Spirit of Modern Consumerism*. Durham, NH: U of New Hampshire P, 2013.

CRITICAL
READINGS

Lost in the Vortex: The Problem of Genius in the Fiction of Nathaniel Hawthorne and Louisa May Alcott

Christopher Fahy

There was a time when Nathaniel Hawthorne and Louisa May Alcott were seldom paired in literary criticism. This is not surprising: Alcott was a friend of Hawthorne's children, not a contemporary of their father. Aesthetically, this is also fitting: many earlier critics tended to interpret Hawthorne as an ironic explorer of the Calvinist heritage,[1] while pre-feminist critics viewed Alcott as a cheerful purveyor of domestic fiction.[2] In the past forty years, more extensive treatment of Hawthorne's "feminine" themes has narrowed the gap between the two authors.[3] Moreover, Madeleine Stern's discovery of Alcott's anonymous thrillers indicated an interest in crime, obsession, and subversive sentiment not unlike Hawthorne's. Similar in their taste for domesticity, sensation, and irony, the two authors shared a common ground.[4]

Some connections have long been evident: Alcott's adolescent diary lists *The Scarlet Letter* among her favorite books (Alcott, *Journals* 63), and the characters in *A Modern Mephistopheles* self-consciously compare themselves to Hester, Dimmesdale, and Chillingworth.[5] A more recent generation of critics has established broader connections. Elizabeth Keyser's 1993 *Whispers in the Dark,* in particular, examines how *The Scarlet Letter* provides a model of womanhood that *Diana and Persis* and *A Modern Mephistopheles* explore.[6]

One link that has not been examined, however, is the authors' mutual ambivalence toward "genius," a concept often discussed in Concord by intellectuals such as Ralph Waldo Emerson, Henry David Thoreau, and Bronson Alcott. Through their artist characters, Hawthorne and Alcott examined the negative effects of genius and its promotion of an anti-social bias. They also personally yearned for genius, even as they mistrusted it, undercutting perhaps their own objective authority on the subject.[7] Importantly, however, both tried to justify the pursuit of authorship and make it socially acceptable through strategies such as the domestication of fiction, the use of an aestheticized notion of the fortunate fall, and (for Alcott), the adoption of Margaret Fuller's concept of celibate apprenticeship.

Genius

The concept of genius has roots that stretch back to ancient times. Before genius took that name, the Greeks explored artistic inspiration in its association with Dionysus, the "ecstatic… merciless" god of wine (Stock 7, 8). In *Ion*, Plato describes how the inspired poet must be mad in order to produce a worthy product (Tigerstedt 63–67). Plato is also wary of the poet's boundless (and amoral) abandonment; in his *Republic*, only when the frenzied element is contained and spiritualized is Dionysus permitted within the state. As chronicled in M. H. Abrams' *The Mirror and the Lamp*, the concept of inspiration continued to evolve in the West. Influenced by Plotinus, for example, the Renaissance era lauded the artist's contemplation of the realm of Ideas, and the artist's work was seen as divine and more real than material reality. At the same time, Renaissance thinkers perceived an internal source of ideas, an intimation of reality buried within what we now consider the unconscious mind (Abrams 43). Not surprisingly, this more subjective source had sexual connotations. By the Romantic era, the artist in touch with such sources of inspiration could be regarded as a "genius," a Latin word linked with male fertility. Like male sexuality, this genius was, in addition to being solitary and individualistic, "powerful, explosive, [and] procreative" (Boyd 129). Genius (like Dionysus himself) also took on androgynous qualities. In *Woman in the Nineteenth Century*, Margaret Fuller described the inspired work originating from the spontaneous union of "male" and "female" aspects of the self. Also sexual was Coleridge's perception of the idea as a mental seed, an unconscious, predetermined form. Taking on a more extroverted form, the erotic metaphor emerges in Wordsworth's and Emerson's rendering of the marriage of mind and world, a coupling that begets an ecstatic moment that is the birthplace of religious experience and inspired creativity.

In short, by the Transcendentalists' era, there was a strong tradition celebrating the genius's spiritual potential, masculinity, and boundless energy. A persistent apprehension was also inherited. R. D. Stock describes Christianity's role in abetting this fear: by the Middle Ages, a goat-hoofed Dionysus, associated with sexuality, violence, and irrationality, had become synonymous with Satan (*Flute* 86). In Puritan New England, the god's Maenads were regarded as witches, and, according to Cotton Mather, even the Muses, ecstatic yet Apollonian, had a "tendency to incite and to foment impure flames" (qtd. in Kelley 112). Witch-hunting ceased with eighteenth-century secularization, but the Enlightenment's distrust of religious enthusiasm bespoke a continuing fear of passionate abandon.

Prominent among Enlightenment thinkers were the Scottish Common Sense philosophers. They emphasized "experience and fact" over idealism, believing that facts were more real than the workings of the imagination and were, consequently, more moral. They wanted literature to be practical and morally efficacious. These philosophers distrusted the emerging romantic emphasis on originality, believing that it blasphemously misrepresented God's creation, overemphasized the individual's role, and brought "intellectual and moral ruin." For them, imagination could be subversive, separating the artist from the (moral) community; in their criticism, they buttressed the old Puritan fear of literature and art (Martin 14, 51, 61, 63).

At the same time, these Common Sense philosophers emphasized both the moral importance of feeling over intellect and the power of the imagination to encourage empathy. In this and their concerns about the imagination, they were emulated by Hawthorne, who had studied them at Bowdoin and Salem. Reflecting both exultation and Common Sense trepidation, Hawthorne relates how "he went to work" on *The Scarlet Letter's* composition "as if the devil were in me" (*Letters* 345). The Common Sense philosophers also indirectly influenced Alcott insofar as they, with their emphasis on feeling and social union, provided the philosophical backbone for Sentimental literature. Both Sentimentalists (a group that arguably includes Hawthorne and Alcott) and Common Sense philosophers believed in the power of empathy; both emphasized the importance of realism (Noble 262–265). They created a cultural climate that was at once optimistic and skeptical, celebratory of emotion and insistent on containment.

Against Society

The solitary genius, imagination fired by communion with the night sky, is a commonplace of the Romantic movement. In his early tale "The Devil in Manuscript," Hawthorne's narrator, the author Oberon, displays an acute understanding of the phenomenon as he peruses his work: "But how many recollections throng upon me, as I turn over these leaves! This scene came into my fancy as I walked along a hilly road, on a starlight October evening; in the pure and bracing air, I became all soul, and felt as if I could climb the sky and run a race along the Milky Way" (Hawthorne, *Tales* 333). This passage, reminiscent of the moment in "Nature" when Emerson confronts the night sky in Boston Common, is a parody of Transcendentalism. Oberon experiences moments of ecstasy, but in the calm light of day, inspired passages are no better or worse than those in which "there were a wall of ice" between writer and subject (334). Worse, such fits abet amoral states. Having decided to burn his unpublishable manuscripts and abandon his craft, Oberon's imagination is seized by the larger blaze his holocaust creates in the town: "'My tales!' cried Oberon. 'The chimney! The roof! The Fiend has gone forth by night and startled thousands in fear and wonder from their beds! Here I stand—a triumphant author! Huzza! Huzza! My brain has set the town on fire! Huzza!'" (337). The Fiend here refers to the Devil but also to Oberon's writing itself. The author does not care that his actions could destroy the town in which he lives—real life is secondary to imaginative life. He continues to desire the fire of imagination, even as it becomes appallingly literal. He lusts for fame, the thrill of knowing that he has affected others, even if that effect is disastrous.

Alcott may borrow from this tale. At the beginning of *A Modern Mephistopheles*, the would-be author Felix Canaris burns his manuscripts and attempts to poison himself with the fumes. In *Little Men,* Demi, the future author, presides over an ecstatic burning of a toy village that resembles Alcott's ideal community of Plumfield (Blackburn 104). But it is *Little Women* itself that provides the most direct parallel. Like Oberon, Jo produces fairy tales and sensation stories. Like him, she is an aspiring author familiar with the inspirational state:

> Every few weeks she (Jo) would shut herself up in her room, put on her scribbling suit, and "fall into a vortex," as she expressed it, writing away at her novel with all her heart and soul, for till that was finished she could find no peace...
>
> She did not think herself a genius by any means; but when the writing fit came on, she gave herself up to it with entire abandon, and led a blissful life, unconscious of want, care, or bad weather, while she sat safe and happy in an imaginary world, full of friends almost as real and dear to her as any in the flesh. Sleep forsook her eyes, meals stood untested, day and night were all too short to enjoy the happiness which blessed her only at such times, and made these hours worth living, even if they bore no other fruit. The divine afflatus usually lasted a week or two, and then she emerged from her "vortex" hungry, sleepy, cross, or despondent. (Alcott, *Little Women* 268)

Despite the disclaimer that Jo did not consider herself a "genius" (265), this passage exemplifies the inspired state. The expression "fall into a vortex" suggests passivity (Stadler 112, 113), surrender to a force involving both violent exterior power and a still interior. Because the vortex is a violent possessing "Other," Jo can only exorcise herself by finishing the work. In contrast, at the still core, Jo "led a blissful life unconscious of want, care, or bad weather." Jo embraces this paradox. Because her private Eden contains spiritual elements, she absorbs the "divine afflatus" and abjures temporal concerns such as food and sleep. Because the vortex implies a sexual component associated with a fall, she works with "entire abandon."[8]

At the same time, this passage's language betrays ambivalence regarding the inspired state. Described as a "fit" and an attack, writing approximates disease. Indeed, Alcott describes intimacy with imaginary friends as productive of an antisocial crossness that could alienate one's own family.[9] In contrast, in 1863, she states that "I hope success will sweeten me and make me what I long to become more than a great writer—a good daughter" (Alcott, *Selected* 258). Abandonment to an eroticized inwardness might produce Eden, but its joy is short-lived, its moral result deleterious.

Alcott makes the anti-social implications of pursuing literature clear through several incidents in *Little Women*. In the chapter "Jo Meets Apollyon," the aspiring author, harboring a grudge after Amy burned her manuscript, deliberately fails to warn her sister of thin ice on the river. In the chapter "Little Faithful," Jo becomes so absorbed in reading a story that she neglects to accompany Beth on a charity visit to the Hummels. Amy survives a near-drowning to teach Jo a valuable lesson in patience and forgiveness, but Beth, visiting the Hummels alone, contracts the disease that will eventually lead to her death. In this way, Alcott shows that literature is not only an exalted calling, but a hunger that can encourage a selfishness that is every bit as harmful as starting a melodramatic holocaust.

Reconcilements

What then, if anything, can be done to redeem the concept of authorship? This article has demonstrated the anxiety Hawthorne and Alcott felt over genius's amoral origins. Believing that dedication to art encourages a passion that may be inimical to morality and social life, the two authors face the task of employing their fictional artists to explore approaches that might reconcile creativity to the needs of their communities.

Here one must understand the cult of domesticity that coexisted with the ethos supporting genius. Ann Douglas describes the former in *The Feminization of American Culture* when she relates how women were expected to embody Christ (128), to represent what Rosemary Ruether calls the passive Christian virtues of "sacrificial love, servanthood, [and] altruism" (*Nineteenth* ix). Expected to redeem men and children's "immortal minds," the Christian wife was considered the "true woman," the "angel in the house" (Welter 20, 21). The moral head of the family, she emphasized compassion rather than a sense of guilt, emotion rather than reason.

With its emphasis on spiritual values, the cult of domesticity shared common ground with the cult of genius. However, where the Dionysian tradition retained its emphasis on passion and extraordinary experience, domesticity stressed meek passivity and the value of the quotidian. Furthermore, while romantic belief in originality tended to laud the inspired male, the religion of the heart extended its values to all humanity. The true woman might be temporarily consigned to a "separate sphere," but she expected maternal values would eventually govern society. Genius tended to celebrate men, self-reliance, and isolation—it could be "pathological" (Stadler xv). Domesticity, refining the quintessential Christian virtues, sought to civilize all.

Hawthorne was himself associated with domesticity. In the 1843 sketch "Fire-Worship," Hawthorne displays his allegiance:

> Wisely were the Altar and the Hearth conjoined in one mighty sentence! For the hearth, too, had its kindred sanctity. Religion sat down beside it, not in the priestly robes which decorated, and perhaps disguised, her at the altar, but arrayed in a simple matron's garb, and uttering her lessons with the tenderness of a mother's voice and heart. The holy Hearth! (*Tales* 848)

The altar and the hearth provide alternative venues for religion. Surprisingly, domesticity is, in some respects, superior: church robes "decorate" and perhaps "disguise"—a matron's garb is always simple; her lessons touch the heart. "Conjoined" with the altar "in one mighty sentence," the hearth takes on the day-to-day labor of salvation.

Alcott's conception of domesticity mirrors Hawthorne's. Marmee in *Little Women*, a character modeled on her own mother, Abba, could serve as the embodiment of "Fire Worship's" "simple matron." After her anger nearly causes Amy's death, Jo comprehends the wisdom of Marmee's teachings:

Jo's only answer was to hold her mother close, and, in the silence which followed, the sincerest prayer she had ever prayed left her heart, without words; for in that sad, yet happy hour, she had learned not only the bitterness of remorse and despair, but the sweetness of self-denial and self-control; and, led by her mother's hand, she had drawn nearer to the Friend who welcomes every child with a love stronger than that of any father, tenderer than that of any mother. (Alcott, *Little Women* 81–82)

Her mother teaches Jo the pre-eminent Christian virtues of self-denial and self-control and draws her close to Christ Himself. Hawthorne's matron taught in a clearer manner than a "disguised" religion; Marmee replaces Father March, her absent minister-husband. Indeed, as Christine Doyle observes, Alcott sees the perfect society as a blend of the Victorian family and a utopian community with a matriarch at its core (*Transatlantic* 130, 131). At once the principle supporter of a traditional faith and the spokesperson for its alternative, Alcott's matriarch possesses all the authority of "the altar."

The first, partially successful approach at justifying authorship, attempts a compromise between the values of genius and hearth. Frequently, this occurs through the influence of a household angel who "tames" the artist's "rage." An example of this occurs in Hawthorne's *The Marble Faun* with the relationship between the sculptor Kenyon and the virginal Hilda: "Kenyon's genius, unconsciously wrought upon by Hilda's influence, took a more delicate character than heretofore. He modeled, among other things, a beautiful little statue of Maidenhood, gathering a Snow-drop" (Hawthorne, *Novels* 1164). Kenyon displays "genius": he is inspired but restrained. His work is all about innocence and springtime; corresponding with Hilda, it is so "airy" and impermanent that it is never put into immortal marble. It is blameless work.

Similarly, in *Little Women* and "Psyche's Art," Alcott depicts the protagonists' vortex as spiritualized by an angelic sister's death. In the latter, Psyche's work is conceived as possessing "power," Alcott's synonym for genius. At the same time, Psyche herself becomes beautiful, through observing duty, a model and inspiration for the sculptor Paul Gage's statue of Eve. And Psyche becomes "rich in the art" that makes life rich for others—domesticity itself becomes a means for duty and art to coexist. The better Psyche behaves, the better her art will be.

Something is lost here. The fire of the muse, the sheer power of genius resists compromise. Art touched by the domestic can seem delicate and diminutive. Yet it should be remembered that these two authors' masterpieces, *The Scarlet Letter* and *Little Women*, are themselves domestic works. Fire remains fire even if confined within a hearth. The source of Kenyon's inspiration continues to be a subtle eroticism (he is in love with Hilda). Alcott describes her artist inspired by the flame of love rather than the anarchy of her thrillers.

At one point in *The Feminization of American Culture,* Douglas states that "Lyman (Beecher) and Harriet (Beecher Stowe) grasped the essential Calvinist truth that Melville understood so well: that sin itself is the sublime, and only its enormity puts men on speaking terms with God" (245). It is this viewpoint that underlies Hawthorne and Alcott's second attempt at humanizing authorship, their employment of the idea of the fortunate fall. This is a theological concept that a greater good occurs through the existence of sin than would have been possible without a fall, as the loss of Adam and Eve's innocence is surpassed by the greater good of Christ's incarnation. Adapting the concept of the fall to the aesthetic realm, Hawthorne and Alcott's fiction indicate that the experience of an eroticized, irrational force may be symbolically linked to the illicit eating of the fruit of knowledge. According to them, the power so generated contributes to the artwork's effect. Not surprisingly, this principle applies to men: Kenyon describes his achievement of molding an inimitable model of Cleopatra as "kind(ling) a great fire within my mind, and (throwing) in the material—as Aaron threw the gold of the Israelites into the furnace—and, in the midmost heat, uprose Cleopatra, as you see her" (Hawthorne, *Novels* 958). Aaron's act of forging the golden calf is idolatrous, and Kenyon may be seen as idolizing his own art. Yet the result of this "fall" is a masterpiece.

In Alcott's novel *A Modern Mephistopheles*, the genius and writer, Jasper Helwyze, is figured as both Satan and the demonic Chillingworth from *The Scarlet Letter.* Helwyze utilizes the innocent young girl Gladys as an inspiring muse, an action that Gladys resists, refusing to wear a bracelet depicting the nine Muses. Helwyze's poem is powerful and tragic, the work of a genius, but enabled by his heartless prying into the psychology of others. It is fallen work.

More surprising, given the period's emphasis on female saintliness, fallenness may also be pertinent for women's creativity. A passion born of transgression inspires Hester Pyrnne's embroidery; her needlework "might have been a mode of expressing, and therefore soothing, the passion of her life" (Hawthorne, *Novels* 190). That needlework is gorgeous and overwrought, parallel to Hester's own passionate nature. Her sin enables her art, deepens it, even as it monetarily sustains her physical existence.

In Alcott's novel *A Modern Mephistopheles*, the virginal Gladys is notable for her cheerful songs and needlework. She becomes an inspired singer when she unknowingly imbibes hashish. Her subsequent performance as Elaine in an Arthurian tableau is impassioned, ending with the shriek, "let me die." Its overall effect is powerful but mixed: her songs terrify her husband and sexually excite him. Fallen without being fallen, Gladys performs her songs as an original genius.

The artist's "fall" may synthesize the power of genius with domesticity's communalism. Hester's embroidery serves a sacerdotal purpose: it invests clerical and government vestures with dignity, power, and sacredness. Gladys' erotic performance effects the true consummation of her marriage; she becomes a saintly mother. The authors, however, retain moral reservations regarding passionate abandon. Reflecting one aspect of Hawthorne's thinking, Hilda praises the murderer Donatello's bust as "the Faun advancing towards a state of higher development" (*Novels* 1169), but condemns Kenyon's belief that sin may be "an element of human education" (1236). As sin and inspiration are commingled in *The Marble Faun*, this bodes ill for a certain type of art. The *felix culpa* might be a fitting subject for a sculpture, but personal adoption of its principles is forbidden. Similarly, though Helwyze's inspired metrical tragedy makes its "dramatic point" with the death of the hero, Gladys perceives that the "moral point" would be lost if the hero does not live and reform his life. Her suggestion that the heroine die in his stead (which is her ultimate fate) shows the primacy of the domestic virtues.

Indeed, examination of the two authors' female artists reveals a more extreme withdrawal from passionate experience's moral implications. For all its power, Hester's work reveals an immoderate, inharmonious nature that affects her art's symmetry. Gladys's intentions are pure, her song perfect, but her capacity for eroticized abandon does not satisfy Alcott. Recasting the girl as a selfless victim and Madonna-like figure, the author expiates sexuality by having Gladys die in childbirth.

There is a double standard here, then, as these authors accord the male artist greater freedom to experience the reality of sin. An explanation of this contradiction might begin with the fact that both Hawthorne and Alcott, to some extent, share their culture's expectations that women be selfless angels, the redeemers of men. In her domestic fiction, Alcott pushes this concept still further by indicating that among the many forms of catalyzing loss (loss of innocence through sin and experience, for example), the most morally efficacious is grief. Experiencing a deepening of character through sorrow, heroines such as Psyche, Diana from *Diana and Persis,* and Jo are all inspired to create a more impressive art.

Hawthorne's situation is somewhat different, according to his own accounts. In "The Custom-House," he indirectly accepts the principle of the artist's "fall." For the narrator's donning of the scarlet emblem signals an embrace of both Dimmesdale's institutional authority and Hester's rebelliousness. Fallen by analogy, the author, for once, fully authorizes his imagination. Allowing Dionysian energy to pervade his work, he achieves the kind of power that can send his genteel wife to bed sick "with a grievous headache" (Hawthorne, *Letters* 311) when she hears *The Scarlet Letter* read aloud.

While Hawthorne has a partner prone to worship him, Alcott must accommodate her moralistic father Bronson, a figure represented in the censorious aspects of both Father March and Professor Bhaer. Moreover, both her publisher and fans desirous of "happy marriages" expect her plots to soothe rather than stimulate. To allay them, Alcott curtails the creative aspirations of Jo, the figure most resembling herself. In so doing, she, unlike Hawthorne, applies the general prohibition against the aesthetic fall to herself and internalizes her father's and her culture's morality. This has a mixed effect on Alcott's fiction: where Hawthorne in his prime possesses the inner assurance to attempt a masterpiece (Baym 107), the author of *Little Women* distrusts her own "vortex." This ambivalence explains much of the enduring interest of the March trilogy. In *Jo's Boys*, having transformed her double Jo into a tamed (though feisty) "domestic angel," the author feels the impulse to destroy her in an earthquake. Tired of the self she has become, Alcott can no longer bear the sight of her fictional image even as Jo, in a feminist gesture, returns to writing.

A third means of validating genius and authorship is the path of temporary transcendence extolled by Margaret Fuller. Here, the woman forsakes early marriage in order to develop the powers of analysis needed to balance her innate sense of intuition. Potentially a genius herself (though Fuller sees a greater female propensity for *inspiring* genius), the mature woman can form a true egalitarian union (19). Hawthorne seems to disagree with this progressive approach. In Hilda, he depicts a celibacy that leads to artistic sterility. Writing of his wife Sophia's career, or lack thereof, he declares it improper for a woman to strive for both artistic accomplishment and domesticity. Alcott, in contrast, embraces Fuller's teachings (see Rigsby 109). Early in *Diana and Persis,* unions of equals seem almost fairy-tale like, in Diana's reaction to Persis's ideal marriage, for example (Alcott 425). Later, she does retain hope, visualizing a European situation in which the female artist Diana produces work that may be *improved* by an egalitarian relationship with a male sculptor (Boyd 114–116). Such a situation is not possible in America, however. And maybe not at all. *Diana and Persis* is unfinished. How

Alcott would have resolved her protagonist's relationships with her love of art is uncertain.

Hopeful, yet unclear on whether these women achieve genius, Alcott reserves her greatest enthusiasm for the joining of woman to woman (Stadler 126). This replaces the old system of mentor and student that Alcott saw resulting in an abuse of the female follower by the teacher.[10] Whether in supportive bands of sisters (as in *Work* and *Diana and Persis*) or in a Boston marriage (*An Old-Fashioned Girl*), Alcott foresees individuals who combine power and wisdom with tenderness. While Hawthorne does portray female friendship in his rendering of Zenobia and Priscilla, Miriam and Hilda, he perceives such unions as imperfect and temporary. He is sympathetic to women's plight, but he believes in neither reforms that could ameliorate it nor new modes of living. Where Alcott hopes to satisfy the demands of genius and domesticity by changing the latter's conditions, Hawthorne perceives them as universal and largely immutable.

Despite their suspicions about genius, both authors wanted to be a genius and to lessen its amoral effects. Fear of genius gives way to a belief that inspiration may be purified and that the authors' characters may successfully serve the hearth. Mere sinfulness, in turn, is replaced by an aesthetic, fortunate fall, inexperience by a celibate apprenticeship. All of these developments complicate the authors' relationship to Common Sense philosophy as it comes into contact with Romanticism. Drawn back to Concord, Alcott interrogates her roots, while Hawthorne takes the measure of his adopted town. Alarmed by their vocation, they negotiate a way to continue writing and find redemption. Through their fiction, they validate their work and their lives. Through their writing, they find a way home.

Notes

1. Bell, for example, discusses how Harry Levin, Paul Elmer More, and Austin Warren each emphasize Hawthorne's Puritanism (26–27).

2. See, for example, the essays by Ednah Cheney, G. K. Chesterton, Cornelia Meigs, and Edward Wagenknecht in Madeleine Stern's *Critical Essays on Louisa May Alcott*.

3. See Person and Erlich, among others.

4. Reynolds' *Beneath the American Renaissance* (249–274, 407–409) chronicles both writers' transformation of pulp fiction.

5. Johnson also notes interesting points of connection between the novelists (113).

6. In addition, Bevan explores the authors' fictional treatment of families; Chapman compares *The Blithedale Romance* and *A Modern Mephistopheles* (167); and Van Buren links Alcott's dark heroines to Hester and Zenobia (291).

7. Doyle notes that women of Alcott's generation often saw the conflict between artists and professional writers through notions of "talent" and "genius" (19).

8. Saxton, Michie, and Showalter have all noted the sexual connotations of Jo's fall into the vortex. In this context, the girl's "fall" suggests a relationship between transgression, sexuality, and art.

9. A February 13, 1882 letter to Mary Mapes Dodge reveals how Alcott feared that composition would make her "fractious as a teething child" (*Selected Letters* 209).

10. Barker observes that Yorke in "The Marble Woman" takes his pupil Cecil and transforms her into a repressed wife who can no longer create art. Barker also notes, however, that Diana and the male artist Stafford in *Diana and Persis* serve as equals whose presence inspires the other (97).

Works Cited

Abrams, M. H. *The Mirror and the Lamp: Romantic Theory and the Critical Tradition.* London: Oxford UP, 1953.

Alcott, Louisa May. *Alternative Alcott.* Ed. Elaine Showalter. New Brunswick: Rutgers UP, 1988.

_____. *A Double Life: Newly Discovered Thrillers of Louisa May Alcott.* Ed. Madeleine B. Stern, Joel Myerson, and Daniel Shealy. Boston: Little, Brown, 1988.

_____. *The Journals of Louisa May Alcott.* Eds. Joel Myerson, Daniel Shealy, and Madeleine B. Stern. Boston: Little, Brown, 1989.

_____. *Little Women.* Ed. Elaine Showalter. 1868. New York: Penguin, 1989.

_____. *A Modern Mephistopheles and Taming a Tartar.* Ed. Madeleine B. Stern. New York: Praeger, 1987.

_____. *Plots and Counterplots: More Unknown Thrillers of Louisa May Alcott.* Ed. Madeleine B. Stern. New York: Morrow, 1976.

_____. *Selected Letters of Louisa May Alcott.* Eds. Joel Myerson, Daniel Shealy, and Madeleine B. Stern. Boston: Little, Brown, 1987.

Barker, Deborah. *Aesthetics and Gender in American Literature.* Lewisburg: Bucknell UP, 2000.

Baym, Nina. "Revisiting Hawthorne's Feminism." *Hawthorne and the Real: Bicentennial Essays.* Ed. Millicent Bell. Columbus: Ohio State UP, 2005. 107–124.

Bell, Millicent. "Introduction." *New Essays on Hawthorne's Major Tales.* Ed. Millicent Bell. Cambridge: Cambridge UP, 1993. 1–35.

_____. *Hawthorne's View of the Artist.* New York: SUNY P, 1962.

Bevan, Ellen Sternberg. "Family Matters: The Fiction of Hawthorne, Alcott, and James." Diss. U. of Rochester, 1991.

Blackburn, William. "'Moral Pap for the Young'? A New Look at Louisa May Alcott's *Little Men.*" *Proceedings of the Seventh Annual Conference of the Children's Literature Association.* New Rochelle, NY: Dept. of English, Iona C., 1982. 98–106.

Boyd, Anne E. *Writing for Immortality: Women and the Emergence of High Literary Culture in America.* Baltimore, MD: Johns Hopkins UP, 2004.

Chapman, Mary. "'Living Pictures': Women and *Tableaux Vivants* in Nineteenth-Century Fiction and Culture." Diss. Cornell U, 1993.

De Shazer, Mary K. *Inspiring Women: Reimagining the Muse.* New York: Pergamon, 1986.

Douglas, Ann. *The Feminization of American Culture.* 1977. New York: Anchor Doubleday, 1988.

Doyle, Christine. *Louisa May Alcott and Charlotte Brontë: Transatlantic Translations.* Knoxville: U of Tennessee P, 2000.

Erlich, Gloria. *Family Themes and Hawthorne's Fiction: The Tenacious Web.* New Brunswick: Rutgers UP, 1984.

Fuller, Margaret. *Woman in the Nineteenth Century.* 1855. New York: Norton, 1971.

Hawthorne, Nathaniel. *The Letters 1843–1853. The Centenary Edition of the Works of Nathaniel Hawthorne.* Vol. XVI. Gen. Eds. William Charvat, Roy Harvey Pearce, Claude M. Simpson, and Thomas Woodson. Columbus: Ohio State UP, 1985.

_____. *Novels.* New York: Library of America, 1983.

_____. *Tales and Sketches.* New York: Library of America, 1982.

Herbert, T. Walter. *Dearest Beloved: The Hawthornes and the Making of the Middle Class Family.* Berkeley: U of California P, 1993.

Johnson, Claudia Durst. "Discord in Concord." *Hawthorne and Women: Engendering and Expanding the Hawthorne Tradition.* Eds. John L. Idol, Jr. and Melinda M. Ponder. Amherst: U of Massachusetts P, 1999. 104–120.

Kelley, Mary. *Private Woman, Public Stage: Literary Domesticity in Nineteenth-Century America.* New York: Oxford UP, 1984.

Keyser, Elizabeth Lennox. *Whispers in the Dark: the Fiction of Louisa May Alcott.* Knoxville: U of Tennessee P, 1993.

Martin, Terence. *The Instructed Vision: Scottish Common Sense Philosophy and the Origins of American Fiction.* Bloomington: U of Indiana P, 1961.

Michie, Helena. *The Flesh Made Word: Female Figures and Women's Bodies.* New York: Oxford UP, 1987.

Noble, Marianne. "Sentimental Epistemologies in *Uncle Tom's Cabin* and *The House of the Seven Gables.*" *Separate Spheres No More: Gender Convergence in American Literature 1830–1930.* Ed. Monika Elbert. Tuscaloosa: U of Alabama P, 2000. 261-281.

Person, Leland. *Aesthetic Headaches: Women and a Masculine Poetics in Poe, Melville, and Hawthorne.* Athens, GA: U of Georgia P, 1988.

Pfister, Joel. *The Production of Personal Life: Class, Gender, and the Psychological in Hawthorne's Fiction.* Stanford, CA: Stanford UP, 1991.

Ruether, Rosemary Radford, and Rosemary Skinner Keller, eds. *The Nineteenth Century, Women and Religion in America.* Vol. 1. San Francisco: Harper, 1981.

Reynolds, David. *Beneath the American Renaissance: The Subversive Imagination in the Age of Emerson and Melville.* Cambridge, MA: Harvard UP, 1988.

Rigsby, Mary. "So Like Women: Louisa May Alcott's *Work* and the Ideology of Relations." *Redefining the Political Novel: American Women Writers 1797–1901.* Ed. Sharon M. Harris. Knoxville: U of Tennessee P, 1995. 109–127.

Saxton, Martha. *Louisa May: A Modern Biography of Louisa May Alcott.* Boston: Houghton Mifflin, 1977.

Showalter, Elaine. "Introduction." *Little Women.* 1868. New York: Penguin, 1989. vii–xxviii.

Stadler, Gustavus. *Troubling Minds: The Cultural Politics of Genius in the United States, 1840–1890.* Minneapolis: U of Minnesota P, 2006.

Stock, R. D. *The Flutes of Dionysus: Daemonic Enthrallment in Literature.* Lincoln: U of Nebraska P, 1989.

Tigerstedt, Eugene Napoleon. *Plato's Idea of Poetical Inspiration.* Helsinki, FI: Centraltryckeriet, 1969.

Van Buren, Jane. "Louisa May Alcott: A Study in Persona." *Psychohistory Review* 9 (1981): 282–99.

Welter, Barbara. *Dimity Convictions: The American Woman in the Nineteenth Century.* Athens: Ohio UP, 1976.

Alcott and the Work of Nursing_____

Emily Waples

In the final chapter of *Woman's Work in the Civil War*—an 1867 account of the efforts of noteworthy women like Dorothea Dix and Clara Barton and the collective service of ladies' aid societies—a "Miss Louise [*sic*] M. Alcott, of Concord, Mass" is numbered among the "Faithful But Less Conspicuous Laborers."[1] Under the shadow of illustrious figures like Dix, Alcott's work as a Union Army nurse was inconspicuous; her tenure at the Union Hotel Hospital in Washington, D.C., lasted only six weeks and was truncated when she contracted typhoid, the treatment for which—involving mercury— would weaken her for the rest of her life. However, her fictionalized account of her wartime experience, *Hospital Sketches*—serialized in Boston's abolitionist newspaper *The Commonwealth* in May and June 1863 and published as a single volume that same year— brought conspicuous attention to Civil War nurses, doctors, and their relations with patients. Upon its republication in 1869, one reviewer predicted that Alcott's *Sketches* would "retain the first place among the memorabilia of these times" (qtd. in Clark 19).

This essay addresses a fundamental tension in *Hospital Sketches*: Alcott's presentation of Civil War nursing as, on the one hand, an exercise in feminine sentiment and sympathy, as it was commonly conceived in the nineteenth-century popular imagination, and, on the other, as prosaic and drudging labor: an extension of the often-taxing domestic duties typically assigned to nineteenth-century women. An analysis of *Hospital Sketches'* most pervasive analogical tropes—nurses as mothers, soldiers as children, soldiers as domestic objects, and doctors as housewives—shows how Alcott upends essentialized gender identities and obligations, revising sentimental depictions of women's wartime contributions by drawing attention to the exacting and enervating *work* of nursing. Complicating the dichotomized view of female nurses as sympathetic caregivers and male doctors as dispassionate scientists, *Hospital Sketches* illustrates how both nurses and doctors mediate emotional and professional "duties" as they negotiate their relationships to patients. Through her narrative persona, Nurse Tribulation Periwinkle, Alcott critiques the gendered associations of "work" in the nineteenth century, while simultaneously exposing women's invisible labor in the domestic sphere.

By the time the thirty-year-old Alcott embarked upon her assignment as an army nurse, she had developed an expansive understanding of the practical and psychological importance of work. As a child, she had been an unwitting participant in her philosopher-father's ill-fated utopian experiment, Fruitlands, which eschewed a more quotidian definition of "work" in favor of "aesthetic labor," a system that encouraged community members to perform pleasurable tasks to which they were ideally suited. As Alcott would later illustrate in her satirical sketch "Transcendental Wild Oats," the ultimate failure of Fruitlands exposed the necessity of difficult and unpleasant work—work that was often the province of women. Indeed, it was Alcott's mother Abba who supported the family through sewing.[2] Heartened by the example of her long-suffering mother—to whom she would dedicate her aptly-titled 1873 novel *Work*—Alcott aspired to become "a truly good and useful woman," as she wrote at sixteen. Of course, this hunger for industry took its toll; in nearly the same breath, she confessed to being "so tired I don't want to live, only," she added, "it's cowardly to die till you have done something" (Alcott, *Journals* 62).

This persistent drive to "do something" remains an animating force in much of Alcott's writing. "When I was eighteen I wanted something to do," she recalled in her 1874 autobiographical narrative "How I Went Out to Service" (350); yet her demoralizing experience of domestic labor illustrates the ways such occupations remained unsatisfactory outlets for women's energies.[3] Alcott's acute desire for "usefulness" could find expression only within a limited range of occupations available to American women: housekeeping; sewing; teaching; nursing; and, eventually, writing. Throughout her life, Alcott reflected upon these various careers with equal parts exultation and exhaustion. "Sewing won't make my fortune," she noted in 1856, "but I can plan my stories while I work, and then scribble 'em down on Sundays"; nine months later, she complained of feeling "rather tired of living like a spider—spinning my brains out for money" (*Journals* 78, 81). In October 1858, her eagerness for industry was rekindled when she attended a sermon by the Reverend Theodore Parker on the topic of "Laborious Young Women."[4] It was, Alcott asserted, "[j]ust what [she] needed." Taking to heart Parker's advice to "accept the humblest work till you can find the task you want,'" Alcott came to see "work of head and hand" as "my salvation when disappointment of weariness burden and darken my soul" (*Journals* 90–91).

For one who professed to "dread debt more than the devil" (*Journals* 158), work indeed supplied an economic "salvation" for Alcott and the family who depended upon her efforts in the marketplace. Beyond its practical rewards, though, as Alcott realized, work offered the possibilities of more self-reliant lives for women who "wanted something to do." Alcott's alter-ego Tribulation Periwinkle crystallizes her desire in the opening line of *Hospital Sketches*: "I want something to do" (4). But if Alcott crafted "Trib" as "a fictional example of Reverend Parker's sermons," as Sarah Elbert suggests (165), the figure of the industrious spinster as embodied in Nurse Periwinkle is simultaneously exemplary and cautionary. While *Little Women*'s Marmee would extol the manifold virtues of women's work—"Work is wholesome," she insists, "and there is plenty for everyone; it keeps us from ennui and mischief, is good for health and spirits, and gives us a sense of power and independence better than money or fashion" (129)—Nurse Periwinkle exposes its underside. Like Alcott, Trib falls ill as a result of her hospital work; like Alcott, she negotiates her ambition against the difficult realities produced by gender expectations. As we shall see, *Hospital Sketches* casts a critical eye toward popular valuations of women's labor as it explores the nineteenth-century pursuit of "something to do."

During the opening years of the Civil War, Alcott "[w]rote, read, sewed, and wanted something to do." From her family's home in Concord, she set to work "sewing and knitting for 'our boys' all the time"—activities that, to Alcott, seemed to pale in comparison

---

to the efforts of "our boys": "I long to be a man," she admitted, "but as I can't fight, I will content myself with working for those who can." Organizations like the U.S. Sanitary Commission mobilized women's efforts on the home front with such success that Alcott teased, "[i]t seems as if a few energetic women could carry on the war better than the men do it so far" (*Journals* 105–106).[5] As the war progressed, certain "energetic women"—white, unmarried, and over thirty—were recruited, under the supervision of Dorothea Dix, to work directly for the Union cause as army nurses. In late 1862, Alcott set down needle and thread and embarked for Washington to join their ranks.

"I never began a year in a stranger place than this," she wrote from Georgetown in January 1863; "five hundred miles from home, alone among strangers, doing painful duties all day long, & leading a life of constant excitement in this greathouse surrounded by 3 or 4 hundred men in all stages of suffering, disease, and death." While Alcott's "trying ... situation" was tempered by a sense of satisfaction "comforting tending & cheering these poor souls who seem to love me," the reality of "doing painful duties all day long" nevertheless proved tiresome (*Journals* 113). Wrote the "worn out" Alcott:

I trot, trot, giving out rations, cutting up food for helpless 'boys,' washing faces, teaching my attendants how beds are made or floors swept, dressing wounds, taking Dr. Fitz Patrick's orders (privately wishing all the time that he would be more gentle with my big babies), dusting tables, sewing bandages, keeping my tray tidy, rushing up & down after pillows, bed linen, sponges, books & directions, till it seems as if I would joyfully pay down all I possess for fifteen minutes rest. (114)

Had Alcott harbored any high-flown ideas about her new occupation, the reality of its quotidian tasks—washing, dusting, sewing— must have smacked discomfitingly of the kind of domestic labor to which she was already accustomed; as historian Stewart Brooks has bluntly claimed, nineteenth-century nursing "was just about on the same par as scrubbing floors" (55). But if *Hospital Sketches* shows that nursing is a species of housekeeping, it also illustrates that housekeeping—in the words of *Little Women*'s housekeeper, Hannah— "ain't no joke" (122).

The association of women and housework solidified in the American popular imagination in the mid-nineteenth century, as the rise of "separate spheres" ideology posited the household as a feminized space apart from the capitalist marketplace. As Ruth Schwartz Cowan has explained, the "separate spheres" paradigm invested the American home with "a particular emotional tone, 'warmth' ... a particular public stance, 'morality'; and ... a particular form of behavior, 'passivity,'" while, conversely, "'work' became associated with 'men,' 'hardheartedness,' 'excitement,' 'aggression' and 'immorality'" (18–19). In turn, as critics like Gillian Brown have observed, the realities of domestic labor were often erased or disguised by the rhetoric of sentimental Transcendentalism. Ralph Waldo Emerson, for instance, argued for a kind of spiritual transmutation of labor: "Let the great soul incarnated in some woman's form," he intoned, "go out to service, and sweep chambers and scour floors...[and] to sweep and scour will instantly appear supreme and beautiful actions" (93).[6] Of course, as Bronson Alcott's ill-fated Fruitlands experiment had shown, the elevation of labor to the realm "supreme and beautiful" did not necessarily have any bearing on one's aptitude or alacrity for performing it, leading to the community's reputation as "a place where Mr. Alcott looked benign and talked philosophy, while Mrs. Alcott and the children did all the work" (qtd. in Sears 173).

The imaginative alliance of "woman's sphere" with its "particular emotional tone" is notably performed in the popular genre of the sentimental novel, which sought to effect change by eliciting emotional reactions from its readership; to note a famous example, in her conclusion to *Uncle Tom's Cabin* (1852), Harriet Beecher Stowe implores her readership to "*feel right*" in response to the moral wrongs of slavery (624). Nineteenth-century nurses were similarly expected to "*feel right*" by engaging in the kinds of sympathetic identification imagined to be the particular domain of their sex. Authors of popular domestic advice literature—like Catharine Beecher, for instance—counted nursing among the most essential of a woman's duties: "it is *woman* who should interest herself to secure such a comfort for the sick," wrote Beecher, "who are especially commended to her benevolent ministries" (214). According Dr. William Alcott—a cousin of Louisa May Alcott's father, Bronson—women's innate aptitude for caregiving ideally suited them for the profession of nursing. Dr. Alcott argued in an 1834 essay published in the *American Ladies' Magazine*, "females are better calculated, by nature and providence, for attending the sick than males," as:

> [t]hey have more fortitude in scenes of trial and distress; their manners and methods are more gentle; their devotion to whatever they undertake greater; their thoughts less engrossed by other objects, and especially the cares and presence of business; and what would seem to follow, their attention is more constant and unremitted. (W. A. A. 303)

If women were to augment this natural aggregate of hardiness, gentleness, and attentiveness with professional training, Alcott suggested, "[t]hey would thus have the pleasure of being employed, and, at the same time, of bestowing a charity"—and, he added, there was no small attraction in "the fact that they can be employed much cheaper" (W. A. A. 301).

During the American Civil War, the influx of women into nursing occasioned what historian Lori Ginzberg terms "the professionalism of benevolence": an institutionalization of the "benevolent ministries" that had hitherto been the domain of the domestic sphere (142).[7] But business and benevolence—what Dr. Alcott had identified as the dual opportunities of "being employed" and "bestowing a charity"—often proved difficult to reconcile, as nurses "came to epitomize the tension between the traditional emphasis on sentiment and womanly feeling on the one hand and the new values of the scientific care on the other" (143). In *Hospital Sketches,* Alcott exposes this central tension between the gendered territories of feminine sentiment and masculine science through a series of interchanges and reversals. Nurses, as Alcott illustrates with the brash and pragmatic Tribulation Periwinkle, are not necessarily naturally endowed with stores of benevolence simply by virtue of their sex. In fact, she suggests, the work of nursing at times requires the kind of affective detachment more commonly associated with the "scientific care" of surgeons. At the same time, the work of surgeons is not sacrosanct in its scientificity; characterized as "a little needle-work" (*Hospital Sketches* 51), for example, surgery is presented in terms the kind of domestic labor typically associated with women. Thus, Alcott shows, "home" and "work" are neither mutually exclusive nor essentially gendered categories.

Upon her arrival at "Hurly-burly House," Tribulation Periwinkle quickly learns that nursing "ain't no joke." Faced with a succession of trying and unromantic tasks—"washing faces, serving rations, giving medicine"— Trib assumes the role of a nurse who "suffered untold agonies, but concealed them under as matronly an aspect as a spinster could assume, and blundered through her trying labors with a Spartan firmness, which I hope they appreciated," she adds, "but am afraid they didn't." Trib not only flaunts associations of feminine benevolence by adopting a "Spartan firmness" in the face of these "trying labors," but disrupts sentimental expectations by admitting to a decidedly unladylike "taste for 'ghastliness'"— "for rheumatism wasn't heroic," she explains; "neither was liver complaint, or measles; even fever had lost its charms since 'bathing burning brows' had been used up in romances, real and ideal" (20). Avoiding the stale sentimental tropes that had hitherto been "used up in romances"—in the romanticized depictions of the war and its casualties, as well as in the sentimental fiction of Alcott's literary contemporaries—Trib aspires to the more "heroic" pursuit of unflinchingly facing battlefield gore.

With the arrival of casualties from Fredericksburg, Trib corrects her "most unpatriotic wish that I was safe at home again" (20) by reassessing her situation from a more dispassionate perspective; the sight of the wounded soldiers "admonished me that I was there to work, not to wonder or weep," she notes; "so I corked up my feelings, and returned to the path of duty" (21). Here, the newly-initiated Nurse Periwinkle delineates between the "work" of nursing and the "wondering" and "weeping" characteristic of nineteenth-century sentimental fiction. For authors like Stowe, the performance of civic duty depended upon the mobilization of emotion, "feeling right," but for Nurse Periwinkle, the "path of duty" instead demands that she "cork up" her feelings. She resists emotional response in order to render the practical work of nursing possible—in this case, washing soldiers' muddied and bloodied bodies in preparation for medical treatment. Although initially "staggered" by the suggestion of "scrub[bing] some dozen lords of creation," Nurse Periwinkle quickly reasons that "there was no time for nonsense": "I drowned my scruples in my wash-bowl, clutched my soap manfully, and, assuming a business-like air, made a dab at the first dirty specimen I saw, bent on performing my task *vi et armis* if necessary." Armed with the quotidian accoutrements of domestic labor, she approaches her soiled "specimen[s]" and "scrub[s] away like any tidy parent on a Saturday night" (22).

Assigning Nurse Periwinkle the role of "tidy parent," Alcott appeals to the familiar figuration of nurse-as-mother that circulated in contemporary accounts of women's war efforts.[8] However, rather than mobilizing the image of the mother for its suggestions of sentimental tenderness, Alcott invokes another set of associations, presenting the mother as the "business-like" household manager who admits "no time for nonsense." Nurse Periwinkle not only de-sexualizes, but de-humanizes—and accordingly de-sentimentalizes—the scene of soldiers' bodies by objectifying them as "dirty specimen[s]." By the time she reports "[h]aving done up our human wash, and laid it out to dry" (25), the reader realizes that, in Nurse Periwinkle's performance as "tidy parent," the wounded soldiers have played the role not of "sleepy children," but of soiled laundry.

If criticism of nineteenth-century women's writing is often plagued by an "unremarked elision between *sentimental* and *domestic*" (231), as June Howard has observed, Alcott aptly illustrates here that the rhetoric of *domesticity* need not invoke associations of *sentimentality*. In this sketch, domestic imagery serves to signify not Nurse Periwinkle's emotional attachment to, but rather her pragmatic detachment from, the scene of suffering. Trib thus assimilates the blood, dirt, disease, and death of the Civil War into a paradigm of domesticity that is as much about unpleasant and alienating labor as it is about sympathetic tenderness. In this way, Nurse Periwinkle's vision of hospital work aligns, at least initially, with that of the resident surgeon, Dr. P.—who, she explains, "seemed to regard a dilapidated body very much as I should have regarded a damaged garment." Envisioning Dr. P. as "a very unpleasant looking housewife, cutting, sawing, patching and piecing, with the enthusiasm of an accomplished surgical seamstress" (*Hospital Sketches* 28), Alcott unites the ideal of scientific objectivity with the gendered performance of domestic duty, exploiting a seemingly jarring disconnect between the objects of surgeons' labor (bodies) and seamstresses' (garments). While critics like Mary Cappello have argued that here, "[a] doctor's mending means something infinitely more important than that of nurse/seamstress" (68), we might alternatively read Alcott not as establishing a hierarchy of gendered labor, but as exposing the ways in doctors and nurses mutually participate in a kind of hospital housekeeping, "cutting, sawing, patching and piecing" in support of the Union cause.

Initially, Trib treats "feeling" as an impediment to "the path of duty." In her treatment of the Fredericksburg causalities, she appears a far cry from the ideal nurse Florence Nightingale described in in her influential *Notes on Nursing* (1860): "a woman of delicate and decent feeling" (182). She comes to understand, however, that for the nurse, "feeling" and "duty" cannot be ultimately separated. For example, addressing the issue of whether "nurses are obliged to witness amputations and such matters, as a part of their duty," Trib illustrates the ways in which the "duties" of hospital labor are apportioned: "Our work begins afterward," she explains; "Then we must sooth and sustain, tend and watch" (Alcott, *Hospital Sketches* 69). As Trib increasingly realizes, to "sooth and sustain, tend and watch" is also to *work*.[9] She thus comes to re-evaluate the sentimental trope of "bathing burning brows," incorporating the unspoken obligations of affective engagement into her estimation of the work of nursing. No longer solely "human wash," the wounded soldiers eventually assume some sentimental signification for Nurse Periwinkle. She professes a "motherly affection for them all" (31), for instance, likening herself to "Rachel mourning for her children" (69) when they are discharged from her "little household" (68).

Trib's appeal to the kinds of sentimental rhetoric she has previously dismissed is most pronounced in her account of the death of John the blacksmith in the fourth sketch, "A Night"—a scene which, tellingly, garnered attention from contemporary reviewers who praised this "noble and touching" element of Alcott's text (qtd. in Clark 9).[10] In her presentation of John— "the manliest man" among her charges, who appears on his deathbed "like a little boy" (*Hospital Sketches* 41)—Alcott makes deliberate use of the "sentimental soldier" trope, a widely-recognizable Civil War-era literary figure that historian Alice Fahs says sought to "mak[e] sense of the bodily sacrifices of soldiers within an explicitly Christian framework" (Fahs 96). On the one hand, Alcott's invocation of the "sentimental soldier" helps render John's death legible for her readership.[11] On the other hand, Alcott's narrative exposes precisely how sentimentality functions as an expectation for, rather than an essential attribute of, the gendered work of nursing. While John's death might be cited as evidence of Alcott's mounting conformity to the generic demands of sentimentality, a careful analysis will illustrate that Nurse Periwinkle negotiates the expectation of gendered sentiment while simultaneously upholding what she sees as the nurse's principal responsibility for sober and composed service.

The task of informing John that he will die is laid upon Nurse Periwinkle because, Dr. P. explains, "women have a way of doing such things comfortably." Thus far, Nurse Periwinkle has demonstrated no special aptitude for gentleness, and yet, she confesses, "[t]he Doctor's words caused me to reproach myself with neglect, not of any real duty perhaps, but of those little cares and kindnesses that solace homesick spirits, and make the heavy hours pass easier" (39). Realizing that even the robust blacksmith "might long for the gentle tendance of a woman's hands, the sympathetic magnetism of a woman's presence," Nurse Periwinkle performs the expected office of her sex, comforting John "as if he had been a little child" (39). She comes to see herself from the perspective of the patient, who interprets her business-like resistance to sympathetic identification as a kind of neglect:

> To him, as to so many, I was the poor substitute for mother, wife, or sister, and in his eyes no stranger, but a friend who hitherto had seemed neglectful. This was changed now; and, through the tedious operation of probing, bathing, and dressing his wounds, he leaned against me, holding my hand fast, and, if pain wrung further tears from him, no one saw them fall but me. (39–40)

Trib's sympathetic offering, does not, to her mind, constitute "real duty." Instead, she comes to see such "little cares and kindnesses" as part of an ethic of care that augments rather than replaces what she understands to be the essential *work* of nursing: "the tedious operation of probing, bathing, and dressing his wounds." Such tasks are "tedious" not only for the patient on whom they are performed, she suggests, but for the nurse who performs them. To acknowledge the tedious realities of "real duty," however, is not to preclude the possibility of sympathetic engagement for the explicit sake of "mak[ing] the heavy hours pass easier." However, rather than reproducing the notion that this kind of "gentle tendance" is essentially a woman's function—as Dr. P. believes—Trib suggests that both nurses and doctors should strive to achieve this balance between practical "duty" and personal care. She critiques, for instance, Dr. P.'s "somewhat trying habit of regarding a man and his wound as separate institutions"—"which though no doubt entirely scientific," Trib concedes, "was rather startling than soothing, and highly objectionable as a means of preparing nerves for any fresh trial." If the "entirely scientific" approach to surgery consists of "whipping off legs like an animated guillotine" (70), Trib suggests, perhaps the "scientific" might benefit from a more harmonious relationship with the "soothing." Indeed, "the pleasures of contrast" are aptly illustrated by Dr. P.'s successor, Dr. Z.—a surgeon who, Trib suspects, "suffered more in giving pain than did his patients in enduring it, for he often paused to ask: 'Do I hurt you?'" (71). In short, Nurse Periwinkle espouses what might today be deemed a holistic approach to medical care: the view that sees "a man and his wound" not as "separate institutions," but as inseparable constituents of the human experience.

Ultimately, as a result of "a sharp tussle with typhoid" (60), Nurse Periwinkle is not just the purveyor, but the recipient of this kind of care, becoming a patient in the very hospital in which she has been employed. For critics like Cynthia Davis, Trib's (and Alcott's) contraction of typhoid speaks to "the empathy endemic to nursing," since "sympathy brought patients and healers so closely together that the latter could easily be exposed to devastating disease" (55). However, this precarious proximity is not simply a condition of sentiment; nurses would maintain physical closeness to their patients regardless of their emotional investment. Accordingly, nurses' vulnerability to disease might be read not simply as an extension of sympathetic exchange, but as an occupational hazard exacerbated by poor working conditions. As Alcott noted in her wartime journal, in spite of her best efforts to "keep well" at the hospital, "bad air, food, water, work & watching are getting to be too much for me" (*Journals* 115). Trib's sickness gestures toward the dangers of *over*work—a condition of which Alcott would become increasingly aware. Upon her return to Concord, Alcott admitted to being "[v]ery tired" and "full of pain from overwork"—a feeling that, reviewing her journals in 1876, she would grimly assess: "Too much work for one young woman," the older Alcott noted: "No wonder she broke down" (*Journals* 166).

Tellingly, Trib embarks upon her hospital duties "to be treated by [the surgeons] like a door-mat, a worm, or any other meek and lowly article, whose mission it is to be put down and walked upon; nurses being considered as mere servants, receiving the lowest pay, and, it's my private opinion," she adds, "doing the hardest work of any part of the army, except the mules" (71). Given her assertion that no one works harder "except the mules," it is significant that, as she observes carnivalesque environs of Washington from the window of her sickroom, she claims, "The mules were my especial delight" (55). Yet if Trib intimates an affinity between animal labor and her own, she also draws attention to the marginalized work of free black women, in whom she takes a strange kind of comfort:

"I liked their cheerfulness," she explains, "for the dreariest old hag, who scrubbed all day in that pestilential steam, gossiped and grinned all the way out, when night set her free from drudgery" (57).

Noting the ways in which domestic "drudgery" might be countered by "cheerfulness," Trib does not sentimentalize the work of "scrubb[ing] all day," but in fact calls explicit attention to both its toilsome nature and to the unsanitary conditions ("that pestilential steam") in which it is performed. At the same time—in anticipation of what the experienced matriarch of *Jo's Boys* would call "the satisfaction of a duty cheerfully performed" (645)—she expresses admiration for the ways in which these marginalized subjects find strategies for survival. Indeed, ever desirous of "something to do," Trib attempts to make what use of her convalescence she can: "Being forbidden to meddle with fleshly arms and legs," she notes, "I solaced myself by mending cotton ones" (54). Here, Alcott once again underscores the interchangeable nature of hospital labor; swapping wounded bodies for damaged garments, Nurse Periwinkle comes full circle to the kinds of work that women performed in both war and peace.

In *Hospital Sketches,* Alcott offers an alternative to sentimental depictions of nursing as an exercise in benevolence, one positioned in stark contrast to the serious and stoic work of surgeons. While both nurses and doctors must mediate emotional detachment and sympathetic care, their "real duty," Tribulation Periwinkle suggests, consists of trying, thankless, and prosaic labor. In this way, her trenchant assessment of the work of nursing also functions as critique of the invisible labor of nineteenth-century domestic sphere. Rather than dissociating women's work from the harsh realities of circumstance, *Hospital Sketches* incisively examines the multifaceted "path of duty" from the perspective of a heroine who resolves "not to wonder or to weep," but—for all its many meanings—"to work."

Notes

1. Brockett and Pierpont note that Alcott, "herself the author of a little book on 'Hospital Scenes,' as well as other works, was for some time an efficient nurse in one of the Washington hospitals" (793). When this text was amended for republication in 1888 under the title *Heroines of the Rebellion*, these "faithful but less conspicuous laborers" were excised.

2. For a discussion of "aesthetic labor" and its implications at Fruitlands, see Brown 108–110.

3. For additional analysis of Alcott's relationship to domestic service, see Maibor.

4. In his 1853 *Sermon on the Public Function of Woman*, Parker suggested that woman's work outside of the domestic sphere fell into in three categories: "Intellectual Pursuits," philanthropy, and "Practical Works." According to Parker, "the various Philanthropies of the age" were those self-abnegating services performed by "angels of mercy," like "Miss Dix, in our day" (10).

5. For an account of the U.S. Sanitary Commission, see Geisberg.

6. In his 1860 essay "Domestic Life," Emerson argues that to "put domestic service on another foundation" would be to "correct the whole system of our social living" (592).

7. For discussions of Civil War nursing, see Long, Shultz, Reverby, Wood, and Young.

8. For additional analysis of gendered rhetoric in *Hospital Sketches*, see Shultz and Young.

9. As Alcott illustrates in *Hospital Sketches*, the nurse's capacity for collectedness in the face of medical gore often surpasses that of men. For instance, when a soldier is instructed to hold a fellow patient's wounded arm during surgery, he "faint[s] quietly away," whereupon Trib assumes his task (70).

10. Brockett also elected to include this scene in his 1866 collection of Civil War narratives, praising the "graphic power" of Alcott's depiction of "the life, heroism, and death of some of our brave fellows, wounded in the struggle for the nation's life." "Among these descriptions of life and death in the hospital," Brockett contends, "none surpasses, in beauty and pathos, the story of John, the West Virginia Blacksmith" (304).

11. For further discussion of *Hospital Sketches* and Alcott's reading public, see Entel.

Works Cited

Alcott, Louisa May. *Hospital Sketches.* 1863. Mineola, NY: Dover, 2006.

_____. "How I Went Out to Service." 1874. *Alternative Alcott.* Ed. Elaine Showalter. New Brunswick: Rutgers UP, 1988. 350–363.

_____. *The Journals of Louisa May Alcott.* Eds. Joel Myerson, Daniel Shealy, and Madeleine B. Stern. Athens: U of Georgia P, 1997.

_____. *Little Women, Little Men,* and *Jo's Boys.* New York: Library of America, 2005.

Beecher, Catharine Esther. *Miss Beecher's Domestic Receipt-Book.* 3rd ed. New York: Harper, 1856.

Brockett, Linus Pierpont. *The Camp, the Battle Field, and the Hospital: Or, Lights and Shadows of the Great Rebellion.* Philadelphia: National Publishing Company, 1866.

Brockett, Linus Pierpont, and Mary C. Vaughn. *Woman's Work in the Civil War: A Record of Heroism, Patriotism and Patience.* Philadelphia: Ziegler, McCurdy, 1867.

Brooks, Stewart. *Civil War Medicine.* Springfield, MA: Charles C. Thomas, 1966.

Brown, Gillian. *Domestic Individualism: Imagining Self in Nineteenth-Century America.* Berkeley: U of California P, 1990.

Cappello, Mary. "'Looking About Me With All My Eyes': Censored Viewing, Carnival, and Louisa May Alcott's *Hospital Sketches.*" *Arizona Quarterly* 50.3 (Autumn 1994): 59–88.

Clark, Beverley Lyon, ed. *Louisa May Alcott: The Contemporary Reviews.* Cambridge: Cambridge UP, 2004.

Cowan, Ruth Schwartz. *More Work for Mother: The Ironies of Household Technology from the Open Hearth to the Microwave.* New York: Basic, 1983.

Davis, Cynthia J. *Bodily and Narrative Forms: The Influence of Medicine on American Literature, 1845–1915.* Stanford, CA: Stanford UP, 2000.

Elbert, Sarah. *A Hunger for Home: Louisa May Alcott's Place in American Culture.* Philadelphia: Temple UP, 1984.

Entel, Rebecca. "Writing 'En Masse': Louisa May Alcott's Civil War Experience and the *Commonwealth*." *American Periodicals* 24.1 (2014): 45–60.

Emerson, Ralph Waldo. "Domestic Life." *The Dial* [Cincinnati, OH] 1.10 (Oct. 1860): 585–602.

_____. "Spiritual Laws." 1841. *Essays: First and Second Series*. New York: Library of America, 2010. 75–93.

Fahs, Alice. *The Imagined Civil War: Popular Literature of the North and South, 1861–1865*. Chapel Hill: U of North Carolina P, 2001.

Howard, June. *Publishing the Family*. Durham, NC: Duke UP, 2001.

Geisberg, Judith Ann. *Civil War Sisterhood: The U.S. Sanitary Commission and Women's Politics in Transition*. Boston: Northeastern UP, 2000.

Ginzberg, Lori D. *Women and the Work of Benevolence: Morality, Politics, and Class in the Nineteenth-Century United States*. New Haven, CT: Yale UP, 1990.

Long, Lisa A. *Rehabilitating Bodies: Health, History, and the American Civil War*. Philadelphia: U of Pennsylvania P, 2004.

Maibor, Carolyn R. *Labor Pains: Emerson, Hawthorne, and Alcott on Work and the Woman Question*. New York: Routledge, 2004.

Nightingale, Florence. *Notes on Nursing: What It Is, and What It Is Not*. London: Harrison, 1860.

Parker, Theodore. *A Sermon on the Public Function of Woman, Preached at the Music Hall, March 27, 1853*. Boston: Robert F. Wallcut, 1853.

Reverby, Susan M. *Ordered to Care: The Dilemma of American Nursing, 1850–1945*. Cambridge, UK: Cambridge UP, 1987.

Sears, Clara Endicott. *Bronson Alcott's Fruitlands*. 1915. Bedford, MA: Applewood Books, 2004.

Shultz, Jane E. "Embattled Care: Narrative Authority in Louisa May Alcott's *Hospital Sketches*." *Legacy* 9.2 (1992): 104–118.

_____. *Women at the Front: Hospital Workers in Civil War America*. Chapel Hill, NC: U of North Carolina P, 2004.

Stowe, Harriet Beecher. *Uncle Tom's Cabin: or, Life among the Lowly*. 1854. Ed. Ann Douglas. New York: Penguin, 1981.

W. A. A. [William A. Alcott], "Female Attendance on the Sick." *American Ladies' Magazine* 7.7 (1834): 301–305.

Wood, Ann Douglas. "The War within a War: Women Nurses in the Union Army." *Civil War History* 18.3 (Sept. 1972): 197–212.

Young, Elizabeth. *Disarming the Nation: Women's Writing and the American Civil War.* Chicago: U of Chicago P, 1999.

_____. "A Wound of One's Own: Louisa May Alcott's Civil War Fiction." *American Quarterly* 48.3 (Sept. 1996): 439–474.

Louisa's Civil War

A. Waller Hastings

"What is the Civil War doing in the first volume of *Little Women*?" scholar John Limon asks (183). Insofar as the first half of *Little Women* is framed by two contrasting Christmases—that of 1861, with Mr. March's absence due to the conflict, and that of 1862, with his return—the war clearly provides the backdrop for this first, separately published, part of the novel. Daniel Shealy writes that the novel "gives readers an alternative Civil War novel, one that depicts the family on the home front" (37n2). Other critics, including Elizabeth Young and Alice Fahs, have also seen this part of the book as a "war novel," albeit one focused on the domestic, feminine experience of war (Fahs 1482). But the very domestic nature of *Little Women* highlighted by these critics militates against readers identifying it with the Civil War. The war is never specifically named; as Harriet Reisen notes, the war is simply "where the fighting was, a vague danger, far away" (266–267). The Marches' domestic arrangement seems to keep the actual experience of war on the home front at arm's length. It is not difficult to forget for chapters at a time that a war is going on.

In 1868, when she was persuaded by her publisher to write a "girls' book," Alcott famously decided to write about her and her sisters' "queer plays and experiences"; when the book turned out better than she expected, she recorded in her journal that it was "simple and true, for we really lived most of it" (*Journals* 166). And so it was, with this notable exception: rather than placing her adolescent experiences in their proper time (the later 1840s and early 1850s), she positions the novel during the first year of the war. As Limon claims, "The Civil War causes the farthest straying from autobiography in a book that claims to alter nothing essential but names" (183).

Critics have seen Alcott's decision to set the novel during the war as way of establishing a metaphor for the protagonist's personal conflicts, as well as her own. According to Judith Fetterley, "The Civil War is an obvious metaphor for internal conflict and its invocation as background to *Little Women* suggests the presence in the story of such conflict" (370). Jo and her three sisters must learn to sublimate their desires in the interest of becoming "little women." Achieving this goal requires the girls to accept their socially ordained position as subordinates to the men in their lives (376). From a significantly less feminist position, Limon similarly argues that the "looming absence" of the Civil War in *Little Women* reflects the need for Jo to become more realistic, to attain a sense of discipline (183). Sarah Elbert sees the novel as a retreat from Alcott's war-era literary works that directly engage with issues of slavery and racial reconciliation ("Reading" 45).

Is Alcott's decision to shift her story forward in time, a shift that necessarily creates a chronological disconnect between Alcott's life and those of her characters, truly a departure from the novel's autobiography, as Limon suggests? It is tempting to assume the setting as an attempt to make the story more "relevant" to a readership that, in 1868, had just come through the actual war—but can it be that simple? Is *Little Women* set during the war years to teach its heroine a lesson that its author steadfastly refused to learn? Or is it possible that the presence of the Civil War in this novel in fact includes autobiography in a broader sense? To put it another way, *Little Women* may demonstrate the war's effect on its author; without the Civil War, there might not have been a *Little Women* at all.

When South Carolina troops fired on Fort Sumter on April 12, 1861, thus starting the Civil War, Louisa May Alcott was twenty-eight years old. She had already established herself in a modest way as a writer, although she had yet to achieve literary fame and fortune; that would come over the next several years. At various points during the war years, she would live with her family in Concord or independently in Boston and Washington, D.C.; in the latter, she would have close personal contact with wounded soldiers. In short, Alcott's experience of the war was entirely that of an unmarried adult woman—a spinster in the terminology of the day. And insofar as her first taste of literary fame came with works written during and about the war, she experienced it as a professional writer, not as the author manqué that her fifteen-year-old avatar, Jo March, is through most of the novel.

After watching the first group of Concord volunteers depart for Washington, Alcott wrote, "I've often longed to see a war, and now I have my wish. I long to be a man, but as I can't fight, I will content myself with working for those who can" (*Journals* 105). Jo March echoes her concern early in *Little Women*: "I can't get over my disappointment in not being a boy, and it's worse than ever now, for I'm dying to go and fight with papa, and I can only stay at home and knit like a poky old woman" (13). In the real world, Alcott did indeed sew for the soldiers, joining other Concord women in making uniforms for them (Elbert, "Introduction" xxviii) and alluding to sewing and knitting several times in her journal for 1861 (105–106).

Such war-related domestic activities do occur in *Little Women*, notably in Mrs. March's participation in the soldiers' aid society and in Chapter 13, "Castles in the Air," when Laurie intrudes on the sisters' "Busy Bee Society," where Jo is knitting and Meg is sewing for the Union troops. These vignettes, along with the various exchanges of letters between family members, indicate that the novel is not set in the Concord of Alcott's own youth. But we might expect activities such as sewing, fundraising for the troops, and offering support to the families of soldiers, all of which were common elements of life on the Northern home front, to occupy even more of the novel. After all, according to historians Nina Silber and Mary Beth Sievens, "the war altered every aspect of New England life, including family and financial matters, women's roles, local elections, and the local economy" (17). In contrast, other than Father March's absence, much of the Marches' lives proceeds as it would have without a war: Meg dances at a ball, Amy goes to school, Jo devotes herself to writing, shy Beth plays her music.

Gender bars both Alcott and her heroine from "going for soldiers"; while boys of Jo's age often found their way into the army, she has no real pathway to the kind of service for which she chafes. As a grown woman, though, Alcott did have a way to serve in a more substantive way: by going to Washington as a nurse, which she did in December of 1862. Alcott fit the requirements for the job: thirty years old, presumably creating little risk of romance between the nurses and their much younger charges (Reisen 209); literate, since a major part of nurses' duties involved reading and writing letters for patients (Nelson 49); and, ideally, skilled in caring for the sick.[1] Alcott had acquired experience nursing members of her family, and she also had studied nursing in preparation for this task. Unfortunately, her tenure as a nurse was short-lived, because she contracted typhoid and had to return home early in 1863.

However, the nursing experience exposed Alcott to aspects of life she had not previously encountered, and this enabled her to enter into her most substantive activity in support of the war: that of a writer conveying military experience to the Northern public. Initially, she described her travels to Washington and her experiences at the Union Hospital in letters to her family. Though brief, her nursing experiences encompassed significant exposure to the true nature of war; she arrived shortly before a heavy influx of casualties from the Battle of Fredericksburg taxed the hospital staff. Invalided out of active service, Alcott then turned her letters into a lightly fictionalized book, *Hospital Sketches* (1863), which became her first major literary success.

Hospital Sketches, although inherently episodic, plots out the trajectory of Northern response to the war, from initial optimism to the stern realization that a long and damaging conflict lies ahead before peace is restored. The initial tone of the *Sketches* is light, as the absurdly named Tribulation Periwinkle prepares to set off as a nurse, casting herself and her family as comic characters. For instance, on learning she has been accepted into the army nursing corps, "Old Trib" comments:

> As boys going to sea immediately become nautical in speech, walk as if they already had their "sea legs" on, and shiver their timbers on all possible occasions, so I turned military at once, called my dinner my rations, saluted all new comers, and ordered a dress parade that very afternoon. Having reviewed every rag I possessed, I detailed some for picket duty while airing over the fence; some to the sanitary influences of the washtub, others to mount guard in the trunk; while

the weak and wounded went to the Work-basket Hospital, to be made ready for active service again. (Alcott, *Civil* 2)

Similarly, *Little Women* employs military language in unconventional contexts. Amy's teacher responds to her possession of limes "like fire to powder," having previously declared such treats "contraband," a term used during the war to designate slaves liberated from their owners (Alcott, *Little Women* 58); defiant Amy bears her punishment without flinching (59). Later, with a conviction reminiscent of John Brown's fanaticism, Jo is willing to oppose Meg's engagement with "any measures, however violent" (163) and stands sentinel outside the study when Laurie is being interrogated by Marmee, "having some fear that the prisoner might bolt" (165). Once the engagement has been finalized, Jo is taken aback: "going in to exult over a fallen enemy, and to praise a strong-minded sister for the banishment of an objectionable lover, it certainly *was* a shock to behold the aforesaid enemy serenely sitting on the sofa" (183). These mock-serious uses of warlike language align themselves with Nurse Periwinkle's initial, humorous reaction to the very serious world of the army hospital in *Hospital Sketches*.

If the early *Sketches* reflect the optimistic exuberance that the North felt at the beginning of the war, later chapters find the humor being modulated by images of the soldiers' plight. Alcott's chronicle is often credited as one of the first documents to bring home to Northern readers the suffering of the hospitalized soldiers, most notably with the arrival of wounded troops from Fredericksburg. At first, Nurse Periwinkle sees this as an opportunity to indulge her fancies about war service: "Having a taste for 'ghastliness,' I had rather longed for the wounded to arrive, for rheumatism wasn't heroic, neither was liver complaint, or measles..." (Alcott, *Civil* 20). She is quickly disabused, however, first by the nasty smell of a ward full of untreated wounds, then by her recognition of the men's bravery as they bear "suffering for which we have no name" (21). As the hospital fills with the wounded and more keep coming, she observes the closest civilian equivalent to the confusion that reigns in battle:

All was hurry and confusion; the hall was full of these wrecks of humanity, for the most exhausted could not reach a bed till duly ticketed and registered; the walls were lined with rows of such as could sit, the floor covered with the more disabled, the steps and doorways filled with helpers and lookers on; the sound of many feet and voices made that usually quiet hour as noisy as noon; and, in the midst of it all, the matron's motherly face brought more comfort to many a poor soul, than the cordial draughts she administered, or the cheery words that welcomed all, making the hospital a home. (Alcott, *Civil* 21)

The more sober tone of this chapter doesn't completely banish Tribulation's wit, however, as she manages to make a pun—"my ward was in truth a *ball-room*, if gunshot wounds could christen it" (21)—and recite a parody of "The Charge of the Light Brigade" set in the hospital (25–26). But there is too much horror at hand for laughter, from the surgeon who treats the wounds as so many puzzles to solve to the gut-shot soldier who dies unattended while waiting for a drink of water. The latter provokes the nurse to meditate on his passing: "I felt bitterly indignant at this seeming carelessness of the value of life, the sanctity of death; then consoled myself with the thought that, when the great muster roll was called, these nameless men might be promoted above many whose tall monuments record the barren honors they have won" (28).

As a child and young woman, Alcott had associated with the great intellects of her time, her father's friends, such as Ralph Waldo Emerson and Henry David Thoreau. One of the great achievements of her war stories, however—both those in *Hospital Sketches* and other stories published in magazines—is their insistent focus on these "nameless" ones and their smaller, intimate moments, as well as the omnipresence of death in soldiers' lives. In the same way, *Little Women* insists on the importance of domestic arrangements rather than the sweeping heroics of a traditional war epic, on ordinary people who pass through life unnoticed by all but close friends and family rather than on the great and powerful: "Everyone missed Beth ... even those who knew her best, were surprised to find how many friends shy little Beth had made (146–47). And while the

Sketches acquaint wartime readers with the omnipresence of death in the army, *Little Women* reminds them that the risk of death is a serious concern of everyday life, as well. The plight of the German children who contract scarlet fever and Beth's near-death encounter with the same disease, even while Father March lies close to death in Washington, brings war and home together in a particularly somber way. As Alcott acknowledges in Chapter 18, "[h]ow dark the days seemed now, how sad and lonely the house, and how heavy were the hearts of the sisters as they worked and waited, while the shadow of death hovered over the once happy house!" (146).

The most powerful of the *Sketches* is the fourth, "A Night," with its depiction of a stoic, fatally wounded Virginian. Despite some initial self-mocking humor, the register of this story is serious, even tragic, its true focus on the wounded soldiers. Trib explains, "Wherever the sickest or most helpless man chanced to be, there I held my watch" (Alcott, *Civil* 32). Logically enough, this means that several of her charges will die, and she piously observes, "a virtuous and useful life untimely ended is always tragical to those who see not as God sees" (34)—a sentiment that would function as well for Beth's death in *Little Women*.[2] After a few other patients are briefly mentioned, John's story takes over the narrative. At first, Trib is somewhat afraid of him, a large man and former blacksmith with an attractive face and a generally composed mien; he acts so contented with his lot that the nurse is surprised when a doctor informs her that he is the patient who most likely suffers more than any other:

> Every breath he draws is like a stab; for the ball pierced the left lung, broke a rib, and did no end of damage here and there; so the poor lad can find neither forgetfulness nor ease, because he must lie on his wounded back or suffocate. It will be a hard struggle, and a long one, for he possesses great vitality; but even his temperate life can't save him; I wish it could. (Alcott, *Civil* 39)

Elizabeth Young finds the *Sketches'* center in John's story ("Wound" 442), and it is hard to argue with this logic; certainly he is the most fully developed character of all the patients Alcott describes, and his stoic acceptance of suffering and death, which

Young elsewhere characterizes as akin to that of Christ (*Disarming* 91), comes to represent the dedication of the nation as a whole to the sacred cause of union. Stories of nursing in an army hospital perhaps helped to make a connection between the war and traditional caring activities such as women at the time might have done at home.

Significantly, John's heroic death in the *Sketches* suggests a possible rationale for one aspect of *Little Women* that vexed many of its first readers, Jo's refusal to marry Laurie—for while the experience of the war and the adjustment to temporary fatherlessness sobers and matures the March girls, Laurie remains essentially a spoiled child in many ways. His fundamental inability to understand the seriousness of the war is demonstrated by the use to which he puts military terms. Unlike the more serious examples of military language in Amy's tribulation over the limes and Jo's response to Meg's engagement, Laurie's use of this language shows little awareness of the realities that Alcott had observed firsthand. At "Camp Laurence," the outing that Laurie organizes in Chapter 12, he assigns military roles to his tutor and himself (commander-in-chief and commissary-general, respectively) and designates the girls as the "company." The food tent is the "mess-tent" and the croquet game between Yankees and British visitors is a battle in which "every inch of the ground" is "contested" and "several skirmishes" nearly break out (Alcott, *Little Women* 104). It is all a mock-serious conceit, a child's playing at war. Laurie's letter on hearing that Mr. March is recovering similarly attempts a humorous mimicry of military language, reporting to Mrs. March, the "Head Nurse of Ward II," that "All [is] serene on the Rappahannock," and signing it "Colonel Teddy" (140), leading Limon to comment, "We can only hope that this letter is destroyed lest mutilated soldiers at the hospital get a look at it" (187). Laurie's references to the language of war trivialize genuine suffering.

During the war, Alcott also wrote several other stories about soldiers and nurses,[3] exploring issues that do not make their way into *Little Women* as readily. While the majority of the Northern populace favored restoring the Union, not all agreed with the radical abolitionism of the Alcott circle. Alcott's family and Transcendentalist friends greeted the war as an opportunity to end the practice of slavery in America. They had entertained prominent anti-slavery proponents and assisted some escaped slaves on the Underground Railroad before the war, and Alcott saw the violent John Brown as a hero, calling his unsuccessful raid on the arsenal at Harper's Ferry, Virginia, "the last heroic act in" the anti-slavery movement, alluding to him as "Saint John the Just" when he was hanged for his actions and publishing a heroic poem about him following his execution (Alcott, *Journals* 95).

Unlike these short stories written for adults, *Little Women* pays little attention to the slave issue, but this may reflect its Massachusetts setting, where Jo and her sisters are unlikely to encounter slaves or, for that matter, very many free African Americans. And, Alcott's early conversion to abolition notwithstanding, it is perhaps not surprising that the adolescent March girls give little thought to the issue. Finally, in the spirit of reconciliation, avoiding mention of slavery might ease the acceptance of the novel by the defeated South. Beverly Lyon Clark suggests that *Little Women* "could very much be considered a national novel," emphasizing soon after the conclusion of hostilities "a family stressed by war and also metaphorically represent[ing] the reunification of the country as a whole" (26), and Elizabeth Young sees it as "continuing the narrative of national recovery that *Hospital Sketches* only begins to imagine…Alcott's first full-scale version of a reconstructed body politic" ("Wound" 463).

If emancipation makes no appearance in *Little Women*, there is significant representation of life on the home front. Alcott had extensive experience with this aspect of the war. As elsewhere in the North, Alcott's home communities of Concord and Boston were highly supportive of the war in its early days. Alcott described Concord at this time as being "in a high state of topsy turviness … when quiet Concord does get stirred up it is a sight to behold" (qtd. in Young, *Disarming* 79). Alcott alludes to a similar military bustle in Boston in her postwar story, "My Red Cap":

> The Common was all alive with troops and the spectators who clustered round them to say God-speed, as the brave fellows marched

away to meet danger and death for our sakes.... Every one was eager to do something; and, as the men stood at ease, the people mingled freely with them, offering gifts, hearty grips of the hand, and hopeful prophecies of victory in the end. (n.p.)

One might expect some elements of this "topsy turviness" to impinge on the awareness of the March girls. So where is this militant spirit in the community inhabited by the Marches?

The close family circle of the Marches suggests that it has never been one for public demonstration. Veronica Horwell observes that in *Little Women*, there are only a few instances of life outside the family circle. The Marches' primary interaction is with Laurie and Mr. Laurence next door, who, like them, avoid most social obligations: "old Mr. Laurence" is "very proud, and don't like to mix with his neighbors" (Alcott, *Little Women* 26). The nature of the family's domestic life, then, offers little opportunity to introduce public spectacle; to do so might seem gratuitous. Within the confines of the family home, both Marmee and the girls do take part in communal activities supporting the war: foregoing Christmas splendor "when our men are suffering so in the army" (11); participating in packing boxes for the troops (15); sewing jackets for the soldiers while learning of a sacrifice of four sons lost in the war (42); knitting socks and sewing for the troops (17, 121). That they do these things within their own domestic sphere and not in the company of their neighbors does not reduce their involvement with or awareness of the war effort.

The significant role of letter-writing in *Little Women* also reflects wartime conditions on the home front. A letter from Father March at the first Christmas reminds the girls that their difficulties pale in comparison with those of soldiers, even though "very little was said of the hardships endured, the dangers faced, or the homesickness conquered" (16) and letters continue to be sent back and forth throughout the novel.[4] The importance of these letters reflects data gathered by Silber and Sievens on New Englanders' letter-writing during the war. They estimate that a tenth of the total population of the region served (8), resulting in an enormous exchange of letters—

an estimated ninety thousand letters a day between soldiers on the Eastern front and their families, and a similar number in the West (2).

I initially shared Limon's skepticism about the presence of the war in *Little Women*, but closer examination of the novel and greater awareness of Alcott's own involvement in the war effort has resulted in my conviction that the war references reflect both Alcott's family history and her firsthand wartime experiences, including her subsequent and successful publication on events affecting the nation. Had Alcott chosen to more closely reflect the period of her own childhood, *Little Women* undoubtedly would have found success as a "girls' book," but it would have remained distinct from her body of adult work—truly something designed for children's entertainment and edification. However, by shifting her chronology forward, and by infusing her novel with her own immediate experience of the Civil War, she is able to develop a continuity between her much-admired wartime writing and her most famous work, one that moves it beyond the "children's literature ghetto" into the realm of the literary classic.

Notes

1. In one crucial respect, Alcott departed from the preferred norm: she was single, and authorities preferred married women as another preventative to romance between nurse and patient.

2. An even more explicit link to Beth's death, or rather to the death of her real-life model, Elizabeth Alcott, in 1858, occurs as John approaches death later in this sketch: "I had been summoned to many death beds in my life, but to none that made my heart ache as it did then, since my mother called me to watch the departure of a spirit akin to this in its gentleness and patient strength" (Alcott, *Hospital Sketches* 43).

3. Specifically, 'My Contraband' and 'An Hour,' both included in subsequent editions of *Hospital Sketches*, address aspects of slavery, and "On Picket Duty" presents soldiers' feelings about those left at home.

4. For an alternative perspective on letter-writing in *Little Women*, see Gaul.

Works Cited

Alcott, Louisa May. "An Hour." 1864. *Louisa May Alcott on Race, Sex, and Slavery*. Ed. Sarah Elbert. Boston: Northeastern UP, 1997. 47–68.

_____. *Civil War Hospital Sketches*. Mineola, NY: Dover Books, 2006.

_____. *The Journals of Louisa May Alcott*. Eds. Joel Myerson, Daniel Shealy, and Madeleine B. Stern. Boston: Little, Brown, 1989.

_____. *Little Women*. Ed. Anne K. Phillips and Gregory Eiselein. New York: Norton, 2004.

_____. "My Contraband." 1863. *Short Stories*. New York: Dover, 1996.

_____. "My Red Cap." *The Literature Network*. Jalic Inc, 2015. Web. 21 May 2015.

_____. "On Picket Duty." *The Literature Network*. Jalic Inc, 2015. Web. 26 Mar. 2015.

Clark, Beverly Lyon. *The Afterlife of* Little Women. Baltimore: Johns Hopkins UP, 2014.

Elbert, Sarah. "Introduction." *Louisa May Alcott on Race, Sex, and Slavery*. Boston: Northeastern UP, 1997.

_____. "Reading the Unwritten War: Renaissance Tales, Nella Larsen's *Passing* and Louisa May Alcott's 'M. L.,' 'My Contraband,' and 'An Hour.'" *Irish Journal of American Studies* 2 (Dec. 1993): 33–127.

Fahs, Alice. "The Feminized Civil War: Gender, Northern Popular Literature, and the Memory of the War, 1861–1900." *Journal of American History* 85 (March 1999): 1461–1494.

Fetterley, Judith. "*Little Women*: Alcott's Civil War." *Feminist Studies* 5 (Summer 1979): 369–383.

Gaul, Theresa Strouth. "'The Precious Home Letters:' Letter-Writing in *Little Women*." *Critical Insights:* Little Women. Ed. Gregory Eiselein and Anne K. Phillips. Ipswich, MA: Salem P, 2015. 97–112.

Horwell, Veronica. "Families in Literature: The March Sisters in *Little Women* by Louisa May Alcott." *The Guardian*. The Guardian News and Media Limited, 22 Dec. 2014. Web. 23 Dec. 2014.

Klimasmith, Betsy. "Slave, Master, Mistress, Slave: Genre and Interracial Desire in Louisa May Alcott's Fiction." *ATQ* 11 (Jun. 1997): 115–35.

Limon, John. *Writing After War: American War Fiction from Realism to Postmodernis*m. New York: Oxford UP, 1994.

Nelson, Michael C. "Writing During Wartime: Gender and Literacy in the American Civil War." *Journal of American Studies* 31 (Apr. 1997): 43–68.

Reisen, Harriet. *Louisa May Alcott: The Woman Behind* Little Women. New York: Picador/Henry Holt, 2009.

Shealy, Daniel, ed. *Little Women: An Annotated Edition.* Cambridge, MA: Belknap-Harvard UP, 2013.

Silber, Nina, and Mary Beth Sievens. *Yankee Correspondence: Civil War Letters between New England Soldiers and the Home Front.* Charlottesville: UP of Virginia, 1996.

Young, Elizabeth. *Disarming the Nation: Women's Writing and the American Civil War.* Chicago: U of Chicago P, 1999.

_____. "A Wound of One's Own: Louisa May Alcott's Civil War Fiction." *American Quarterly* 48 (Sept. 1996): 439–474.

Divas, Drugs, and Desire on Alcott's Gothic Stage

Monika Elbert

> Perhaps it is acting, not writing, I'm meant for. Nature must have a
> vent somehow. (Alcott, *Journals*, June 1858)

Looking at Alcott's fiction and her inner life as quintessentially and
dramatically Gothic, this essay examines her Gothic stories about
dramatic impersonations and drug-induced states, activities that take
the True Woman out of the "normal" woman's realm. In her own
life, Alcott was drawn to the Gothic and wanted to emulate such
exemplary Gothic writers as Charlotte Brontë. In a June 1857 journal
entry, Alcott revealed her desire to emulate Brontë: "I can't be a
Charlotte Brontë, but I may do a little something yet" (*Journals* 85).
On the American Gothic side, she admired Hawthorne (especially
The Scarlet Letter) for his "lurid" writing, although her mother
recommended the more sedate Fredrika Bremer. Certainly, "bad"
girls attracted her, whether they were governesses, adulteresses, or
actresses. Alcott herself had short stints as governess/servant and
as actress. The Gothic governess, like the Victorian actress, had a
dubious reputation, and musings about sexuality could be made
through their stories. For Alcott's fictional characters, though,
poverty was the common denominator; the price of such poverty
might be freedom of expression, as they took on forbidden roles in
society. Moreover, role-playing was liberating for Alcott. Early on as
an adolescent, Alcott enjoyed playing the role of male Gothic villains
or swashbuckling heroes in the melodramas she wrote or performed
with her sisters, episodes that are fictionalized in *Little Women*. The
use of Gothic motifs in her fiction allows Alcott to experiment with
ideas about androgyny and gender (s)exchanges, so that the male
Gothic figure is often overpowered by a stronger female. In the two
influential Gothic texts I mention above, for example, the roles are
reversed, so that Rochester is finally feminized and seen as weaker

than the governess Jane, and at the end of *The Scarlet Letter*, Hester has unmanned both of her lovers. Alcott would follow a similar pattern in investing her female Gothic protagonists with the ability to undo the males who would try to overpower them.

In the 1860s, there was a proliferation of American women writers composing Gothic thrillers in opposition to earlier formulaic Gothic stories that had, at their center, the dark, threatening, sexual male villain and the easily subdued female of the Radcliffean mold.[1] Responding to the threat of male sexuality in early Gothic, writers like Alcott and Harriet Spofford created dramatic women, who project their own sexual desires onto would-be villains and, making most of their acting abilities, become overpowering femmes fatales. If supernatural hauntings and male desire were the mainstay of horror in late eighteenth- and early nineteenth-century Gothic, in the late nineteenth century, women Gothic writers would depict the female will to power, through the use of her body, as far more devastating. In Alcott's "Behind a Mask: Or, A Woman's Power" (1866)," *A Modern Mephistopheles* (1877), and "Pauline's Passion and Punishment" (1862), and Spofford's "The Amber Gods" (1863), male sexual desire is rendered passive compared to women's desire to control men through dramatic tableaux, which capitalize on the female body as the locus of desire. Spofford's female-centered Gothic writing was often compared to Alcott's. When Alcott penned her *A Modern Mephistopheles* in the anonymous "No Name Series," many reviewers erroneously attributed Alcott's Gothic thriller to Spofford. One reviewer for *The Independent*, in particular, was adamant that only Spofford could have "produced the story" because of its conventions: "a field of romance, and weirdness, and mystery, and glamor, and rich color, and musky perfume" (qtd. in Clark 291). When the identity of the author was revealed after Alcott's death, one of the reviewers applauded the book as being one of Alcott's best and surprisingly believed her future reputation would rest on this masterpiece: "It is quite probable that Miss Alcott's fame as an author will in the end rest more on this novel than on any other she has written. It has more imagination, more of creative power, more plot, more scope" (*Boston Evening Traveller*, qtd. in Clark 304).

In these Gothic thrillers of the 1860s and 70s, Alcott and Spofford, caught between the era of the True Woman and the New Woman, create female protagonists who use their sexuality or femininity to unman the men who seek to control them. These male characters initially appear to be the sexualized villain type of Gothic fiction—male figures who imprison a woman in a domestic space or haunt her footsteps in pursuit of her innocence. Yet this stereotype is ultimately overturned, and the female protagonist, through her acting ability, renders the male passive as he is too engrossed with the staged effects and the sexual fantasy rather than the actual woman concocting the show, an early type of peep show perhaps.[2]

Though I do not wish to go the way of Camille Paglia and suggest that these women are empowered through pornographic display, I would like to suggest that in constructing male sexualities, these women writers have shown men to be effete and exposed male physical desires as more of an encumbrance than a sign of danger or power. Thus, if women find their voice through exploiting their bodies in quite visual ways, men abdicate power by giving in to sexual desires. The dangerous Gothic villain who will take advantage of woman's innocence, either by turning her into an *objet d'art* or by seducing her, becomes a pawn to the orchestrating woman/actress. The women are often forced into these acting roles as a result of class differences or in reaction to the oppressive cult of True Womanhood. By focusing on the male spectators, who watch but do not act, Alcott and Spofford implicitly see male sexuality as a liability. They do not own their bodies, but must watch women, as the women make spectacles of their own bodies to claim their power in an almost vampire-like manner. Even when the male protagonists attempt to subdue the women first with hashish and then sexually, as in *A Modern Mephistopheles* or "The Marble Woman," the women ultimately loom larger than life and have the last word, even if it is in a tableau mort, as in *A Modern Mephistopheles*. Responding to the initial threat posed by the dark, sexual villain, the female Gothic heroine projects her own repressed sexuality onto the Gothic male and then outdoes the male in the battle of the sexes by conquering what the demonic male has unleashed. In a convoluted way, she exploits her newly found sexual power to conquer her seducer.

Alcott's and Spofford's presentations of female tableaux counter Laura Mulvey's idea of the empowered male gaze, a cinematic term explored by Mulvey on the male spectator/voyeur's ability to control or possess women's image. In the scenes I discuss, the roles are reversed, and men are reduced to passive spectators who are disconnected from their bodies (their source of power, creativity, and sexuality) and become captive to the female gaze. Even when the female protagonists, as in *A Modern Mephistopheles* and "The Amber Gods," appear to participate in, if not stage, their own deaths, it is the tableau of the beautiful, dead, revenant body that wins the day—not the male voyeur. Especially in the tableaux scenes, women are empowered as they seduce unassuming males: Gladys acts the part of the enchantress Vivien (from the Merlin story) in *A Modern Mephistopheles*, and Jean Muir in "Behind a Mask" plays Judith (the biblical slayer of Holofernes) as well as a damsel in distress, who triumphs over male pursuers and redeemers. So convincing is Jean's art that Gerald, the head of the household and participant in the tableau, "for the first time in his life … felt the indescribable spell of womanhood and looked like the ardent lover to perfection" (Alcott, "Mask" 149). Gerald even accuses Jean of possessing witchcraft, so under her (acting) spell has he become: "You make a slave of me already. How do you do it? I never obeyed a woman before. Jean, I think you are a witch" (183). In Spofford's "The Amber Gods," the self-possessed Yone imagines herself to be Venus or Isis and plays the part convincingly, seducing the artist Rose, who, beguiled by her charms, calls her "Circe" and the "Witch of Atlas" (49). Sometimes, the female protagonist is not simply the subject to be gazed at, but the director of the drama. For example, Pauline in Alcott's "Pauline's Passion and Punishment," creates her own drama as she makes pawns of her male admirers through her seductive art and as she rids herself of her female rival in the process.

Certainly, the rise of the actress in the nineteenth century as representative of sexual license or promiscuity was helpful in reformulating the notion of the Gothic heroine. Alcott, for example, had always thought of acting as a means by which women could become self-reliant and by which they could subvert conventional gender roles. Not only did she stage plays and tableaux vivants at home with her sisters, but she also acted with a local theater troupe in Walpole, New Hampshire, in the 1850s. She met the celebrated actress Fanny Kemble in 1855 and, sometime later, acted as a way of raising money for charitable causes. In February of 1868, somewhat wearied, Alcott notes her excessive stage activity during the preceding two months: "Acted for charity twelve times" (*Journals* 165). In her journals, Alcott evinces her fascination with the actress figure, as a type to admire and to aspire to. In June 1858, she "saw Charlotte Cushman, and had a stagestruck fit" (90). In the spring of 1868, she played the part of Mrs. Pontifex in "Naval Engagements" and dreamed that night that she was "an opera singer" and so "waked up prancing" (163). Shortly thereafter, she heard Fanny Kemble reading from *The Merchant of Venice* and commented on her grandeur: "She was a whole stock company in herself. Looked younger and handsomer than ever before" (163).

Alcott's love for the stage inspired many of her melodramatic writings, which would fend off the family's penury. Significantly, shortly after being "stagestruck" by Charlotte Cushman, Alcott is prompted to "work off [her] stage fever" by "writing a story" (July 1858), which culminated in "Marion Earle; or, Only an Actress," (published 1858), a story about the trials of the actress figure in fending off the negative stereotypes associated with her art. Not only is Marion Earle a talented artist, but she is a kind-hearted soul, whose acts of charity are able to convince a hard-hearted aristocratic woman that her prejudices about acting woman as "weak, frivolous, and vain" (Alcott, "Marion" 254) are wrong. Indeed, we hear that Marion has become an actress in an effort to stave off poverty and to care for her orphaned little sister: "Marion had the courage to enter the profession for which her talents fitted her. She knew the dangers and the labor through which she must pass, but for the child's sake she ventured it" (255). Mrs. Leicester, the snobbish aristocrat, feels that the elderly gentlemen defending Marion is blinded by her beauty: "With you gentlemen, beauty veils so many blemishes" (254). The story will have Mrs. Leicester renounce her earlier prejudice as she learns of her "good and tender heart." The conflict arises when Mrs. Leicester's dilettante son, Robert, is about to marry Marion. Agnes, a poor and honest girl of the streets, crashes the wedding and announces that Robert has fathered her illegitimate child. Marion, who is known for her acts of charity (especially after the devastating death of her sister) and who has already helped Agnes, unbeknownst to her, when she gave her money and shelter in her time of need, now forces Robert to marry Agnes to give the child a name. But the elder Mrs. Leicester and son Robert soon disappear from the scene and relinquish their responsibilities as they embark on travels to Europe. Marian continues acting and caring for Agnes and child, but eventually Robert and his privileged mother return, having squandered their fortune. Marion receives the now homeless but penitent aristocrats into her care, and Marion nurses the disease-ridden Robert back to health, though the price of her generosity is her own death. Having bequeathed her property to Agnes, Robert (the child), and Robert's mother, Marion comes to a "noble end," though the narrator sarcastically adds, "though she was but an actress" (274). Alcott sentimentalizes the acting woman here, but in her Gothic, she is able to liberate the actress protagonist.

In "Behind a Mask," Alcott shows how the masks Gothic heroines wear are liberating; the upper-class men who try to outwit and exploit the lower-class servant, the governess Jean Muir, are finally outdone by the consummate actress, who woos and wins the wealthy Sir John Coventry. As Jean reveals to a friend from her former life as an actress, she uses her acting experience and charms to bring the Coventry family down and to marry the oldest and most established Coventry, the bachelor neighbor, the uncle, Sir John. She explains her disdain for the arrogance of the two young classist brothers, Ned and Gerald, and vows vengeance. She complains about Ned's rudeness at her arrival, "Through the indolence of Monsieur the young master, no carriage was sent for me, and I intend he shall atone for that rudeness by-and-by" (Alcott, "Mask" 195). Similarly, she finds fault with Gerald for his pride, "Monsieur … was unapproachable, and took no pains to conceal his dislike of governesses" (195). Indeed, Jean plans to make Gerald fall out of love with his betrothed, his cousin Lucia, and to "teach him how to woo a woman by making his heart ache" (195). Ned and Gerald are like the "sporting men" of mid-century, the middle- and upper-class men who were prone to gambling and felt that they could swagger and play with women's emotions because of their wealth (Horowitz 23–26). These "sporting men" were similar to the Gothic villains and might be seen as cads, rogues, or ne'er-do-wells, who took advantage of unassuming women. Women of a certain class, who seemed available, in venues such as brothels and the theater, seemed easy prey; to the sporting men, "women were merely instruments of men's pleasure to be used and discarded freely" (Horowitz 23–24). Like the "monstrous male[s]," whom Marysa Demoor finds in the atavistic males John Reed and the clergyman Brocklehurst or in the seductive Sir John in *Jane Eyre*, the Coventry men are used to making women their prey. As Jean knows, Lucia "worships" Gerald, "like an inanimate idol as he is" (Alcott, "Mask" 195). Using "stage looks" (195) to provoke and ensnare the Coventry men, she has all three finally falling in love with her.

Ironically, it is in the tableaux scenes where Jean Muir is most revealing of her true self. When she poses as Judith, the slayer of Holofernes, the Coventry family is stunned by the dark hatred in her eyes, which Gerald detects as genuine: "It was not at all art: the intense detestations mingled with a savage joy that the object of her hatred was in her power was too perfect to be feigned; and … Coventry felt as if he caught a glimpse of the truth" (147). "The intensity of expression" in her eyes seemed to match that of the biblical Judith: "Hatred, the deepest and bitterest was written on her sternly beautiful face, courage glowed in her glance, power spoke in the nervous grasp of the slender hand that held the weapon, and the indomitable will of the woman was expressed" (147). One of the Coventrys says, prophetically (as Jean represents the downfall of the upper class), "She looks as if she'd use her sword well when the time comes" (147). In the second tableau scene, Gerald is asked to play a fugitive cavalier fighting the Roundheads in the English Civil War, as depicted in a hallway painting; moreover, he is to rescue

---

Jean, who ends up rescuing him from the Roundheads in pursuit. Before the scene starts, Jean symbolically unmans him by making him kneel before her, disheveling his hair, pulling off his lace collar, untying his cloak, and removing his gloves and sword, all for the sake of verisimilitude: "you are too elegant for a fugitive" (148), she admonishes him, with an obvious jab at his class privilege. As she tries to hide the "cavalier" Gerald under her cloak, she uses looks backward with "such terror in her eyes" that the young male spectators had an urge to "hurry to her rescue" (149). At this moment, too, Gerald is smitten with Jean: "Many women had smiled on him, but he had remained heart-whole, cool, and careless, quite unconscious of the power which a woman possesses and knows how to use, for the weal or woe of man" (149). Gerald is totally transformed in this tableau, "looking as he had never looked before" (149).

In the second part of the tableau, Jean, as the redemptive woman, suffers a beautiful death at the hands of the Roundheads; still embracing Gerald, as cavalier, she lays her head on his breast, and "her eyes looked full into his, no longer wild with fear, but eloquent with the love which even death could not conquer. The power of those eyes thrilled Coventry with a strange delight" (149). Looking into his eyes, Jean knows she has ensnared Gerald through her acting, "She felt his hands tremble, saw the color flash into his cheek, knew that she had touched him at last, and when she rose, it was with a sense of triumph which she found hard to conceal" (149). Though others in the audience feel is its "fine acting," the rival Lucia, with her discriminating eyes, knows that Jean is seducing her beau, and hurrying behind the scenes, she is "bent on putting an end to such dangerous play" (149). Lucia is definitely the loser when she entreats Gerald to stay with her, but he responds, "I've done my part—no more tragedy for me tonight" and subsequently follows Jean Muir to the garden. He leaves the rival Lucia before "she could entreat or command"; the only imposing woman in these tableaux and in the domestic drama is Jean, who has her vengeance, as Gerald now treats her as an equal and not as a servant.

Moreover, in the private garden scene, Gerald opens up to her in a way that is almost embarrassing, as he candidly admits that he has worn a mask and as he is totally unaware of Jean's duplicity. Like a fallen aristocrat, he admits, "I am not what I seem, and my indolent indifference is but the mask under which I conceal my real self. I could be as passionate, as energetic, and as aspiring as Ned, if I had any aim in life" (153). Jean sets up him for a fall, playing the role of the misunderstood and wronged maiden. "Tears streamed down her cheeks, sobs choked her words, and she turned toward the young man in all the abandonment of sorrow, fear, and supplication" (155). Moved by her crocodile tears, Gerald feels "he knew not how to play his part" and falls victim to "romantic nonsense" and "most of all, the presence of a beautiful, afflicted woman" (155). However, when he tries to play the role of the protective knight, she mocks him by calling him "Fainthearted knight" (157). The final moment of the tableau chapter has Gerald offering his new-found love Jean a rose, but Jean refuses to allow Gerald to act the part of gallant lover and rebukes him "imperiously": "There has been enough of this folly. You forget yourself" (157), as she casts him off. Not only has Jean created enmity between Lucia and Gerald, but between the two brothers, who are now rivals for Jean's love, so much so that Gerald sends Ned away.

The final moment of triumph comes for Jean when she orchestrates the love match between her and old Sir John. In a private tableau meant only for Sir John's eyes, she strikes a pose of maiden love for John, as she gazes, most artfully, at the miniature picture of Sir John. The old uncle, sitting at his desk, casts "covert glances" at the maiden figure (ironic in itself, as she daily puts on fake hair and teeth to feign being nineteen when she is already thirty), and Jean affects "unconsciousness" of his glances. Although he feels in control, as he thinks Jean is rendered the object of his gaze, Jean is most certainly the actress aware of her effect on the male spectator: "suddenly, as if obeying an irresistible impulse, she took it [the miniature] down, looked long and fondly at it, then, shaking her curls about her face, as if to hide the act, pressed it to her lips and seemed to weep over it in an uncontrollable paroxysm of tender grief" (178). All of the Coventry men have now fallen victim to her beguiling ways and her tender, but spurious, displays of emotion. She plays the Coventry men against each other so they all feel as if they have to protect her. Indeed, once she has Sir John propose to her, she displays true feeling for the first time in the narrative: "the blessed sense of safety ... filled Jean Muir with such intense satisfaction that tears of *real* feeling stood in her eyes" (181, emphasis mine). In this story as well as in *A Modern Mephistopheles*, the acting women want nothing more than the security of home.[3] This view of the Gothic heroine actually trying to establish domestic security through her sexuality goes against the conventional notion of Gothic critics that women are actually entrapped in a domestic prison.

Gladys, the female Gothic protagonist in *A Modern Mephistopheles*, is a different type of empowered acting woman. As Rena Sanderson explains, "While Gladys...enjoys the kind of control typically exerted by the seductive and vengeful females who often direct the action in Alcott's early potboilers, Gladys differs from other seductresses" (51). Sanderson views Jean Muir, of "Behind a Mask," in a judgmental and misguided way, when she asserts, "Such femmes fatales as Jean Muir use their erotic powers for evil, selfish ends that imitate the competitive male drive for power" (51). Certainly, Muir is ambitious, but she is eager to find a safe haven in a world that derides her because of her class station. Gladys, Sanderson believes, shows the maturity of Alcott as she "represents Alcott's attempt to legitimize a woman's libidinal potential as an untapped resource for national leadership and regeneration" (51). This may be going a bit far; after all, Gladys dies the death of a True Woman—as a redeeming mother—and the sanctity of motherhood is celebrated in the tableaux morts of mother and child. It is true, however, that her effect on others is ennobling: she saves the soul of her husband and her rival Olivia. And she reconciles the warring men, Felix and Helwyze, at the moment of her death, "Forgive each other for my sake" (196). It is true, too, that Gladys does incorporate some of the more proactive qualities of the New Woman, as she actually works to make a living, when her writer husband finds himself in need of money, and finally teaches him the need to work, to do any "honest work" (203). What drives her is the desire to make a home; even in her death, she looks forward to a heavenly home and ghoulishly invites her husband to that other home: "Remember, love, remember, we shall be waiting for you. The new home will not be home to us until you come" (196).

However, what interests me, in the context of the Gothic power struggle, is the role reversal of the empowered devil/tempter figure, Helwyze, and the seemingly innocent and disempowered Gladys. Felix Canaris, Gladys's husband, had made a pact with the devil figure, Jasper Helwyze, in order to gain fame through his writing. Initially, Helwyze feels an almost homoerotic bond towards Felix and secures him a wife in order that he may stay put in his villa. But gradually, the angel of the household, Gladys, is more attractive in her innocence than the fallen Felix, and the devil Helwyze falls in love with her. Indeed, he becomes so obsessed that he falls ill when Gladys dies and bemoans his future without her. The imperial and imposing Olivia, regretting her earlier unkindnesses to Gladys, becomes a nursemaid to her erstwhile lover, Helwyze: "now the haughty queen had changed to a sad woman, wearing for her sole ornaments constancy and love" (200). The devil figure, Helwyze, who tried to control Gladys, now is tortured with loving thoughts of her; the final words of the book are his, and are filled with agony, "Life before was Purgatory, now it is Hell, because I loved her, and *I* have no hope to follow and find her again" (206). The devil has been outwitted. He recalls how he brought Gladys there as a "plaything" for Felix, but realized, to his chagrin, that "this girl whom he had expected to mould to his will, exerted over him, as well as Canaris, a soft control which he could neither comprehend nor conquer (157). Gladys has a "soft control" in contradistinction to that of Jean Muir, with her almost dominatrix type tactics. The unrelenting Helwyze tries to take control of that situation by giving Gladys hashish. Olivia, who knows Helwyze so well because, as his girlfriend, "she had so often seen his face without a mask" (144) now scolds him for being so power-hungry: "You were always prying into things, even as a boy, when I caught butterflies for you to look at" (145). Helwyze flatly denies that he has done anything evil to Gladys; in fact, he feels he has liberated her, "I do not regret it [drugging her] for it showed what the woman is capable of" (145). This leads to a difficult question—is Helwyze ultimately a liberating figure of Gladys, even as he is undone by his machinations?

There is one dramatic tableau, which reveals that Gladys is leading a double life, as her sexual self is represented in her reenactment of Cleopatra, albeit under the influence of hashish, with which Helwyze had drugged her, unbeknownst to her. Like a mesmerized actress, Gladys encounters a "doubled identity": she "moved and spoke as she was told,—a pale, dim figure, of no interest to any one; the other was alive in every fibre, thrilled with intense desire for something, and bent on finding it, though deserts, oceans, and boundless realms of air were passed to gain it" (140). Olivia, her rival, is jealous of "her enchanting gift," and the men are totally mesmerized by her intensity. Indeed, in her drugged state, Gladys, like Poe's Ligeia, has eyes that are "luminous and large," and her face grows paler and her manner less agitated, "yet unnaturally calm" (140). She plays various parts—as Vivien, Cleopatra, and a nun—and both her husband (the Faust figure) and Helwyze (the devil figure) are intoxicated with desire. When she passes out and is brought to bed, they discuss her physical charms and appeal. Helwyze feels that she could have been "a cantatrice to be proud of," Felix, insulted by such an idea, comments, "Fancy that modest creature on a stage for all the world to gape at. She was happiest in the nun's gown tonight, though simply ravishing as Vivien" (143). But Felix is still enthralled thinking about her "pretty bare feet," and Helwyze actually makes a pass at her in the drug-induced state, hoping for a kiss. Helwyze, acting as mesmerist, forces a conversation out of the sleeping Gladys, who admits, to his dismay, that she fears his love and prays to God she may "never know" it. Shortly after, Gladys finds herself pregnant, and there is some possibility that Helwyze is the demon father, but the baby's death—and, shortly, Gladys' own—foil the devil's plan. Her tableau mort is the moment of moral victory, as she passes out words of wisdom to the three standing around her deathbed.

Long before Hollywood and the larger-than-life fleshy women of the silver screen, the women of these Gothic texts, whether apparent ingénue or femme fatale, create images of female beauty and sexuality with which to seduce the males. Gothic male desire is easily manipulated by fantasies of female beauty/sexuality, images that are artificial/artistic and easily contrived by apparently even weak or innocent women. Alcott bravely shows how the male protagonists are controlled by their fantasies, as they become prisoners to their desires—whereas the female protagonists remain in control of the situation, as they see beneath the men's addictive nature and remain centered, in an inviolable feminine sphere of their own. If the women activate and agitate, creating several persona and reinventing themselves, the men simply respond to visual stimuli. This view overturns the conventional notion of Gothic female passivity. It could be argued that in Alcott's rendering of the Gothic hero, the males are more romantic and the females more pragmatic, as the latter are forced to confront their body as a sexual commodity to be bartered on the stage or in the marketplace driven by male fantasies. However, these women are emancipated by their art as they enact multiple personalities on and offstage, and if they cannot outwit the male spectators, they finally stage the outcomes of their own drama. As actress Meryl Streep realizes about women even today, acting is a way to survive: "Women are better at acting than men. Why? Because we have to be. If successfully convincing somebody bigger than you of something he doesn't know is a survival skill, this is how women have survived through the millennia. Pretending is not just play. Pretending is imagined possibility. Pretending or acting is a very valuable life skill, and we all do it. All the time" (qtd. in Longworth 7).

Notes

1. Several studies trace the model of the passive female Gothic heroine back to Horace Walpole and Ann Radcliffe. See Ellis, Aguirre, and Demoor.

2. Indeed, tableau-vivant spectacles outside the American middle-class parlor did border on the pornographic in public theaters and operas of the mid-nineteenth century, starting in 1847 with the exhibit at Palmo's Opera House in New York City (Gilfoyle 127).

3. Compare, for example, the actress Anna Cora Mowatt, who decided to go on stage to keep her family afloat when her husband's business failed. To keep her "sweet home" safe, she capitulated to the world of acting (142).

Works Cited

Aguirre, Manuel. "The Roots of the Symbolic Role of Woman in Gothic Literature." *Exhibited by Candlelight: Sources and Developments in the Gothic Tradition.* Ed. Valeria Tinkler-Villani and Peter Davidson. Amsterdam: Rodopi, 1995. 57–64.

Alcott, Louisa May. "Behind a Mask." *Alternative Alcott.* Ed. Elaine Showalter. New Brunswick, NJ: Rutgers UP, 1988. 97–202.

_____. *The Journals of Louisa May Alcott.* Ed. Joel Myerson and Daniel Shealy. Boston: Little, Brown, 1989.

_____. "Marion Earle; Or, Only an Actress!" *The Early Stories of Louisa May Alcott, 1852–1860.* Intro. Monika Elbert. New York: Ironweed P, 2000. 264–274.

_____. *A Modern Mephistopheles.* Intr. Octavia Davis. New York: Bantam, 1995.

_____. "Pauline's Passion and Punishment." *Behind a Mask: The Unknown Thrillers of Louisa May Alcott.* Ed. Madeleine Stern. New York: Quill, 1995. 105–152.

Clark, Beverly Lyon, ed. "Reviews of *A Modern Mephistopheles.*" 1877. *Louisa May Alcott: The Contemporary Reviews.* New York: Cambridge UP, 2004. 283–306.

Demoor, Marysa. "Male Monsters or Monstrous Males in Victorian Women's Fiction." *Exhibited by Candlelight: Sources and Developments in the Gothic Tradition.* Ed. Valeria Tinkler-Villani and Peter Davidson. Amsterdam: Rodopi, 1995. 173–182.

Dickerson, Vanessa D. *Victorian Ghosts in the Noontide: Women Writers and the Supernatural.* Columbia: U of Missouri P, 1996.

Ellis, Kate Ferguson. "Can You Forgive Her? The Gothic Heroine and her Critics." *A Companion to the Gothic.* Ed. David Punter. Oxford: Blackwell, 2000. 257–268.

Gilfoyle, Timothy J. *City of Eros: New York City, Prostitution, and the Commercialization of Sex, 1790–1920.* New York: Norton, 1994.

Horowitz, Helen Lefkowitz, ed. *Attitudes Toward Sex in Antebellum America: A Brief History with Documents.* Boston: Bedford, 2006.

Longworth, Karina. *Meryl Streep: Anatomy of an Actor.* New York: Phaidon, 2014.

Mowatt, Anna Cora. *Autobiography of an Actress; or, Eight Years on the Stage.* Boston: Ticknor, Reed and Fields, 1853.

Mulvey, Laura. *Visual and Other Pleasures.* 2nd ed. New York: Palgrave, 2009.

Paglia, Camille. *Sexual Personae: Art and Decadence from Nefertiti to Emily Dickinson.* New York: Vintage, 1991.

Reviews of *A Modern Mephistopheles.* 1877. *Louisa May Alcott: The Contemporary Reviews.* Ed. Beverly Lyon Clark. New York: Cambridge UP, 2004. 283–306.

Sanderson, Rena. *"A Modern Mephistopheles*: Louisa May Alcott's Exorcism of Patriarchy." *American Transcendental Quarterly* 5.1 (1991): 41–55.

Spofford, Harriet. *"The Amber Gods" and Other Stories.* Ed. and intro. Alfred Bendixen. New Brunswick, NJ: Rutgers UP, 1989. 37–83.

Stern, Madeleine. *Louisa May Alcott: A Biography.* 1950. Boston: Northeastern UP, 1996.

Tinkler-Villani, Valeria, and Peter Davidson, eds. *Exhibited by Candlelight: Sources and Developments in the Gothic Tradition.* Amsterdam: Rodopi, 1995.

"A Loving League of Sisters": The Legacy of Margaret Fuller's Boston Conversations in Alcott's *Work*

Katie Kornacki

Work: A Story of Experience (1873) is arguably "the most feminist of Alcott's novels" (Showalter xxxi), following its self-reliant heroine, Christie Devon, through roughly twenty years of her working life, as she discovers her true vocation as a woman's rights activist, speaker, and mediator. Experiencing a variety of different types of employment available to women, including "service" as a maid, acting, being a governess, and working as a seamstress, Christie ultimately finds "the task [her] life has been fitting [her] for" (Alcott 334) in her women's rights activism. What is more, in a "remarkable feminist conclusion" (Showalter xxxv), the reader is presented with an image of the power of feminist sorority. Having gathered her female friends round her, ready to embark on her new vocation, "with an impulsive gesture, Christie stretched her hands to the friends about her, and with one accord, they laid theirs on hers, a loving league of sisters, old and young, black and white, rich and poor, each ready to do her part to hasten the coming of the happy end" (Alcott 343). Christie serves as the link binding this diverse group of women together into one "loving league of sisters": the rich Bella; Christie's Quaker mother-in-law, Mrs. Sterling; Hepsey, a former slave and Underground Railroad conductor; Christie's young daughter, Ruth; Mrs. Wilkins, a working-class "laundress"; and even a redeemed "fallen woman," Christie's sister-in-law, Rachel/Letty. While Christie's independence, insistence on her right to work, search for a vocation, and resistance to the conventional heterosexual marriage plot all mark the text as feminist, it is the powerful vein of sorority and its vision of a diverse feminist community that transcends age, class, race, and conventional morality that make *Work* so radical a feminist text.

What is more, in this feminist vision, especially Alcott's insistence on the need for women to cultivate a sense of sorority (as Christie puts it, "trying to know and help, love and educate one another" [Alcott 348]), we can clearly see the influence of Margaret Fuller's earlier Boston Conversations for women (1839–1844)—conversations that centered on a woman's right to education, self-reliance, vocation, and sorority. Through her formal Conversations and her feminist texts, Fuller provided a model of feminism discernable in novels written in the early years of organized woman's rights reform activity that feature activist heroines, including Alcott's Christie.[1] As a young girl, Alcott knew Fuller personally. Although too young to have attended her Conversations, Alcott would later recall Fuller's visits to her family home in Concord. Indeed, Fuller's formative influence on Alcott is a connection frequently noted by contemporary women writing about the famous author's early life. Alcott's "earliest teacher was Margaret Fuller" (Lillie 156), one woman wrote in a tribute written following Alcott's death. Another author noted that as a girl, Alcott was "especially fond of reading Shakespeare, Goethe, Emerson, Margaret Fuller, Miss Edgeworth, and George Sand" (Bolton 442). Not only does *Work*'s emphasis on sorority resonate with Fuller's own feminist project, but Christie's women's rights work, including her speaking, resembles Fuller's conversational practice. Furthermore, the work that Christie and her "loving league of sisters" (Alcott 343) set out to do at the end of the novel bears a close resemblance to the real-life work of a group of women who had collaborated with and known Fuller, through her Conversations or otherwise, and who, in 1868, had formed the New England Woman's Club, of which Alcott herself had been an early member.

It might seem unlikely that Fuller, who had published the majority of her (nonfiction) work in the 1840s and died in 1850, was a presence looming large in feminist novels published in the 1870s.[2] However, her feminist advocacy for reform from within (self-culture and self-reliance) as a crucial step toward social engagement and change was a project that could unite feminists on either side of the suffrage question and was particularly adaptable to fiction. Central to Fuller's feminism in the Conversations and in *Woman in the Nineteenth Century* [*Woman*] (1845) is her insistence that women act to help one another, not only through organized reform activity or political action, but also in more intimate, woman-centered ways, making self-reliance a communal activity amongst women. "I believe that, at present," she proclaimed, "women are the best helpers of one another" (Fuller, *Woman* 344). More explicitly, Fuller argued for the need for women to help their sisters who have "fallen"—victims of seduction and, more radically, prostitutes—a call that the heroine of Alcott's *Work* takes up, responding, it could be argued, to Fuller's earlier call to "seek out these degraded women, give them tender sympathy, counsel, employment" (Fuller, *Woman* 329). Through this model of feminist self-reliance, women help one another to attain education and vocation, thereby building sorority or sisterhood—a hallmark of the feminist community building that Fuller saw as so necessary.[3] Such a vision of sorority that Fuller envisioned and practiced was one that worked to construct horizontal alliances between women across lines demarcating class, race, and sexual "purity." Moving beyond simply talking about sorority, Fuller insisted that, whether practiced in public or in private, sisterhood necessitated taking action.

Beginning in November of 1839, Fuller held a series of thirteen weekly Conversations for Boston women in the parlor of Elizabeth Palmer Peabody's bookshop. This first series, on Greek mythology, proved so successful that Fuller would conduct subsequent Conversations, beginning the following spring with a series on the fine arts and continuing over the course of the next several years. Over the whole course of the Conversations, more than one hundred women participated at one or more series. Each Wednesday, usually at noon, a group of approximately twenty-five women met for two hours to discuss, initially, mythology and the fine arts. In subsequent series, the topics continued to include literary and aesthetic subjects, such as the fine arts and Greek mythology (the only series to which men were also invited and which Fuller considered to be the least successful), but also broader social considerations, such as ethics (including the Family, the School, the Church, Society, and

Literature), Woman, and Education (with weekly topics on Culture, Ignorance, Vanity, Prudence, and Patience). Other subjects included Demonology, Influence, Roman Catholicism, and the Ideal.

To better understand Fuller's radical work in these Boston Conversations, it is helpful to look at the "prospectus" that she laid out in a letter to Sophia Ripley, describing her intentions for the first series. In addition to stimulating "conversation of a better order than is usual," calling attention to the very real limits placed on women's formal education, Fuller expressly formulated the Conversations as an opportunity for women to "pass in review the departments of thought and knowledge and endeavor to place them in due relation to one another in our minds. To systematize thought and give a precision in which our sex are so deficient" (Fuller, *Letters* II: 87). Indeed, she was looking to form a "circle" of women who hoped to answer two "great questions" that women were not usually asked to consider: "What were we born to do? How shall we do it?" (*Letters* II: 87). Anticipating her later call in *Woman* for women's right to a vocation, she wished, through these Conversations, "to ascertain what pursuits are best suited to us in our time and state of society, and how we may make best use of our means for building up the life of thought upon the life of action" (*Letters* II: 87). Indeed, the label "fine arts," usually understood to be the focus of the Conversations, masks the feminist project at the heart of Fuller's endeavor.

As Fuller had astutely recognized, one of the barriers to sorority was that women, as products of a patriarchal society catering to male privilege, were raised to view one another as potential rivals. Thus, one of the goals of her Conversations was to engender a greater sense of community, sisterhood, and friendship among the members of her classes, inviting women to look past these barriers. Her boast to a friend that "there I have real society, which I have not before looked for out of the pale of intimacy. We have time, patience, mutual reverence and fearlessness eno' to get at one another's thoughts" (Fuller, *Letters* II: 118), suggests that she met with some success in realizing this goal. In her Prospectus, Fuller expressed the hope that "what is invaluable in the experience of each might be brought to bear upon all" (*Letters* II: 87), suggesting the community-

or sorority-building work enabled by the Conversations. Thus, as Elizabeth Ann Bartlett has pointed out, "in a very real way, Fuller's Conversations resembled the contemporary consciousness-raising group, in which women are encouraged to express their own truths, and in so doing discover a unity with other women" (116).

Like Christie's league of sisters, the sorority Fuller worked to construct through her quasi-private Conversations and her more public writing was surprisingly diverse in terms of race, class, and sexual mores—a point that is frequently overlooked due to the degree of celebrity she achieved through the paid series of Conversations that she conducted in Boston for a circle of mostly upper- and middle-class women from prominent New England families. In addition to her more famous Boston Conversations, Fuller also led several conversations at the utopian Brook Farm communitarian settlement, and, in an even bolder experiment, conducted conversations for the female inmates of New York's Sing-Sing Prison, where she was also a "featured speaker" on one occasion (Capper II: 206–7). Most of Sing-Sing's predominantly Irish and African American female prisoners were "prostitutes and petty thieves" (Capper II: 174). Although she addressed them from a vertically-oriented position of power and privilege as "featured speaker," Fuller also participated in more horizontal, egalitarian exchanges with the women in Sing-Sing, meeting and "talk[ing] with a circle of women" (Fuller, *Letters* III: 247) and emphasizing their shared experiences as women and as human souls, during which time, according to Fuller, "all passed much as one of my Boston Classes" (*Letters* III: 237). While in New York, Fuller also lent her support in helping to establish the first halfway house for female prisoners, mostly women convicted of prostitution—a cause which she brought to the pages of the *New-York Tribune* during her tenure as literary editor and critic.[4] In calling attention to the plight of "fallen women" and other women of a "rougher sort" and prompting her white, middle-class sisters to donate to, organize, or work towards the women's aid, Fuller extended the consciousness-raising effect of her Conversations to a larger body of women.

As we have seen, Christie's vision of sorority in *Work* is independent of kinship. It is non-elitist and inclusive, and the membership of her small band of sisters transcends age, class, race, and social position. In this sense, Alcott's novel is more progressive and radical than many of the feminist activist novels written in the second half of the nineteenth century which carry an "unspoken racial dynamic," as they "privilege the white, middle-class family as the primary unit of American society" (Petty 33). This dominant model, as Leslie Petty argues, based on familial relations, "prevents those who do not live in these traditional, middle-class families from joining, thereby negating both their potential to influence gender reform as well as their potential to benefit from it" (33). In contrast, the "feminist commune" (Showalter xxxii) Alcott envisions in *Work* allows space for non-white and non-middle-class women to participate on equal terms with their white, middle-class co-laborers in the work of first-wave feminist reform.

Not only is Hepsey, a former slave, a member of Christie's sisterhood, but she maintains a position of equality with Christie and the other members of the group; she is not a subordinate or marginal figure, but a "fellow-worker" (Alcott 101), both in Christie's "loving league" and at Christie's first place of employment, where Hepsey serves as cook and Christie as "table girl" for a well-to-do family. Having escaped from slavery, she later works for the Underground Railroad, through which she "liberated several brothers and sent them triumphantly to Canada" (101). While Hepsey is a minor character in the novel, Alcott suggests that we should read her as another heroine of her story, as Christie's admiring introduction of the fugitive slave to the white, upper-class Bella illustrates. Hepsey, Christie proclaims, "has saved scores of her own people, and is my pet heroine" (341). Written and published at a time when "the woman's rights movement was consciously distancing itself from race activism" (Petty 14), *Work* argues for the continuity between the two movements, stressing the need to include African American women in the sisterhood of first-wave feminist reform. Through her novel, Alcott "attempted to reforge the reformist alliance between women and blacks" (Kasson xxiii).

The novel also argues against the conflation of true womanhood with middle-class values. Sorority (or sister-feeling) and charity, as is demonstrated through the character of the working-class Mrs. Wilkins, are not the special province of genteel middle-class women. Working-class women are shown to be capable of an equal, or even greater, degree of honorable treatment towards their fellow women. When Rachel/Letty deposits a forlorn and desperate Christie at Mrs. Wilkins's door, Christie is astonished by the woman's unquestioning hospitality. "But you don't know any thing about me," she says to her hostess, "and I may be the worst woman in the world" (Alcott 131). To which Mrs. Wilkins replies, "I know that you want takin' care of, child, or Rachel wouldn't a sent you. Ef I can help any one, I don't want no introduction; and if you be the wust woman in the world (which you ain't), I wouldn't shet my door on you, fur then you'd need a lift more 'n you do now" (131). Unlike middle-class women, whom Fuller and other feminist writers had criticized for their refusal to help less fortunate women—women who "dare not cross [their] guarded way" (*Woman* 329)—this "laundress" presents a model of womanhood worthy of emulation. Mrs. Wilkins's unconditional sisterly love and assistance highlight the hypocrisy of a middle-class value system that taught the "true woman" to remain pure and pious by not associating with "bad" women, lest she become contaminated herself. Mrs. Wilkins practices sorority in her home, but there is also an important place for the Mrs. Wilkinses of the world in Christie's feminist reform community.

Making Christie's feminist circle even more revolutionary is the fact that there is also room for fallen women. Christie first encounters Rachel (later revealed, in a Dickensian plot twist, to be David's sister, Letty) while working as a seamstress and, despite Rachel's initial resistance, the two become close friends, with Christie finding in Rachel a "female soulmate" (Showalter xxxiii). When a fellow seamstress discovers Rachel's past, she exposes her as a fallen woman, insisting that their female employer fire Rachel. Christie arrives at the sweatshop just after Rachel's past has been revealed and finds her friend standing "alone, before them all ... a meek culprit at the stern bar of justice, where women try a sister woman" (Alcott 106). Met with a hostile, un-sisterly reception, Rachel almost falls again. Looking for sympathy, Rachel sees only "pity, aversion, or contempt, on every face," and even "Christie's eyes were bent thoughtfully on the ground, and Christie's heart seemed closed against her" (109). It is the treatment that Rachel receives from other women, even more than her fall itself, which seems insurmountable and "as she looked her whole manner changed; her tears ceased to fall, her face grew hard, and a reckless mood seemed to take possession of her, as if finding herself deserted by womankind, she would desert her own womanhood" (109). Rachel tells the women:

> It's no use for such as me to try; better go back to the old life, for there are kinder hearts among the sinners than among the saints, and no one can live without a bit of love. Your Magdalen Asylums are penitentiaries, not homes; I won't go to any of them. Your piety isn't worth much, for though you read in your Bibles how the Lord treated a poor soul like me, yet when I stretch out my hand to you for help, not one of all you virtuous, Christian women dare take it and keep me from a life that's worse than hell. (Alcott 109).

Rachel's denunciation of these unsympathetic women thus serves as a poignant illustration of the need for a new type of feminist reform.

This pivotal scene provides Christie with the opportunity to practice her feminist activism, and in treating Rachel as a sister Christie takes her first steps towards the sorority that later becomes one of the hallmarks of her feminist reform activity. Although "grieved and disappointed" at the discovery of her friend's past, Christie defends Rachel, telling her "I'll stand by you still" (Alcott 108). Christie appeals to the shop owner's sympathy and, in words reminiscent of Fuller's plea in *Woman* for her middle-class female readers to "take the place of mothers" to "degraded women" (329), she implores Mrs. King to "think of your own daughters, and be a mother to this poor girl for their sake" (Alcott 108). Here, Alcott imaginatively enacts Fuller's radical feminist sorority through her heroine, Christie. Taking Rachel's hand with a "touch, full of womanly compassion" (110), Christie is able to discern "the unfallen spirit of the woman" (111) in her eyes; she "took Rachel in her arms, kissed and cried over her with sisterly affection, and watched her prayerfully, as she went away to begin her hard task anew" (112). Although Christie is unable to save Rachel's job, through this heroic act of sisterhood she succeeds in saving Rachel from a second fall.

Furthermore, Christie's act of sorority has a ripple effect and Rachel, the fallen woman, becomes a feminist activist heroine as well; just as Christie had saved Rachel, she in turn rescues Christie when she is on the brink of committing suicide. As Rachel later reveals to Christie, after leaving Mrs. King's sweatshop in disgrace, she begins to practice the feminist activism Christie had displayed to her, telling her friend, "I went away where I was not known. There it came into my mind to do for others more wretched than I what you had done for me" (Alcott 125). Rachel's experience as a fellow fallen woman positions her in an egalitarian, horizontal relationship with the women she works to help, enabling her to succeed where a more "pure" woman might fail. As her words to Christie reveal: "I had no fear, no shame to overcome, for I was one of them. They would listen to me, for I knew what I spoke; they could believe in salvation, for I was saved; they did not feel so outcast and forlorn when I told them you had taken me into your innocent arms, and loved me like a sister" (126).

Seduced and subsequently abandoned, Rachel is ultimately redeemed and reinstated within her family, marking another of Alcott's radical breaks with conventional fictional portrayals of fallen women. Even when presented sympathetically, the fate of the fallen woman was almost always death, as was the case in Susanna Rowson's popular *Charlotte Temple* (1791), which helped to establish the formula that would be repeated in many subsequent seduction novels. Reflecting the social realities of nineteenth-century America, novelists struggled to imagine a social world where such women would be accepted without judgment. Thus, as Hawthorne tells the reader at the conclusion of the *Scarlet Letter* (1850), in a passage highly evocative of Fuller's *Woman*, Hester Prynne recognized that the world must wait for "some brighter period, when ... a new truth would be revealed, in order to establish the whole relation between man and woman on a surer ground of mutual happiness" (241). Throughout the era, even novels featuring a feminist activist as heroine and advocating the type of sorority enacted by Christie struggled to accept without judgment the fallen woman. For example, in Laura Curtis Bullard's *Christine* (1856), the eponymous heroine believes in aiding fallen women and demonstrates sorority with a friend, Annie, who "falls," but Annie's fate remains nonetheless conventional.[5] Similarly, in Elizabeth Boynton Harbert's *Amore* (1892), Hester Baird, the victim of rape, is shunned by a society that "thought that somehow she must have been at fault" (148), despite being treated as a sister by the novel's feminist heroine, Theodora; Hester is only restored years later when her repentant (and now-sober) attacker marries her.

In contrast, initially cast off by her brother David, Rachel has, after "years of patient well-doing, washed away her single sin" (Alcott 268). Suffering remorse for having abandoned his sister, David is resolved to find and restore her within the family. As he later explains, he "knew [his] home must be hers" (272). Finally reunited with Rachel/Letty, David boldly reclaims his sister, "sin" and all, telling Christie, "if any one dares think I am ashamed to own her now, let him know what cause I have to be proud of her; let him come and see how tenderly I love her; how devoutly I thank God for permitting me to find and bring my little Letty home" (268). Letty has a place in David's family, remaining in Christie's home as daughter, sister, and aunt. That Rachel/Letty is allowed to re-enter the family and take up her place within the domestic circle at Mrs. Sterling's house was, indeed, a radical departure from nineteenth-century norms, as was her membership in Christie's "loving league of sisters," through which she is on equal footing with the other members of this sorority.

While such intimate and informal "leagues" were one important way in which women could enact Fuller's feminist vision of sisterhood, the larger, better-organized, and more public women's clubs that were established after the Civil War were another vital legacy of Fuller's earlier work and one which feminist authors, including Alcott, depicted in their fiction. Clubwomen originally sought to come together in cultural organizations that echoed

Fuller's Boston Conversations (with their emphasis on self-culture, education, vocation, and sorority), later extending their efforts to include larger public reform projects, including women's suffrage. Often dismissed as apolitical and elitist, the women's club movement, much like Fuller's Conversations, served as a catalyst for feminist intellectual exchange, affirmation of woman's right to vocation and education, and broader reform initiatives. While the founders of the New England Woman's Club (NEWC)—one of two clubs that vied for the distinction of being the first to organize—most directly and explicitly drew on the Conversations, Fuller's influence on the origins and development of the woman's club extended far beyond the Boston women of the NEWC.

In the final chapter of *Work*, Christie attends "one of the many meeting of working-women, which had made some stir of late" (Alcott 330), where she is first moved to speak out, finding her true vocation and planting the seed for her future work as a woman's rights speaker, activist, and mediator. Discovering a network of middle-class women looking to help their working sisters, this organization, it could be argued, is a fictional representation of the NEWC and thus linked to Fuller's legacy. In addition to being a literary and cultural club, the NEWC was interested in reform projects, including its early work towards the establishment of the Women's Horticultural School in Newton, Massachusetts; a campaign to elect women to the Boston school boards; and involvement in dress-reform initiatives. One of the NEWC's earliest projects was the Friendly Evenings Association, through which working-class women could safely and comfortably meet (New England Women's Club Records, Folders 1–5: M-145, Reel 1). These Friendly Evenings were likely a real-world model for the meeting that Christie attends. The novel closes with Christie ready to embark upon her work in helping to organize and advocate for working women and in serving as mediator between classes. Like the early leaders and organizers of the NEWC, whose club work originates in Fuller's Conversations, Christie also picks up the threads of Fuller's feminist conversations and carries on her legacy.

Another way in which we can see this legacy of Fuller's conversations in Alcott's novel is through Christie's desire to serve as a mediator between women of different classes and backgrounds. Recognizing "how difficult it was for the two classes to meet and help one another in spite of the utmost need on one side and the sincerest good-will on the other" (Alcott 330), Christie is moved to speak at the meeting. Her speech is a success, largely due to her ability to successfully mediate between the working women and the "ladies." Both groups are "grateful" for her words, and the ladies invite her to return:

[They] had begged her to come and speak again, saying they needed just such a mediator to bridge across the space that now divided them from those they wished to serve. She certainly seemed fitted to act as interpreter between the two classes. (Alcott 334)

Like Fuller, whose work as conversationalist and writer was premised on cultural mediation, translation, and interpretation, which she employed in *Woman* to argue for the establishment of "the right relation between the sexes" (312), Christie has "a strong desire to bring the helpers and the helped into truer relations with each other" through her feminist activism (Alcott 331).

Desiring to serve as a mediator, facilitating multi-directional horizontal exchanges, Christie rejects the one-directional, vertical position of lecturer or orator, adopting a role more in line with that of Fuller in her Conversations. Speaking *with*, or *among*, the women in her audience, rather than *to* them, Christie declines an offer to ascend the platform, choosing to deliver her speech among the crowd, saying "I am better here, thank you; for I have been and mean to be a working-woman all my life" (Alcott 332). The other ladies who, "with kindliness, patience, and often unconscious condescension," had, like one well-meaning woman, "talked over the heads of [their] audience," delivering a "charming little essay," giving a "political oration," reading "reports of sundry reforms in foreign parts," and offering a "cheerful budget of statistics" (330–31), Christie adopted a more conversational tone, speaking with a "spirit of companionship" (333) as a sister working-woman. It is this position of sorority and equality, coupled with her own experiences as a working-woman, through which Christie gains authority, making her speech more effective than that of the middle-class speakers. Her audience felt that "more impressive than anything she said was the subtle magnetism of character, for that has a universal language which all can understand. They saw and felt that a genuine woman stood down there among them like a sister, ready with head, heart, and hand to help them help themselves; not offering pity as an alms, but justice as a right" (333).

Furthermore, *Work* highlights the importance of conversation (with its ability to change the status quo and lead to reform) as a valuable tool for feminist activism. Conversation is not only a means of bridging the gap *between* disparate classes, but it is also as a powerful method for consciousness-raising *among* the leisure class, as Christie's plan to give Bella something to "do" illustrates. The well-to-do Bella, too, needs a vocation. Coming to Christie for advice, Bella explains that while her brother Harry, with whom she shares a home, "has his work and loves it," she has "nothing after [her] duty to him is done" (Alcott 336). Christie's plan for Bella includes another sort of club as well, a genteel conversational club for men and women "in [her] own class" (338), hosted by Bella at her brother's home. Recognizing that this class of wealthy men and women "need help quite as much as the paupers, though in a very different way" (338), Christie believes that this reform work is better adapted to conversation, which can "quietly insinuate ... a better state of things into one little circle," than to the lecture platform, political convention, or public oration (339).

Like conversation, imaginative literature might also "quietly insinuate ... a better state of things into one little circle." Through novels such as *Work*, Alcott aimed to inspire a circle of readers to seek their right to vocation and education and their right (or duty) to construct feminist communities based on mutual cooperation, shared personal experiences, and the cultivation of sorority. Thus we can begin to trace a genealogy of feminist community-building from Fuller to the succeeding generation of American women, including Alcott, who had known Fuller personally as a young girl. Through their fiction, feminist writers such as Alcott responded to the two "great questions" that Fuller had asked and aimed to answer through her Boston Conversations: "What were we born to do?" and "How shall we do it?" (*Letters* II: 87).

Notes

1. I am indebted to Leslie Petty for the term "feminist activist heroine," which captures the diversity of reform activity that fell under the rubric of "feminism" in the 1870s and reflects the diverse body of women whose imaginations were sparked by Fuller's earlier life and writing. These fictional heroines served as inspiration for female readers, "bringing [them] to self-knowledge" (Petty 8) through which they might build real-world communities of women or become feminist activists themselves.

2. Fuller's place in the tradition of women's imaginative and feminist fiction remains largely unexplored. That the body of literary work Fuller produced did not include imaginative fiction (at least, not any stand-alone texts) has served as a barrier to the study of the relationship of Fuller to feminist fiction produced in the second half of the nineteenth century. Indeed, as Christina Zwarg has pointed out, feminist scholars have often struggled to place Fuller within a tradition of American women writers, primarily because she did not work within the dominant "women's" genres, sentimental and domestic fiction. There are exceptions to this general trend. For example, Annette Kolodny's reading of Fuller's *Summer on the Lakes, in 1843* connects it to American women's experience of the land; Nina Baym includes Fuller in her *American Women Writers and the Work of History*; and Sherry Lee Linkon situates Fuller within the context of other nineteenth-century American women essayists in *In Her Own Voice*.

3. In using the term "sorority," I draw on Bartlett's *Liberty, Equality, Sorority*.

4. See, for example, Fuller's "Asylum for Discharged Female Convicts."

5. Fleeing an abusive husband, Annie becomes a "sinner" (Bullard 293), after she begins a relationship with a free-love advocate, and eventually dies, leaving Christine to adopt her young daughter.

Works Cited

Alcott, Louisa May. *Work: A Story of Experience*. 1873. Ed. Joy S. Kasson. New York: Penguin, 1994.

Bartlett, Elizabeth Ann. *Liberty, Equality, Sorority: The Origins and Interpretations of American Feminist Thought: Frances Wright, Sarah Grimké, and Margaret Fuller*. Brooklyn: Carlson, 1994.

Baym, Nina. *American Women Writers and the Work of History, 1790–1860*. New Brunswick, NJ: Rutgers UP, 1995.

Bolton, Sarah K. "Louisa M. Alcott." *Friends' Intelligencer* 10 July 1886: 442–444. *American Periodicals*. 23 May 2014.

Bullard, Laura Curtis. *Christine: Or Woman's Trials and Triumphs*. 1856. Ed. Denise M. Kohn. Lincoln: U of Nebraska P, 2010.

Capper, Charles. *Margaret Fuller: An American Romantic Life, Volume II: The Public Years*. New York: Oxford UP, 2007.

Fuller, Margaret. "Asylum for Discharged Female Convicts." *New-York Tribune* 19 June 1845: 1. *Margaret Fuller, Critic: Writings from the New-York Tribune, 1844–1846*. Ed. Judith Mattson Bean and Joel Myerson. New York: Columbia UP, 2000. 134–137.

_____. *Letters of Margaret Fuller*. Ed. Robert Hudspeth. 6 vols. Ithaca: Cornell UP, 1983–1994.

_____. *Woman in the Nineteenth Century*. 1845. *Essential Margaret Fuller*. Ed. Jeffrey Steele. New Brunswick, NJ: Rutgers UP, 1992. 243–378.

Harbert, Elizabeth Boynton. *Amore*. Chicago: New Era Publishing, 1892.

_____. *Out of Her Sphere*. Des Moines, IA: Mills, 1871.

Hawthorne, Nathaniel. *The Scarlet Letter*. 1850. Intro. Michael J. Colacurcio. Cambridge, MA: Belknap P of Harvard UP, 2009.

Kasson, Joy S. "Introduction." *Work: A Story of Experience*. 1873. By Louisa May Alcott. Ed. Joy S. Kasson. New York: Penguin, 1994. ix–xxxi.

Kolodny, Annette. *Land Before Her: Fantasy and Experience of the American Frontiers, 1630–1860*. Chapel Hill: U of North Carolina P, 1984.

Lillie, Lucy C. "Louisa May Alcott." *The Cosmopolitan: A Monthly Illustrated Magazine* Apr. 1888: 156–64. *American Periodicals*. 23 May 2014.

Linkon, Sherry Lee, ed. *In Her Own Voice: Nineteenth-Century American Women Essayists*. New York: Garland, 1997.

New England Women's Club Records. Schlesinger Library, Radcliffe College.

Petty, Leslie. *Romancing the Vote: Feminist Activism in American Fiction, 1870–1920*. Athens: U of Georgia P, 2006.

Rowson, Susanna Haswell. *Charlotte Temple* (1794). Ed. Cathy N. Davidson. New York: Oxford UP, 1986.

Showalter, Elaine. Introduction. *Alternative Alcott*. Ed. Elaine Showalter. Brunswick: Rutgers UP, 1988. ix–xliii.

Zwarg, Christina. *Feminist Conversations: Fuller, Emerson, and the Play of Reading*. Ithaca: Cornell UP, 1995.

Polly, Pygmalion, and the (Im)practicalities of an Independent Womanhood⎯⎯⎯⎯⎯⎯⎯⎯⎯⎯

Marilyn Bloss Koester

Louisa May Alcott's *An Old-Fashioned Girl* (1870) offers a late nineteenth-century American version of the classic tale of the country mouse and the city mouse, where fourteen-year-old Polly Milton travels to the city and joins her fashionable and wealthy urbanite friend, Fanny Shaw. Despite her rejection by other sophisticated characters, Polly's charming and warm personality wins over the Shaw family. Six years after this initial visit, Polly returns to the city to pursue a career as a music teacher and reunites with Fanny, whose family now teeters on the brink of bankruptcy. Her friend's precarious financial situation allows Polly to introduce Fanny to a world outside wealth and fashion. This essay focuses on a particular scene during this secular education in which Polly introduces "real" women artists whose lives and work impact the sheltered sensibilities of fashionable Fanny. In this scene, we encounter a circle of five muses who embody the arts: Rebecca, the sculptor; Elizabeth, the engraver; Kate, the writer; Polly, the musician; and Fanny, the embodiment of high society charms. Here, Alcott celebrates the value of feminine community and incorporates symbols of women's rights and autonomy. This circle of imaginary women artists foretells the existence and activities of real women's artist groups who successfully navigate the male-dominated American art scene in the later nineteenth century and beyond. At the same time, Alcott creates a complex, ambiguous masculine/feminine dichotomy through the characters Becky and Bess. These women illustrate Alcott's view of women as artistic and independent, in both their attractive freedoms and their harsh realities. They (nearly) function independently of men, although their feminine agency remains tempered by Alcott's necessary reminders of propriety and domesticity in a text that must meet the demands of a conservative readership.

The scene appears in the chapter entitled "The Sunny Side," suggesting that readers will encounter a positive, hopeful message within its text. Like Jo's subversive maneuvers amid traditional trappings in *Little Women*, Polly's embrace of this atypical community remains within an otherwise traditional tale of girlhood. Couching the scene in the safe space of a domestic girl's book that exalts the "old-fashioned" virtues of hard work and selflessness enables Alcott to envision an artistic, communal womanhood in which she herself may have desired to belong. Parallels emerge between other novels, such as *Moods* (1864) and *Work* (1873), where Alcott's heroine steps outside of the conventional and accepted confines of young adult life. Polly becomes our guide to this world of subversive and creative femininity.

Before formal introductions to the characters Rebecca and Elizabeth, the protagonist Polly gives us a description of the pair as the embodiment of Damon and Pythias, symbols of loyal friendship in Greek legend. The two artists live in their studio and go "halves in everything" (Alcott, *Old-Fashioned* 239). Polly notes that the women are "all alone in the world, but happy and independent as birds—real friends, whom nothing will part" (239). Fanny contends that a lover will come between the women at some point and their partnership will not last. Polly answers, "Take a look at them and you'll change your mind" (239). What readers then see is a vision of an unbreakable, but unconventional, relationship between two female characters. It is not until the latter part of this scene that we discover Bess is going to be married, and Becky will also live with the couple, an arrangement with its own suggestive subversiveness. When asked if the two are going to "dissolve partnership," Bess quickly retorts, "Never! George knows he can't have one without the other, and has not suggested such a thing as parting us" (245).

Polly describes Rebecca Jeffrey, or Becky, as a "regularly splendid girl, full of talent" whom she believes will be famous one day (Alcott, *Old-Fashioned* 238). The use of the masculine surname "Jeffrey" is indicative of Rebecca's appearance and personality. She is described as being "tall, with a strong face, keen eyes, short curly hair, and a fine head" (239). This physical description could be easily read as one of many male figures in nineteenth-century texts. At first glance, she is also a "great clay figure," dominant, powerful and also non-human, a woman who perhaps could not exist in reality, but must be fashioned into clay herself (239). Alcott's descriptors entangle Becky with her current project, the clay sculpture of a woman. Both are literally covered in clay, as well as metaphorically covered in an aesthetic material that distances them from the reality of the average woman in Alcott's culture. Becky represents all that can be thought of as masculine, strong and dominant, juxtaposed with her partner, Elizabeth.

A "dreamy, absorbed little person" with large eyes, pale hair and a wan face, Becky's cohort, Elizabeth Small, also known as Bess or Lizzie, sits at a table by the window (Alcott, *Old-Fashioned* 239). Bess is the epitome of idealized femininity: small (in surname and stature), weak, pale, and talented in creating dainty artworks. Her looks and meek personality provide a feminine complement to Rebecca's masculine persona, just as Rebecca's powerful sculptures contrast with Lizzie's "delightful little pictures" (239). In this scene, "feminine" creations are figured as tiny delights, lacking the depth, strength and literal large size of masculine creations. Bess speaks quietly and rarely, reinforcing her idealized femininity. Alcott treats the pair with warmth and optimism, however, and the reader remains confident in their mutual affection and partnership.

Same-sex female friendships within nineteenth-century fiction have been romanticized as both socially acceptable and emblematic of virtuous conventionality.[1] This positioning does a disservice to the subversive and novel illustrations of female partnerships within Alcott's works, such as *An Old-Fashioned Girl*, *Little Women* (1868), *Diana and Persis* (1879), and *Work*, all of which contain same-sex relationships that have undertones of feminine eroticism. Jo and Beth March from *Little Women* echo the relationship of Becky and Bess, particularly in physical descriptions and loving endearments. The unpublished and unfinished *Diana and Persis* illustrates a similar relationship between two women, the sculptor Diana and her sensual partner Percy. We see this relationship yet again in *Work*, where working-class Christie woos the fallen woman Rachel. Marylynne Diggs argues that the typical "romantic friendship model," a model often seen in Alcott's works, continually "overlooks both the pathologizing and the resistant discourses that emerged in the United States well before the turn of the century" (320). In particular, Diggs uses this scene from *An Old-Fashioned Girl* as an example of how female friendships could be viewed as problematic by contemporaries. She quotes Fanny, who states that the circle of women artists are a "different race of creatures," a quotation used in her article's title, to illustrate the unconventional nature of the women surrounding her (Diggs 321).

The continued use of these same-sex relationships demonstrates Alcott's familiarity and reliance on such female partnership tropes, although Alcott adds an underlying element of sensuality. Gregory Eiselein claims that Alcott uses "sentimental discourses to eroticize the representation of women workers and the romantic-erotic possibilities opened up by work" (204). In similar fashion, *An Old-Fashioned Girl* eroticizes the female artist and even art itself. Aside from the tired-looking Kate, the other Sunny Side muses are portrayed as attractive, each in their own way. More telling, Fanny also notes that "men must respect such girls as these ... and love them, too, for in spite of their independence, they are womanly" (Alcott, *Old-Fashioned* 244). Her thoughts demonstrate Fanny's reliance on male validation, despite the independence the three have achieved, but Fanny also sees that women can work according to their own desires and still attract men with their feminine virtues. This consoles Fanny and allows her to cherish her experience in the studio. As Eiselein suggests, sentimental fiction allows readers to identify with non-traditional characters and become more comfortable with progressive ideologies. By encouraging identification with the characters, Alcott makes such "alternative" choices attractive and accessible to readers.

Upon the entrance of Polly and Fanny, Becky asks Polly to pose for her, immediately indicating the interdependence of these women. They are each other's models and muses and an outlet for camaraderie and creativity, echoing Alcott's own use of her female family members as models for her characters. Becky proceeds to lift the veil off the head of her current statue; a move that excites a cry from Fanny, "How beautiful it is!" (Alcott, *Old-Fashioned* 240). Rebecca immediately turns her "keen" eyes to Fanny and asks a question wrought with emotional and aesthetic significance: "What does it mean to you?" (240). Here stands a sculpture of a woman that defies the current aesthetics of femininity that link women with the diminutive, the small, the sexualized, and the passive. Even Fanny, the likeable yet snobbish socialite, sees its brilliance, remarking, "I don't know whether it is meant for a saint or a muse, a goddess or a fate, but to me it is only a beautiful woman, bigger, lovelier, and more imposing than any woman I ever saw" (240). This clay woman treads on the ground. She is no saint, muse, or goddess, but rather a representation of Alcott's idealized "real" woman, large and commanding, yet lovely and attractive. The women approve of Fanny's assessment with smiles, nods, and hand clapping. Despite her lack of arts education and her shallow notions of fashion and class, Fanny has recognized that which is normally lacking in artistic depictions of women. After acknowledging her incorrect assumption that Fanny would fail to recognize the sculpture's value, Polly proudly states that Fanny has paid Rebecca "the compliment of understanding her work" (240).

Polly elaborates on this womanly representation, echoing Fanny's adjectives and adding that "she is a true woman…the mouth is both firm and tender, as if it could say strong, wise things as well as teach children and kiss babies" (Alcott, *Old-Fashioned* 240). This is Alcott's ideal woman as reflected in her juvenile texts, dedicated to domesticity and motherhood, but also educated and robust. As Rebecca explains, "strength and beauty must go together" (241). It is not enough for a woman to be strong, wise, or talented. She must also be beautiful. This mantra tempers Alcott's feminism. In part, Alcott caters to a readership of young, middle-class women brought up in a culture defined by beauty and domesticity. To ignore the role of femininity and motherhood would alienate her readers, potentially resulting in a novel that fares less successfully in the literary marketplace—an unacceptable outcome for Alcott whose family depended on the financial success of her writing.[2]

Alcott returns to Greek allusions with this sculpture to subvert Pygmalion's statue myth. The myth arises in Alcott's works directly, as in *Jo's Boys*, where "Laurie, looking at his tall girl as Pygmalion might have looked at Galatea" (29), and indirectly, as in "A Marble Woman."[3] In the original myth, Pygmalion, disenchanted with the promiscuous women surrounding him, fashions his ideal woman out of ivory and prays for the goddess Venus to grant him a woman as perfect as his statue. The goddess bestows the breath of life into his ivory maiden and the pair marry, living happily ever after. Alcott's women are not so fortunate.

These American women know the ancient Greek mythology their European cohorts cherish, but, living in the New World with its own history and mythologies, they often overturn or reshape those Old World myths. Perhaps Alcott had grown weary with the neoclassicism popular in mid-century aesthetics. Perhaps she wanted to create a new work of art, a visual work embedded in her own literary text that went beyond the traditional historical and mythological narrative. In Alcott's *Psyche's Art*, the heroine Psyche comments on the "genius" statue of sculptor Paul Gage, "It was neither a mythological nor historical character, Psyche thought, and was glad of it, being tired to death of gods and heroes" (6). Like Psyche's awareness of Paul's sculpture's new intentions, Alcott's sculptor in *An Old-Fashioned Girl* breaks new ground, birthing a woman from American clay, one grounded in new freedoms and ideologies.

Nineteenth-century male artists, European or American, often recreated classical mythology in its original context. Sir Edward Coley Burne-Jones's painting *Pygmalion and Galatea* (1878) and Jean-Léon Gérôme's sculpture *Pygmalion and Galatea* (1890) were each visual recreations of the myth. But American women artists often felt the need to create their own foundations and re-envision continental mythology in a way that reflected the reality of their lives. For example, Harriet Hosmer, the Boston-born sculptor who inspired Alcott, created a bust of *Medusa* (1854) that defies neoclassical style and reveals a tender, beautiful version that highlights the dual nature of her existence as both victim and vehicle. The American woman artist embodies the hopes and desires of a "New Woman," a term made popular by nineteenth-century American author Henry James, indicating a woman who advocated equality and freedom, while exercising the right of social and economic independence. Hosmer herself, like many of James' expatriate female characters, moved from Boston to Rome to further her own artistic career and thereby inspired many young American female artists to pursue their own independence.[4] Like Hosmer's *Medusa*, Alcott's statuesque woman does not rely on a male artist to design her according to his desires, and the woman artist does not call on a supernatural source to bestow gifts. No goddess will bring Becky's statue to life; Alcott's women must do this themselves.

The most telling moment comes when the four women decide what to put in the hands of this representation of the New Woman. Rebecca denounces Fanny's suggestion of a scepter and Polly's suggestion of a man's hand, saying "my woman is to stand alone and help herself ... strong-minded, strong-hearted, strong-souled, and strong-bodied" (Alcott, *Old-Fashioned* 241). Quiet, feminine Bess suggests a child be put in her arms, but Rebecca refuses. A new voice from an "odd-looking woman" behind them calls out, "Give her a ballot box" (241).

The new voice belongs to Kate King, a writer with some degree of notoriety, confirmed by Fanny's adoration and Polly's addressing her as "my King" (Alcott, *Old-Fashioned* 242), although Alcott moderates the allusions to royalty by stating that the "shabby" Kate wrote "a successful book by accident and happened to be the fashion just then" (242). The comment downplays Kate's talent and writes off her book as a passing fad. We are told that Kate's life has not been easy, and Fanny wonders if women will ever be able to achieve success or financial benefit "without paying such a heavy price for them, for Kate looked sick, tired and too early old" (246). This description illustrates Alcott's ambivalence towards successful women artists. If they do achieve notoriety and fame, like Kate King, then their feminine beauty seems also to diminish.

Kate's story echoes Alcott's own life, as she had to work exceptionally hard, at the expense of her personal life and health, to provide for her family.[5] Janice M. Alberghene highlights these commonalities, noting that Alcott often described herself as ill and exhausted from work and quoting Alcott's own description of writing *An Old-Fashioned Girl*: "I wrote it with left hand in a sling, one foot up, head aching, and no voice ... I certainly earn my living by the sweat of my brow" (qtd. in Alberghene 42). Alberghene contends that Kate and the other artists are present in this one chapter only because the hardships of their lives were too dreary for young readers. More likely, the subversive nature of their lives could not feature too prominently in a traditional juvenile novel. Another of her artists, Psyche from *Psyche's Art*, echoes Alcott's difficult trial of trying to "serve both masters at once" (8). Like Alcott, she must support and care for her family, often at the expense of her artistic pursuits. The narrator laments this continuous obstacle, noting "Sculpture and sewing, calls and crayons, Ruskin and receipt-books, didn't work well together, and poor Psyche found duties and desires desperately antagonistic" (Alcott, *Psyche* 8).

Kate then announces she will use Polly as a model for her next novel, just as Alcott often used women in her own life as inspiration for her characters. Polly appears shocked, "Me! Why there never was such a humdrum, unromantic thing as I am" (Alcott, *Old-Fashioned* 246). This self-deprecating announcement fails to deter Kate from her decision to include Polly. The move also illustrates the value of the "ordinary" girl, demonstrating that even the common young woman may become involved in an uncommon and entertaining story. Kate doesn't wish to create a character from an unrealistic and imaginary ideal, such as Pygmalion, but desires to shape the actual woman who exists in her lifetime. Furthermore, their creative partnership illustrates that Alcott's women must use a multilayered aesthetic to enact social change through interdependence on each other. Through visual arts, musical arts and writing arts, the women join in a united front of artistic expression to produce public works that inform young women at large of the possibilities available to them, although these possibilities function successfully in the text due to their supportive community.

Although Rebecca has yet to decide what will be placed in her clay woman's hands, she does add Kate's suggestion of the ballot box to her list of symbols at the statue's feet. These symbols—"needle, pen, palette, broom" and now ballot box—prove quite telling, embodying the mitigated feminism of Alcott's women (Alcott, *Old-Fashioned* 241). They may be writers and artists, but they still wield the traditionally domestic feminine tools of the needle and broom. To proclaim the woman's right to vote is certainly a forward step, especially when we remember that the Nineteenth Amendment guaranteeing this right isn't ratified until nearly fifty years later. Nevertheless, insisting on the right to vote and to work and live as independent artists does not liberate these women from "necessary" domestic obligations.

Alcott's own childhood was steeped in suffrage movements. As Madeleine Stern details in her article "Louisa Alcott's Feminist Letters," Alcott's father, Bronson Alcott, attended the First National Woman's Rights Convention of 1850 and supported suffrage and women's rights throughout his life, stating publicly in 1881, "Not until the women of our nation have been granted every privilege would the liberty of our republic be assured" (qtd. in Stern 430). Alcott herself was undoubtedly influenced by her parents' reform work, but she did not participate directly in women's suffrage until the 1870s. Beginning in 1874, she wrote several letters for the women's suffrage paper, *Woman's Journal*. In her journal for July 1879, she notes that she "was the first woman to register my name as a voter" after the Act to Give Women the Right to Vote for Members of the School Committees was approved in Massachusetts (Alcott, *Journals* 216). Stern includes many of Alcott's *Woman's Journal* letters in her article, but one in particular directly relates to the ideas in *An Old-Fashioned Girl*, written thirteen years earlier. In this 1883 letter, Alcott argues against the assumption that suffragists and motherhood are mutually exclusive:

> The assertion that suffragists do not care for children, and prefer notoriety to the joys of maternity, is so fully contradicted by the lives of the women who are trying to make the world a safer and a better place for both sons and daughters, that no defense is needed. Having

spent my own life, from fifteen to fifty, loving and laboring for children, as teacher, nurse, story-teller and guardian, I know whereof I speak, and value their respect and confidence so highly that for their sakes, if for no other reason, I desire them to know that their old friend never deserts her flag. (*Letters* 269)

Like Becky, Alcott argues that womanhood and motherhood go hand in hand. A woman may fight for women's rights, including the right to vote, without sacrificing her own desires for a "traditional" and stable family life. Women must stand together, support each other, and pursue freedoms, thereby honoring their families and children by making the world "a better place." Alcott values domestic labor, a labor that is routinely trivialized or dismissed as not "real" work. According to Beverly Lyon Clark, Alcott is a "domestic feminist," who espouses women's rights personally and values loyalty to family above all else in her books (93). This ambivalence can be seen in the empty hands of Rebecca's statue and in the positive examples of independent women who remain minor characters in a novel that otherwise upholds conservative values. Clark argues that "though Alcott gives some play to subversive ideas of self-expression, her overt message is that girls should subordinate themselves and their language to others," citing the example of Jo being forced to forgive Amy for burning the manuscript of her book (81). Such ambivalence seems to shape not only this scene, but also the remainder of *An Old-Fashioned Girl*, although this ambivalence may also reflect Alcott's wish to deliver what her traditional audience wanted to read.

Returning to the scene following Kate's entrance, the five women in Alcott's chapter pull together a variety of foods and snacks for an impromptu picnic, during which Fanny muses upon the impact this "different race of creatures" has upon her (Alcott, *Old-Fashioned* 244). The artists have opened up a new world to her, one in which shows her that a woman's life can exist beyond those "spent in dress, gossip, pleasure or *ennui*." Going further, Fanny realizes that these women "were girls still, full of spirits, fun, and purpose, which seemed to ennoble her womanhood, to give her a certain power, a sustaining satisfaction, a daily stimulus that led her on to daily effort and in time to some success in circumstance or character" (244). Fanny calls her own worth into question, pondering with "sincerest emotion" whether her life is aimless and stating, "I wish I had a talent to live for, if it would do as much for me as it does for them .... Money can't buy these things for me, and I want them very much" (244). Until this point, wealth and social status have supported Fanny and directed her ambitions. For the first time, she experiences a desire that lies beyond money. One cannot buy talent. Talent must be developed and encouraged, and artistic talents are not the kind the high-society Shaw family seems to value.

The focus of the scene then swings back to the female statue, as Fanny impulsively states that Rebecca should "put that in marble and show us what we ought to be" (Alcott, *Old-Fashioned* 246). Fanny's statement echoes Alcott's use of Michelangelo's famous quotation in *Jo's Boys,* "Clay represents life; plaster, death; marble, immortality" (82). This clay woman represents life, possibility, and hope. She is not ready to be fixed and immortalized in marble, and she may never be, as the role of women in their contemporary society exists in a precarious, ever-changing position. Yet following Fanny's declaration, there is a pause. All five women sit in silence, "looking up at the beautiful, strong figure before them, each longing to see it done and each unconscious that she was helping, by her individual effort and experience, to bring the day when their noblest ideal of womanhood should be embodied in flesh and blood, not clay" (Alcott, *Old-Fashioned* 246). The stillness of the moment invites the reader to participate in contemplating this figure. It also highlights their genuine, internal reflections and their shared kinship in making this woman a reality. Nina Auerbach notes that Alcott seeks to communicate "a community of new women whose sisterhood is not an apprenticeship making them worthy of appropriation by father-husbands, but a bond whose value is itself" (22). She aptly calls Becky's statue the "collective daughter" of the artistic group, emphasizing the communal nature of this piece and pointing implicitly to the lack of female artistic communities at the time.

In this scene, Alcott champions the creation of female-supported artistic communities. Counterparts to traditional male artist groups, such as the Boston Artists' Association or the New England Art Union, simply didn't exist until the mid-late nineteenth century in America. The growing public presence of women artists slowly emerged during the course of Alcott's career. Julie Graham traces the nineteenth-century American women's art scene, noting that groups such as the Women's Art School of the Cooper Union and the Philadelphia School of Design for Women opened mid-century. Despite such communities, the predominant attitude toward women and the arts saw the arts as merely a hobby of pleasure for women, not an actual independent career. Graham cites a report from the 1868 feminist paper *The Revolution* that states of the 160 women enrolled at Cooper Union, only twenty planned professional careers (8). Alcott's own characters from other works, such as Psyche from *Psyche's Art* or May from *Little Women,* exemplify the woman artist as hobbyist economically dependent on outside sources. The Sunny Side artists fall into the minority category of women striving to make a self-sustaining career from their artistic works. The newly formed art schools and groups were not, for the most part, ready to provide the kind of support and exposure female artists like those in Alcott's fictional circle would have needed to enter the overwhelmingly male-dominated world of the arts.

One particular organization, The Ladies' Art Association (LAA) was founded in 1867 and epitomized the traditional role of women in the arts. The LAA failed to challenge the current status of women in the arts and their exhibitions catered to stereotypical female artistic representations as seen in a *New York Times* review of their 1877 annual show, which reported numerous flower paintings "for which women have a constitutional fondness" (qtd. in Graham 9). Twelve years later, however, The National Association of Women Artists arose in 1889 under similar circumstances as those represented in *An Old-Fashioned Girl.* Five young women, like Alcott's group of five women, met in a Washington Square studio on January 31, 1889. The women agreed "that since there was strong discrimination against the work of women in existing exhibitions, something must be done to secure opportunities for them to show their work in dignified, professional auspices" (qtd. in Graham

10). The women of the National Association succeeded in making their vision a reality. These organizations produced few renowned artists, however, leaving these successful women artists to develop within an art world dominated by a masculine majority.[6] To counter this economic and gender dependence, Alcott's Sunny Side muses encourage a female artistic community that has the potential to be self-supporting, and they seek to rectify the lack of support for independent women artists. Captivatingly, the famous American illustrator Jessie Willcox Smith, who illustrated the 1902 edition of Alcott's *An Old-Fashioned Girl*, lived in a similar arrangement as the Sunny Side muses. Collectively called "The Red Rose Girls," Smith and her artistic sisterhood obtained financial independence and fostered creativity amongst themselves, illustrating how Alcott's fictional desire for an independent female artistic partnership could be a reality.

The Sunny Side scene ends with the women parting by shaking hands, unlike the goodbye kisses that Fanny is accustomed to, and with Fanny asking Polly if she may return again and visit these new "creatures," in the hopes that they might make her "better." These foreign "creatures," not quite "women" yet to her, have disrupted Fanny's comfort and reliance on dominant feminine ideals. She wants to grow, a desire that reveals a timid optimism on Alcott's part as well as an awareness of how more "conventional" women can often respond to more "unconventional" women. Fanny reiterates her earlier fears to Polly after leaving, confessing, "I like your friends very much, Polly. I was afraid I should find them mannish and rough, or sentimental and conceited. But they are simple, sensible creatures full of talent and all sorts of fine things" (Alcott, *Old-Fashioned* 247). Polly beams in response, for Fanny "stood the test better than [she] expected," and she hopes that Fanny can learn "what helpful friends girls may be to one another," again reaffirming the importance of a communal sisterhood (247).

Poor Fanny never has the chance to explore her artistic side or meet with the lovely creatures again, as her family's fall in status and wealth requires her to "wrestle with housekeeping, 'help,' and heartache" (Alcott, *Old-Fashioned* 320). Fanny eventually attracts the attention of a long-pined-for suitor, Arthur Sydney, but only because he is a "domestic man and admired housewifely accomplishments" (329). In fact, Fanny hardly believes his declarations of affection and marriage proposal, stating that she is too "weak and poor and silly" (332). Although the visit to the "Sunny Side" may inspire a transformative effect on Fanny's outlook, it fails to alter the traditional trajectory of marriage in Alcott's storyline. The brief interlude does, however, offer readers a glimpse of an alternate life, one that rests on creativity and communal womanhood. Polly declares to Fanny that "'Help one another' is part of the religion of our sisterhood" and that sisterhood exists, even if it remains a small one nearly hidden, nestled amidst a traditional society and story (246).

We never know what Rebecca places in the hands of the statue. Perhaps Alcott herself remained uncertain about which symbol should represent modern femininity. The pen, palette, needle, broom, and ballot box all remain at the clay woman's feet while the space in her hands remains empty, echoing Alcott's own reluctance to embrace, or to portray, a womanly ideal entirely free from the domestic sphere. The resulting ideal reflects Alcott's dedication to her traditional readership. As so many female readers begged of her *Little Women*, a novel is not complete without marrying off the female characters.[7] Alcott's awareness of her audience may be the stultifying force behind her reluctance to fully identify the modern woman developing in Becky's studio with a more radical feminism. Although her female characters remain entrenched in the call of domesticity, Alcott does make a case for female self-sufficiency and interdependence. As Becky stated, her woman must "stand alone and help herself" (Alcott, *Old-Fashioned* 241). Alcott's artists rely on one another for inspiration and support, fostering a female community of artistry and (mitigated) freedom outside of the patriarchal sphere. As the narrator of *An Old-Fashioned Girl* notes, "the 'women who dare' are few, the women who 'stand and wait' are many" (332). Perhaps outside of the space in Alcott's novel, a woman artist, represented by the inspiring Rebecca Jeffrey, would dare to complete her statue and encourage the creation of an independent, fulfilling womanhood.

Notes

1. Smith-Rosenberg brought same-sex female relationships into the critical conversation, and scholars continue to research the subject.
2. Indeed, *An Old-Fashioned Girl* was successful. In an 1877 letter, Alcott writes: "I am thinking of a new book like Old Fashioned Girl, as my publisher tells me that sells better than any other of my immortal tales" (*Letters* 220).
3. "A Marble Woman" (1865), one of Alcott's thrillers, tells the story of an artist, Bazil Yorke, who adopts a child, Cecil, and proceeds to turn her into his "marble woman."
4. For further reading on Hosmer, see Culkin.
5. Alcott's biographers, such as Cheney and Stern, emphasize the difficulties Alcott faced to support her family financially through writing. In addition to financial strain, Alcott frequently acknowledged her declining health (*Journals* 171; 184).
6. Exceptions, particularly in Boston, can be found in Hirshler.
7. In her journal, Alcott bemoans her readers' requests for the March girls to marry: "Girls write to ask who the little women marry, as if that was the only end and aim of a woman's life. I *won't* marry Jo to Laurie to please any one" (*Journals* 167).

Works Cited

Alberghene, Janice M. "Alcott's Psyche and Kate: Self-Portraits, Sunny Side Up." *Proceedings of the Eighth Annual Conference of the Children's Literature Association, University of Minnesota, March 1981*. Ed. Priscilla A. Ord. New Rochelle, NY: [Children's Literature Association], 1982. 37-43.

Alcott, Louisa M. *Jo's Boys*. 1886. Boston: Roberts Brothers, 1891.

_____. *The Journals of Louisa May Alcott*. Ed. Joel Myerson, Daniel Shealy, and Madeleine B. Stern. Boston: Little, Brown, 1989.

_____. *An Old-Fashioned Girl*. 1870. New York: Puffin, 2004.

_____. *Psyche's Art*. Boston: Loring, 1868.

_____. *The Selected Letters of Louisa May Alcott*. Ed. Joel Myerson, Daniel Shealy, and Madeleine B. Stern. Boston: Little, Brown, 1987.

Auerbach, Nina. "Austen and Alcott on Matriarchy: New Women or New Wines?" *NOVEL: A Forum on Fiction* 10.1 (1976): 6–26.

Clark, Beverly Lyon. "A Portrait of the Artist as a Little Woman." *Children's Literature* 17 (1989): 81–97.

Culkin, Kate. *Harriet Hosmer: A Cultural Biography*. Amherst, MA: U of Massachusetts P, 2010.

Diggs, Marylynne. "Romantic Friends or a 'Different Race of Creatures'? The Representation of Lesbian Pathology in Nineteenth-Century America." *Feminist Studies* 21.2 (1995): 317–40.

Eiselein, Gregory. "Sentimental Discourse and the Bisexual Erotics of Work." *Texas Studies in Literature and Language* 41.3 (1999): 203–35.

Graham, Julie. "American Women Artists' Groups: 1867–1930." *Woman's Art Journal* 1.1 (1980): 7–12.

Hirshler, Erica. *A Studio of Her Own: Women Artists in Boston 1870–1940*. Boston: MFA Publications, 2001.

Smith-Rosenberg, Carroll. "The Female World of Love and Ritual: Relations between Women in Nineteenth-Century America." *Signs* 1.1 (1975): 1–29.

Stern, Madeleine B. "Louisa Alcott's Feminist Letters." *Studies in the American Renaissance* (1978): 429–452.

Violence and Confinement in *Little Men*_____

Antoinette M. Tadolini

> The story is not a pretty one. There is violence in it. And cruelty.
> But stories that are not pretty have a certain value, too, I suppose.
> Everything, as you well know (having lived in this world long enough
> to have figured out a thing or two for yourself), cannot always be
> sweetness and light.
>
> (Kate DiCamillo 183)

> I think it is really important to show dark things to kids—and in the
> showing, to also show that dark things can be beaten, that you have
> power.
>
> (Neil Gaiman)

At the conclusion of *Little Women*, formerly rebellious Jo March
marries doughty Professor Bhaer and opens a boy's school at
Plumfield, an estate she has inherited from her Aunt March. *Little
Men* picks up with Jo and the professor well-established. On the
surface, Plumfield is a supportive and peaceful community. A more
discerning reader, however, will recognize that violence is prevalent
and that Plumfield is actually characterized as a sort of prison.
Indeed, Plumfield is actually more akin to what Laurie humorously
refers to at the end of *Little Women* as a "Bhaer-garten" (376) which,
as the note explains, is "an arena wherein bears were baited and
tortured" (Alcott, *Little Women*, 376, n3).

Scholars have previously considered issues of violence and
confinement in *Little Men*. Elizabeth Lennox Keyser and Michael
Moon have concluded that the presence of these themes renders
the novel as a covert horror story or dystopia. Alternately, Gregory
Eiselein considers strands of violence and nonviolence as one of
the numerous paired contradictions in the text that are a part of "a
more general thematic about normative expectations and sanctions"
(10). These and other critical views have not fully addressed the
complexity and nuance of *Little Men*. Close reading of key scenes

of violence and confinement in the novel demonstrates that Alcott, despite her derisive characterization of her children's novels later in her career as "moral pap" (*Journals* 204), deliberately portrays Plumfield as a microcosm of the real world, rife with moral ambiguities and violence. Significantly, the novel acknowledges that chaos and violence do exist, but they can be controlled and are survivable. Moreover, negotiating the violence of childhood, characters are better prepared to face the challenges offered by the world beyond the gates of Plumfield.

Life at Plumfield is represented as everything a "wilderness of boys" could hope for. Violent tendencies seem controlled or channeled: for example, the pillow fights scheduled for Saturday nights. This surface placidity deepens the impact of Alcott's violent scenes, several of which are most unsettling. Child-to-child violence is lavishly described when Dan provokes Emil to fight: "Emil's face was covered with blood from a cut lip and a bruised nose, while a bump on his forehead was already as purple as a plum" (Alcott, *Little Men* 89). Similarly, the children incite Nan to self-abuse in order to demonstrate her toughness, bringing her "tingling hands ... and the purple lump rapidly developing itself on her forehead" (106). Moon concludes that such scenes demonstrate "the displacement of the putative responsibility for wreaking disciplinary violence on child bodies from the adult sphere, where it had long resided, onto the child sphere" (210). This, he argues, is because Alcott represents "physical pain and suffering ... as both necessary and inevitable to child life" (210). Indeed, to the extent that Alcott is depicting the reality of the life of a child in the rough and tumble of a school, the tradition of the school story mandates some sort of violence, whether student-on-student (as in Thomas Hughes' *Tom Brown's Schooldays*) or headmaster-on-student (as recounted by Roald Dahl in *Boy: Tales of Childhood*).

Dan and Nan, the two most inherently volatile of the Plumfield students, provoke the violent incidents described above. Still, to grapple fully with the complexity of the worldview Alcott portrays in the novel, it is important to analyze as well the violence surrounding the more pacific children. Nat, who had regularly experienced physical violence in his pre-Plumfield life, is the key character in several telling incidents of Plumfield violence. "[A]s docile and affectionate as a girl," Nat is often called a "daughter" by Father Bhaer and "thought amiable but weak" by Mrs. Jo, who "liked manly boys" (Alcott, *Little Men* 56). Nat's fault is that he tells lies, primarily to avoid violence and ridicule: "I used to tell 'em because I was afraid of father and Nicolo, and now I do sometimes because the boys laugh at me" (56). Father Bhaer approvingly tells Nat that his own "dear grandmother" had cured him of lying by "[drawing] out my tongue and snipp[ing] the end with her scissors till the blood ran" (56). Leaving that gruesome image implanted in Nat's (and the reader's) mind, Bhaer threatens Nat with a punishment far more severe, from Nat's perspective: "when you tell a lie I will not punish you, but you shall punish me" (57). Nat is properly cowed, "since love of him [Mr. Bhaer] would be more powerful with Nat than fear for himself" (57). Nat stumbles, however, "when peppery Emil threatened to thrash him if it was he who had run over his garden … Nat declared he didn't and then was ashamed to own up that he did do it, when Jack was chasing him the night before" (57). Two incidents of Plumfield violence are embedded in this sentence: Emil's threat and Jack's chasing Nat. The rational conclusions are that Emil would have thrashed Nat had he told the truth and that Jack would have engaged in some sort of physical violence against Nat if he had caught him. These scenarios suggest that Plumfield is awash in physical violence during student leisure times. Bhaer's refusal to credit the validity of Nat's motives for this lie are also instructive: Nat was expected to either endure Jack's thrashing and stay out of the corn or, alternatively, endure Emil's thrashing as retribution for having avoided Jack's physical violence. In either scenario, Nat was expected by the denizens of Plumfield to accept being the victim of physical violence. Nat's lie, even though rationally self-protective, is perceived by Mr. Bhaer as the moral fault requiring correction. As threatened, Mr. Bhaer requires that Nat physically punish him, in a scene that ends with Nat "sobbing out in a passion of love, and shame, and penitence: 'I will remember! Oh, I will!'" (59). This scene is wrenching in its emotional intensity as it portrays the sensitive boy being forced to inflict violence on one he has come to care for. There is no doubt that this punishment is a psychological form of violence much more cruel than an actual physical thrashing. Elizabeth Barnes astutely finds this scene to be another locus of moral ambivalence in the novel, since its avowedly benign intent of sparing the child from the physical abuse results in "the child learn[ing] to internalize other people's pain as, literally, his or her fault" (14). Nat's treatment here seems unfair, but the real world is frequently unjust. Further, Alcott shows that the harsh punishment is effective: Nat not only survives, but remembers not to lie, even later in the book when he endures cruel ostracism rather than lie in order to protect himself from an unjust accusation of theft.

Tommy is missing one dollar, and Nat is presumed to be the only one who knew where it was. When Mr. Bhaer solemnly questions each boy in turn, Nat denies having taken the money with "trembling lips" (Alcott, *Little Men* 205). In an interesting narrative move, Alcott keeps the reader ignorant: Nat is the apparent thief. Mr. Bhaer makes it clear to him and all the boys that suspicion rests on Nat, while setting the stage for Nat's ostracism: "I cannot expect you to feel as kindly toward anyone whom you suspect as before this happened, but I do expect and desire that you will not torment the suspected person in any way" (206). Despite Mr. Bhaer's exhortations to the other boys, Nat suffers: "even the hardest beating he ever received from his father was far easier to bear than the cold looks, the avoidance, and general suspicion that met him on all sides" (206). Daisy, Nat's only believer, "actually slapped her beloved Demi when he tried to convince her that it *must* have been Nat because no one else knew where the money was" (emphasis in original, 207). The tension builds and Nat confides to his protector Dan: "'It's so hard to have 'em hate me for nothing. I don't think I *can* bear it much longer. If I had any place to go to, I'd run away, though I love Plumfield dearly; but I'm not brave and big like you, so I must stay and wait till someone shows them that I haven't lied'" (211, emphasis in original). Dan is moved by his friend's desperation and lies himself, claiming that he stole the missing money (217). The reaction of the Plumfield residents to Dan's confession is instructive about this society: "it was harder somehow to see brave Dan disgraced than timid Nat" (217). At the same time as the Plumfield residents, the reader is informed that Dan is innocent; he has lied to protect his friend Nat. Mr. Bhaer forgives Dan because "it was a kind lie" (221). Mrs. Jo is so exultant that "she wanted to dance a jig for joy" (221). No one ever apologizes to Nat for his "week of slow torture" (206), during which he refuses to lie to free himself from the presumption of guilt. Dan is lavishly rewarded for his lie in the currency of Plumfield, spending a secluded half-hour with Mrs. Jo in the parlor. The boys are so penitent that they get together their meager funds and buy him a longed-for microscope (229). The tangled morality in this entire incident, intermingled with violence, double standards, and social ostracism demonstrates again that the novel is a portrayal of a realistic world, in which the students and the reader must continually engage with moral ambivalence.

Additional challenges are faced by other innocents at the school. Demi, whose spiritual and fanciful attitudes are becoming distorted by his interactions with the other boys, invents an "invisible sprite called 'The Naughty Kitty-mouse,' whom the children had believed in, feared, and served for a long time" (Alcott, *Little Men* 112). In an oft-discussed episode from the novel, Demi notifies Daisy that the Kitty-mouse wants a "'*sackerryfice*' ... we must bring all the things we like best ... and burn them!' he added with an awful emphasis on the last words" (113, emphasis in original). Daisy, anxious at the appearance of the dreaded Kitty-mouse, reluctantly contributes her new paper dolls, since she "never thought of denying the unseen tyrant anything it demanded" (113), anymore than she denied the seen tyrant, Demi. They are joined in this misadventure by Rob and Teddy. The children burn their most treasured toys on the altar, one-by-one, becoming frenzied by the excitement: "the lookers-on enjoyed the spectacle immensely, cheering as each house fell, dancing like wild Indians when the steeple flamed aloft, and actually casting one wretched little churn-shaped lady who had escaped to the suburbs, into the very heart of the fire" (115). Teddy is too young to understand why the children are bringing along toys, but tucks his doll Annabella under his arm, "little dreaming what anguish the latter idol was to give him" (114). When he places the doll on the fire, "she did not blaze, but did what was worse, she *squirmed*. First one leg curled up, then the other, in a very awful and lifelike manner; next she flung her arms over her head as if in great agony; her head itself turned on her shoulders, her glass eyes fell out, and with one final writhe of her whole body, she sank down a blackened mass on the ruins of the town" (115–116, emphasis in original). The reader, like Teddy and the other witnessing children, is repulsed and appalled. Critic William Blackburn describes this scene "as one of the most remarkable moments in the novel, a moment in which Alcott's model children are wondrously transformed," wondering as well whether "[i]t would perhaps be perverse to suggest that the children consciously think of the soldiers as their fellow students, of the village as Plumfield or of 'the little churn-shaped lady' as Mrs. Jo" (104). Aunt Jo is not so affected, however, "laugh[ing] until the tears ran down her cheeks" after "Demi explained their play" (Alcott, *Little Men* 116). She then counsels them that destructiveness is bad, couching the moral in a light-hearted lesson: "'The children of Holland take pleasure in making / What the children of Boston take pleasure in breaking.' Only I shall put Plumfield instead of Boston" (116). It might appear that Aunt Jo laughingly and superficially exonerates Demi for provoking the destruction and trauma.

The Kitty-mouse scene demonstrates that suppression of a child's imagination can result in distortion and violent acting out. It is replete with religious imagery triggered by overheard tales of Greek sacrifices to gods. Alcott refers to Demi as a "high-priest" and to Annabelle as an "idol"; Demi insists, "you have to sacrifice what you like best" (116). These strong religious implications in a scene that is a parody suggest that Alcott is raising serious questions about religion, at least religions that require the sacrifice of that which is most important to an individual. Alcott seems to be critiquing the very nature of a god that demands sacrifice and fear when she has Jo say: "If I had any Kitty-mouse I'd have a good one who liked you to play in safe pleasant ways, and not destroy and frighten" (116). Grover Smith, Jr. believes that D. H. Lawrence was so affected by Alcott's doll-burning scene that he incorporated a similar scene into

Sons and Lovers, perhaps seeing in it "a symbol of male retaliation against female domestic ascendancy" (30). Keyser views the scene as suggestive that "the dark side of male sacrifice, as practiced by John Brooke and extolled by Professor Bhaer, is female immolation" (91). She further observes that "Demi's reference to the Kitty-mouse as 'she' suggests that such 'rites' are an attempt to propitiate and suppress female power" (91). Alcott certainly demonstrates ample ambiguity about her feelings toward female domesticity and male sacrifice in this novel and her other work, lending some credence to these interpretations of the scene. However, these critics overlook the conclusion of the incident, which restores order and normalcy to the Plumfield world.

After Demi explains why he "sackerryfice[d]" the toys, Aunt Jo tells the children that the situation is "something like the bean story" (Alcott, *Little Men* 117), contextualizing the incident into one of the many moralizing cautionary tales she tells in the novel. In the bean story, a poor mother admonishes her children *not* to put beans up their noses during her absence (117). Aunt Jo continues: "Now the children had never dreamed of doing that last thing (putting beans in their noses), but she put it into their heads...and they ran and stuffed their naughty little noses full of beans" (117). Because of Rob's interest in whether the insertion of the beans hurt, Aunt Jo tells another story of her own childish misbehavior. She had inserted little pebbles into her nose, with the dire result that one had to be extracted by the doctor (117). Mapping the Kitty-mouse incident onto this story, Aunt Jo implies that Demi's idea for the Kitty-mouse's predations stemmed from Uncle Fritz, who had put the idea of emulating the Greeks into Demi's mind. The lesson Demi learned, like that of the three children and young Jo who stuffed their noses, was not the lesson intended by the adults. Interestingly, the moral is offered to adults, who should beware the unintended lessons they teach to children. Nonetheless, as often happens in the novel, the bean story and the Kitty-mouse incident close with a return to order. Annabella, that object of so much trauma, is buried. Daisy is consoled by replacement paper dolls. Most importantly, however, "the Naughty Kitty-mouse seemed to be appeased by the last offerings, for she tormented them no more" (118). Demi and Daisy have purged themselves of the spell of the Naughty Kitty-mouse, whether through their "sackerryfices" or Aunt Jo's moralizing. At Plumfield, chaos and violence do exist, but they can be controlled and are survivable.

The students at Plumfield not only mistreat each other and their possessions; there are several incidents in which they mistreat animals. Such violence is in defiance of the rules as Professor Bhaer informs Dan: "one of the first and most important of our few laws is the law of kindness to every dumb creature on the place" (93). This remonstrance is in reaction to the particularly violent abuse of Buttercup, the amiable cow who is incited to leap a wall after being goaded into acting the part of the bull in an impromptu bullfight. Several of the boys, including Demi, willingly participate and watch as the cow is harassed. Mr. Bhaer, of course, does not condone this mistreatment, requiring the boys to forfeit an outing and care for the beleaguered cow (93). In other reported scenes, however, Ned "is discovered tormenting some unhappy field mice" (196); Dan reports on having euthanizing cats by putting their heads in a boot with ether and then drowning them (233); and Tommy feeds the hens rum-soaked bread, with the entire family "convulsed with laughter at their antics" (29). Although not as prevalent nor as violent as the aggressions among the students, the reports of animal abuse contribute to the sense that Plumfield has an underlying and pervasive dark side.

Another significant incident that challenges Alcott's characterization of Plumfield as a sanctuary of domestic bliss occurs when Dan confines the crab family he has collected under the auspices of Mr. Hyde:

> [t]wo little crabs were scuttling about the floor, having got through the wires of the cage. A third was clinging to the top of the cage, evidently in terror of his life, for below appeared a sad yet funny sight. The big crab had wedged himself into the little recess where Polly's cup used to stand, and there he sat eating one of his relations in the coolest way. All the claws of the poor victim were pulled off, and he was turned upside down, his upper shell held in one claw

close under the mouth of the big crab like a dish, while he leisurely ate out of it with the other claw, pausing now and then to turn his queer bulging eyes from side to side, and to put out a slender tongue and lick them in a way that made the children scream with laughter. (151-152)

As with other descriptions of violence, this detail is lavish and laden with (comic) horror. The group of crabs is turned into a family by the narrator's inclusion of the identifying "one of his relations." The narrator calls the scene "funny"; the children "scream with laughter."

Not unlike the cage in which the crabs were imprisoned, Plumfield is portrayed as a sort of prison in which the students in residence at the beginning of the novel are either family members, or boys crippled by circumstance, disability, or innate nature. Emil, Franz, Demi, Daisy, Rob, and Teddy—all March-Bhaer family members—make up nearly half of the school. This portrayal of family as imprisoning device mirrors Alcott's personal experience; she devoted her life to the financial support as well as the emotional and physical support of her family. In the initial description of the non-familial students, each is assigned a characteristic that makes him unable to attend any other school: Dick Brown's "affliction was a crooked back" (25); Adolphus "Dolly" Pettingill stutters (25); Jack Ford's "unboyish keenness and money-loving [was] as much of an affliction as Dolly's stutter or Dick's hump" (26), and he is returned to Plumfield after he flees in disgrace because "the school was cheap" (239); Ned Barker is "all legs, blunder, and bluster ... prone to be easily led astray" (26); George "Stuffy" Cole has been "spoilt by an overindulgent mother"; Billy Ward has been "changed to a feeble idiot ... by his ambitious father" (27); and Tommy Bangs is the "scapegrace of the school" (28). These established students are not escape risks, since their afflictions confine them to Plumfield; either they would not be accepted in other schools due to physical or mental disabilities or their moral deficiencies limit them to Plumfield.

However, the "new" students, Nat, Nan, and Dan, are immediately recognized by Mrs. Jo as flight risks. Mrs. Jo's concern that the new students will want to escape is introduced early in the novel when she puts over-sized slippers on Nat, the first to arrive: "you can't run away from us so fast as if they fitted" (12). The slippers are soon unnecessary, however, because Nat becomes emotionally bonded to Plumfield, unable to leave because he has no place to go and is not "big and strong like [Dan]" (211). After Nan, the second new arrival, insists on going to fetch her own delayed belongings, Mrs. Bhaer warns her "you will get into trouble if you run away" (109). Dan's first escape is actually from Mr. Page's farm, where he had been sent in disgrace after his expulsion from Plumfield (100). He reappears at Plumfield, injured, and is "slowly … tamed by pain and patience" (158). Once healed, he engages in a wild fit of running, explaining to Mrs. Jo, "the devil gets into me sometimes, and then I do want to bolt" (241). She muses to herself, "My wild hawk needs a larger cage; and yet, if I let him go, I am afraid he will be lost. I must try to find some lure enough to keep him safe" (242). Here, Mrs. Jo herself literally refers to Plumfield as a cage. The lure she tries on Dan is emotional coercion: "'I fear that I have not done all I ought, or you would not want to leave me,' she added sorrowfully" (242). This appeal nets Dan: "I don't want to go, and I won't go if I can help it; but every now and then I feel as if I must burst out somehow" (242). Mrs. Jo astounds him, "saying with a look that showed the words cost her something: 'Well, Dan, run if you must, but don't run far; and come back to me soon, for I want you very much'" (243). The narrator approves of Mrs. Jo's reverse psychology: "She felt instinctively that the more the boy was restrained the more he would fret against it; but leave him free, and the mere sense of liberty would content him" (243). Mrs. Jo imprisons Dan by offering him freedom: his prison becomes his emotional connection to her, which she consciously cultivates and exploits.

Mrs. Jo's reaction to Nan's inadvertent "running away" stands in sharp contrast to her "freeing" Dan to lure him into staying. Nan, "thirsting for adventures," leads Rob away from the others during a berry-picking excursion (173). Having been safely found, Nan is resistant to Mrs. Jo's attempts to persuade her that "running away" should prompt remorse. Rather than "freeing" Nan, as she had Dan, Mrs. Jo "ties her up like a naughty little dog"; requiring that she spend the day confined to a room where she can see the other children play, but is unable to join them. Nan learns her lesson, tearfully cautioning a stray bee: "If you have run away, you'd better go right home and tell your mother you are sorry" (191). The lesson is reinforced by Mrs. Jo, and Nan decisively agrees with Teddy that she "ain't going to be naughty again" (192). The conclusion here is not that Mrs. Jo has contained and constrained Nan; it is, as Eiselein perceptively notes, that Nan "has begun, as later chapters show, an education in 'self-control,' which Jo sees as a crucial step in Nan's learning to 'be ready to use her freedom'" (16).

While the students' physical and mental disabilities and Jo's direct actions confine the students to Plumfield, adult confinement at Plumfield is the result of social and economic constraints. As *Little Women* is drawing to a close, Jo and her fiancé, Professor Bhaer, are unable to marry due to their separate, but comparable, poverty. Aunt March's sudden death and the bequest of Plumfield "liberates" them to marry and realize Jo's dream of a school for boys. Plumfield "never was a fashionable school, and the Professor did not lay up a fortune" (Alcott, *Little Women* 376). The long-tamed Jo "was a very happy woman there, in spite of hard work [and] much anxiety, [but] now told no stories, except to her flock of enthusiastic believers and admirers" (377). Mrs. Jo and the Professor are confined to Plumfield by choice and economic necessity.

The final words on confinement at Plumfield are uttered as the novel ends: the Thanksgiving celebration is complete, and Grandfather March has pronounced a benediction on the year's "harvest." Turning the tables on their captors, "the whole flock pranced into the room, joined hands and danced about Father and Mother Bhaer ... the circle narrowed till the good professor and his wife were taken prisoner by many arms" (Alcott, *Little Men* 328–329). While "the bouquet of laughing young faces" seems positive, Beverly Lyon Clark observes that "imprisonment intrudes in this paragraph of love and flowers, an eruption of the effects of armed battle" (337), and Keyser declares it an "image...of constriction and suffocation" (99). Alternately, the image is one of reciprocal confinement. Alcott's suggestion is that Plumfield, like society, like a home, confines the Bhaers as well as their students: they are at risk of being eaten inside the cage, but the world outside the cage is even riskier and more perilous. Importantly, the Plumfield children survive and thrive. Jo tells her father in the final pages of the novel, "I only want to give these children a home in which they can be taught the few simple things which will help to make life less hard to them when they go out to fight their battles in the world" (328). Alcott's approach to violence and containment is thus consistent with the perspectives of psychologist Bruno Bettelheim in the twentieth century that "a struggle against severe difficulties in life is unavoidable, is an intrinsic part of human existence—but that if one does not shy away, but steadfastly meets unexpected and often unjust hardships, one masters all obstacles and at the end emerges victorious" (8). Neil Gaiman similarly argues that "the thing that is so big and so important about the darkness is it's like in an inoculation. You know you are giving somebody darkness in a form that is not overwhelming—it's understandable. They can envelop it, they can take it into themselves, they can cope with it." The readers of *Little Men* imaginatively experience the traumas of the characters in the novel and witness their endurance. Within Plumfield's relatively safe confines, students become prepared to survive, even thrive, in the violent world outside the school.

The world portrayed by Alcott in *Little Men* is very different from and more interesting than that promised by her airy dismissal in 1877 of such work as "moral pap." "Pap" requires no chewing, no engagement, just consumption. The world suggested by Alcott's characterization would present only easy moral choices or none at all. In contrast, Plumfield, like the real world, contains violence, oppression, contradiction, constraint, and moral ambiguity. Children make errors; they suffer consequences, sometimes unjustly; and they are confused. Alcott does not, however, leave them mired in what Moon and Keyser see as darkness. Even confinement to Plumfield is a better option than freedom in the unknown, and presumably even riskier, outside world. As in the real world, there is hope for children to survive in dark and difficult reality. Like the Plumfield students, young readers are prepared for the real world by their exposure to violence in the safety of confinement, in their case within the pages of the novel. In *Little Men*, Alcott provides real nutrition for the mind, and the violence and imprisonment are important components of the banquet she prepares and serves.

Works Cited

Alcott, Louisa May. *The Journals of Louisa May Alcott*. Eds. Joel Myerson, Daniel Shealy, and Madeleine B. Stern. Boston: Little, Brown, 1989.

_____. *Little Men*. 1871. New York: Signet, 1986.

_____. *Little Women, or, Meg, Jo, Beth, and Amy*. Ed. Anne K. Phillips and Gregory Eiselein. New York: Norton, 2004.

Bettelheim, Bruno. *The Uses of Enchantment: The Meaning and Importance of Fairy Tales*. New York: Knopf, 1976.

Barnes, Elizabeth. "The Whipping Boy of Love: Atonement and Aggression in Alcott's Fiction." *Journal X: A Journal in Culture and Criticism* 2 (1997): 1–23.

Blackburn, William. "Moral Pap for the Young?: A New Look at Louisa May Alcott's *Little Men*." *Proceedings of the Seventh Annual Conference of the Children's Literature Association*. New York: Iona College, 1982. 98–106.

Clark, Beverly Lyon. "Domesticating the School Story, Regendering a Genre: Alcott's *Little Men*." *New Literary History* 26 (1995): 323–342.

Dahl, Roald. *Boy: Tales of Childhood*. London: Puffin, 1984.

DiCamillo, Kate. *The Tale of Despereaux: Being the Story of a Mouse, a Princess, Some Soup, and a Spool of Thread*. Illus. Timothy Basil Ering. Cambridge, MA: Candlewick Press, 2003.

Eiselein, Gregory. "Contradiction in Louisa May Alcott's *Little Men*." *New England Quarterly* 78.1 (2005): 3–25.

Gaiman, Neil. "Neil Gaiman on comics and scaring children, with Francoise Mouly and Art Spiegelman." *Toon Books*. TOON Books, Oct. 2014. Web. 3 June 2015.

Hughes, Thomas. *Tom Brown's Schooldays*. 1857. *The Norton Anthology of Children's Literature*. Ed. Jack Zipes, et al. New York: Norton, 2005.

Keyser, Elizabeth Lennox. *Whispers in the Dark: The Fiction of Louisa May Alcott*. Knoxville: U of Tennessee P, 1993.

Moon, Michael. "Nineteenth-Century Discourses on Childhood Gender Training: The Case of Louisa May Alcott's *Little Men* and *Jo's Boys.*" *Queer Representations: Reading Lives, Reading Cultures.* Ed. Martin Duberman. New York: New York UP, 1997. 209–215.

Smith, Grover, Jr. "The Doll Burners: D. H. Lawrence and Louisa Alcott." *Modern Language Quarterly* 19.1 (1958): 28–32.

A Faith Truly Lived: Alcott's Use of Biblical Allusion in *Eight Cousins* and *Rose in Bloom*

Mo Li

Louisa May Alcott lived in an era of exuberant religious activities. On the one hand, early nineteenth-century American culture saw church as separate from state, which "invigorated and reawakened" (Howe 165) religion in American life, engendering numerous choices for religious beliefs and practices. On the other hand, American culture of the era perceived religion as only one of the many feasible means of interpreting the world and structuring lives. Fueled by the Calvinist work ethic, market capitalism, technological and scientific development, and growing individualism, American culture shifted away from belief in an overarching divine power toward a more human-centered perspective. Unitarianism and Transcendentalism, for example, provided versions of religion that championed human nature and human potential (Ronda 58). Alcott's own intellectual and spiritual life was especially influenced by her Transcendentalist and Unitarian family, friends, and mentors, many of whom wrote about faith and social justice.

Most of the critics who address Alcott's religious or philosophical influences focus on her March family trilogy. For instance, Linda K. Kerber claims that the Puritan heritage in Alcott's *Little Women* confines the female characters socially and religiously. Contrary to Kerber's reading, Anne K. Phillips argues that the pilgrim metaphor in *Little Women* grants the characters "freedom from the limitations of nineteenth-century social mores" (214). R. Eric Tippin believes that although *Little Women* "reflects aspects of Puritanism, Unitarianism, and Transcendentalism" (128), it nevertheless shows a "uniquely Alcottian" (136) religion. In contrast, Bruce Ronda questions the religious nature of *Little Women* and argues that it epitomizes the integrated status of "religious talk" and "secular values" (65) in the nineteenth century. Some scholars do more broadly address Alcott's spirituality: for example, Roberta Seelinger Trites examines

Jonathan Edwards's theological legacy as well as Ralph Waldo Emerson's and Theodore Parker's Unitarian and Transcendental influences on Alcott, while Christine Doyle maintains that Alcott advocates a "public" (80) religion of good works and a religious community for "feminine spirituality" (102). Gregory Eiselein contends that Alcott's theology is "distinctly feminist, pluralist, and Pragmatic" (121), a system that resists being overshadowed by either "Protestant orthodoxy" (120) or Transcendentalism. Although the question of Alcott's religion has generated such diverse opinions, little of the inquiry has focused specifically on works published in the later decades of Alcott's career.

This essay addresses Alcott's allusions to the Bible in *Eight Cousins* (1875) and its sequel, *Rose in Bloom* (1876), using those allusions to learn more about Alcott's theology. *Eight Cousins* introduces Rose Campbell, a thirteen-year-old girl orphaned after the death of her father and somewhat adrift in an extended family community until her new guardian, Uncle Alec, introduces her to innovative notions about mind and body. In *Rose in Bloom*, Rose is twenty and beginning to make meaningful life choices. These novels have received minimal critical attention, and few critics have discussed their treatment of religion. In them, Alcott tailors the spiritual significance of the Bible to her own purposes, effecting a primarily lighthearted tone in *Eight Cousins* but establishing a more serious tenor in *Rose in Bloom*. Alcott seems to feel that for children, the Bible should encourage personal connection. For emerging adults, it should be respected as a guide for moral improvement. When incorporating the Bible in both texts, Alcott focuses less on its divine truth than on how it might guide readers' earthly lives.

Eight Cousins and the Bible as an Open Text
In *Eight Cousins*, Rose gradually is liberated by Uncle Alec from constraints regarding her physical, mental, and moral health. The novel celebrates independence, well-being, and vitality. Therefore, it is reasonable to perceive the text's allusions to biblical verses, which deviate frequently from their meaning in the original source to humorous effect, as consistent with Alcott's strategies throughout

the novel. The allusions suggest that Alcott is inviting younger readers, in the interest of emotional and intellectual freedom and health, to think in less orthodox and constrained ways about the Bible.

In *Eight Cousins*, Alcott sometimes reduces the metaphorical meaning of Bible passages to a literal level, tailoring the original's spiritual solemnity to more lighthearted contexts. For instance, Rose tries to show off her riding skills to Uncle Alec, only to fall off her horse. Mac teases her by saying, "pride goeth before a fall" (L. Alcott, *Eight* 155), which alludes to a verse in Proverbs: "Pride goes before destruction, And a haughty spirit before a fall" (Prov. 16.18).[1] In the Bible, "fall" represents a spiritual failure with serious consequences. Here, however, it is reduced to a literal fall, where no greater price is paid except for Rose's sprained ankle—suggesting that the Bible is not orthodox prescription to be followed strictly, but an accessible resource through which people can understand and characterize daily experiences.

Another playful allusion depicts Rose learning from Aunt Plenty "in the good old-fashioned manner, to look well after the ways of the household" (L. Alcott, *Eight* 193). The phrase echoes the first half of Proverbs 31.27. Hayley Miller Lenahan suggests that this allusion demonstrates Alcott's respect for "the importance and sacredness of women's work" (19n7). However, while the reference does celebrate women's work, readers who are familiar with Proverbs might also append the second half of the verse: "and does not eat the bread of idleness" (Prov. 31.27). They might then laugh a little at the pun, recalling Rose's "'many failures and troubles'" (L. Alcott, *Eight* 189) before successfully baking a loaf for Uncle Alec, her equally busy mentor, who has carefully planned this housekeeping curriculum. Neither Rose nor Uncle Alec eats the bread of idleness, literally or metaphorically. Relying on her readers' familiarity with the Bible, Alcott's allusion elicits a pleasant joke.

Alcott also presents biblical allusions to effect hyperbole. After the unpopular Annabel Bliss has visited Rose, Mac reluctantly agrees to escort her home. He "trudged meekly away, wishing the gentle Annabel at the bottom of the Red Sea" (176). In Exodus 15.4, the

Red Sea is where Pharaoh's pursuing army drowns when he refuses to release the Israelites. Characterizing Mac as wishing Annabel at the bottom of the formidable Red Sea, Alcott demonstrates, through hyperbole, how much he dreads the task of escorting her home. The grim biblical connotation makes this situation humorous because, after all, Annabel does not deserve to be drowned.

Most of the biblical allusions already discussed deviate from the original source's purpose or tone to comical effect. However, there is one intriguing exception to this pattern. At the end of *Eight Cousins*, Rose chooses to live with Uncle Alec for another year. After she embraces Uncle Alec, Rose's left cheek is imprinted with "the mark of a waistcoat button" (299). Uncle Alec then kisses Rose and announces that "this is my ewe lamb, and I have set my mark on her, so no one can steal her away" (299). While this declaration can be read as a reference to nineteenth-century livestock management, the image of a shepherd guarding his sheep is quite biblical. Moreover, marking and protecting one's charge echoes three verses in the Bible: "from now on, let no one make trouble for me; for I carry the marks of Jesus branded on my body" (Gal. 6.17); "and do not grieve the Holy Spirit of God, with which you were marked with a seal for the day of redemption" (Eph. 4.30); and "I give them eternal life, and they will never perish. No one will snatch them out of my hand" (John 10.28). The first verse illustrates Apostle Paul's confidence in his permanent connection with Christ through the imprint of salvation. The second verse shows that the Holy Spirit is an emblem of redemption reserved for believers. In the third verse, Jesus promises his followers eternal life and an unbreakable bond with God. Together, these verses convey God's everlasting ownership of His believers. In this instance, the allusion to a mark that solidifies the guardian-charge relationship does not contradict the original biblical context because they both present a relationship in which the master is protective towards his follower. However, even though she refrains from joking, Alcott does not hesitate to put a human in Christ's place, as long as the human resembles Christ in good thoughts and deeds. Uncle Alec gives up smoking to set a good example for his nephews and advocates women's rights, among other good works. Therefore, *Eight Cousins* favorably characterizes Uncle Alec as a proud, Christ-like shepherd for Rose.

Alcott's unorthodox attitude toward the Bible is no doubt influenced by her father, Amos Bronson Alcott. At his controversial Temple School in Boston, Bronson advocated imagination and discussion as the way for his young pupils to understand the sacredness of the Gospels. To many parents' dismay, Bronson invited the children to suggest "emblems of birth" (A. B. Alcott 183) when discussing John the Baptist. The children responded with "a small stream" becoming "large enough to send out other streams" (183), "the rising light of the sun" (184), and "God's wind" coming "upon the ocean of life" (184). These natural images, full of imagination and meaning, yet free from any obscenity or irreverence, vindicated Bronson's theory that free discussion will lead to an understanding of the sacredness of the text, rather than blasphemy. It is likely that Louisa was educated similarly and thus enables her youthful characters to align their feelings and experience with Biblical images and phrases.

More broadly, Alcott's liberty with the Bible was not an isolated practice. In her era, owners of different bibles actively sought to weave their own lives into the grand biblical scheme, both "materially" and "figuratively" (Gutjahr 146). People inscribed their names and verses, bound family records, or sometimes even sewed personal mementos into their bibles. They were also encouraged to employ "[p]ersonal imagination" (Daniell 727) to connect themselves to the narratives. Popular forms of adapting and appropriating the biblical text included dramatized narratives of biblical figures as well as sentimental fiction with religious messages. Among these new creations, the most intriguing were fictional biographies of Jesus, the popularity of which surged during the second half of the nineteenth century. For instance, Joseph Smith, Jr.'s *The Book of Mormon* (1830) presents a resurrected Christ in America "for Americans" (Daniell 730), and Joseph Holt Ingraham's *The Prince of the House of David* (1855) aims to offer a report of the character and life of Jesus, faithful to history, yet more elaborate and personalized than the Gospels. It was common, then, to interact with and adapt biblical phrases, images, and scenes for one's own purposes, but the agendas and measures differed with each author. Alcott's allusions to the Bible in works such as *Eight Cousins* demonstrate that she sees the Bible as an intimate, lively, potentially humorous wellspring for the mind and the heart.

Rose in Bloom and the Bible as Moral Guide

It is even more noteworthy when Alcott resists referring to the Bible in a primarily humorous way. Most of the biblical references in *Rose in Bloom* accord with the Scripture's more earnest tone. For instance, Uncle Alec straightforwardly supports Rose's commitment to philanthropy: "'they who give to the poor lend to the Lord,' and practical Christianity is the kind He loves the best" (L. Alcott, *Rose* 12). This comment echoes the passage, "whoever is kind to the poor lends to the LORD, and will be repaid in full" (Prov. 19.17). In this case, both the biblical verse and Uncle Alec acknowledge the godliness of charity. Uncle Alec also expands the teaching of the Bible by adding, "practical Christianity is the kind He loves the best." In a journal entry written in 1852, Alcott recorded that although her parents "had no money to give," they offered "time, sympathy, help" and provided "a shelter for lost girls, abused wives, friendless children, and weak or wicked men." She characterized this work as "practical Christianity" and praised the "love and happiness" (L. Alcott, *Journals* 67) it brought to those in need. *Rose in Bloom* reiterates Alcott's admiration of "practical Christianity" through Uncle Alec's explicit affirmation that doing charity work accords with the Bible's teaching. As Eiselein has acknowledged, Alcott approves of believers who "practice their faith through altruistic, philanthropic acts" (130).

Eight Cousins and *Rose in Bloom* represent Alcott's perspective in the mid-1870s. The Christmas holiday of 1875, occurring between the novels' publications, expanded and brought new energy to Alcott's idea of "practical Christianity." Visiting New York City, Alcott joined Mrs. Abby Hopper Gibbons in distributing candies, dolls, and pictures to children at an orphanage on Randall's Island, a holiday ritual Mrs. Gibbons had practiced for thirty years. The next March, Alcott published "A New Way to Spend Christmas" (1876) to honor this experience. *Rose in Bloom*, also published in 1876, specifically commends "Abby Gibbons" as one of Rose's new "heroes" (313). Such 1870s experiences strengthened Alcott's belief in philanthropy and reinforced her inclination to sincerely uphold the biblical teaching of giving to the poor.

Not only does the text of *Rose in Bloom* allude to the Bible with greater earnestness, but it also critiques those who take a superficial view of the Bible. Contrary to the hopes of the Campbell family, Charlie, the charming "Prince," resists maturing into a responsible adult and clings to the childish playfulness celebrated throughout *Eight Cousins*. Significantly, he alludes to the Bible flippantly when he tries, preemptively, to secure Rose in a romantic relationship. Alluding to a little agate heart that he had given Rose years earlier, Charlie asks Rose "half in earnest, half in jest," "will you let me take away the heart of stone and give you a heart of flesh?" (75). This speech alludes to God's promise in the Old Testament that the former indifference of the people of Israel will be transformed: "a new heart also will I give you, and a new spirit will I put within you: and I will take away the stony heart out of your flesh, and I will give you a heart of flesh" (Ezek. 36.26). By positioning Rose and himself in the context of this verse, Charlie assumes the role of God while half-accusing Rose of callousness. Rose immediately rejects this usurpation as "irreverent and audacious" (L. Alcott, *Rose* 75). In *Eight Cousins*, collapsing the boundary between divinity and humanity is acceptable, especially in the case of Uncle Alec claiming his shepherd-like guardianship of Rose, since Uncle Alec's merits are not in conflict with those of Jesus. Here, however, the association offered by idle, irresponsible Charlie contradicts the serious, inspiring, and promising relationship described in the original biblical context, rendering Charlie's alignment of himself with God imprudent, self-centered, and immature. Subsequently, despite his efforts to reform, Charlie fails to keep his temperance pledge and dies. This tragedy reinforces Alcott's disapproval of the joking, idle qualities in adults that prevent them from improving themselves or contributing to the good of the society.

However, advocating the seriousness of the Bible does not mean that Alcott fully embraces an orthodox reading of the text. She supplants biblical teaching of the divine and the spiritual with her own instruction on the practical and the moral. As a rich heiress, Rose finds herself surrounded by insincere and potentially harmful friends and lovers. Uncle Alec suggests that she should "try to find wheat among the tares" (L. Alcott, *Rose* 63). The image comes from Jesus's teaching that on Judgment Day, "the wheat" (true believers) will be gathered into his barn while "the tares" (false believers) will be bound "in bundles" and burned (Matt. 13.30). Although Alcott's allusion to the Bible is unorthodox because she puts Rose in the position of Jesus, she agrees with the Bible about the importance of making wise judgments. While Jesus's judgment decides the life and death of the believers in the afterlife, Rose's judgment determines whether she lives in virtue or in vain on earth, a difference comparable to life and death for a maturing young woman. Alcott's reworking of the Bible emphasizes that the Bible provides essential, practical, human advice rather than divine truth.

Another noteworthy allusion occurs when Mac, a follower of Uncle Alec in both the study of medicine and the pursuit of philanthropy, is accompanying Rose and her adopted child. Dulcinea is a three-year-old orphan rescued by Mac and subsequently adopted by Rose. As they travel home, Mac secretly enjoys the image of a contemporary "Flight into Egypt" (L. Alcott, *Rose* 247). In the Bible, Joseph, Mary, and Jesus have to flee to Egypt because King Herod intends to find and kill the baby (Matt. 2.13). Although Mac refrains from verbalizing his comparison because he is "a reverent youth" (L. Alcott, *Rose* 247), his perception produces a humorous exaggeration of his situation, since he and Rose are not traveling as refugees and the child would not seem to be a divine gift to the world. While Mac is too respectful to voice his vision, the narrator certainly encourages readers to dwell on and appreciate its serious implications. While the Holy Family is formed by divine prophecy, Mac, Rose, and Dulcinea represent a family established on human charity and new hope for good works, just as the newborn Jesus was the hope for humans two thousand years ago. In addition, the association with the Holy Family foreshadows romance between Mac and Rose. Contrary to what Charlie had proposed, however, this more genuine romance promises fruitfulness. Therefore, although the reference to "the Flight into Egypt" is not strictly analogous to the biblical context, it does echo the seriousness of the Bible by evoking hope and moral power.

How might we justify the interpretation that Alcott's biblical allusion is mostly lighthearted in *Eight Cousins*, but more serious in *Rose in Bloom*, especially since they were published within a year of each other? Generally, books of the era were enjoyed by both youthful and adult readers (Clark 16), and Alcott recognized the breadth of her readership, acknowledging, "Fathers & mothers tell me they use my books as helps for themselves, so now & then I like to slip in a page for them, fresh from the experience of some other parent, for education seems to me to be *the* problem in our times" (*Selected* 237). Given Alcott's concern for education and her willingness to assist parents, her writings for youth were produced to impart values to their respective younger readers that could be reinforced by parents or guardians who also read the books. Significantly, however, Alcott dedicated *Eight Cousins* and *Rose in Bloom* to two different sets of readers. The dedication page of *Eight Cousins* reflects that the story is intended for "[t]he many boys & girls whose letters it has been impossible to answer." Although "boys & girls" is not age-specific, it is not unreasonable to assume that the term applies to an age group comparable to the characters in the novel. For these readers, then, Alcott suggests that the Bible should not be an unreachable, unchallengeable text whose seriousness smothers the pleasure of its readers. Her attitude may be that the freedom to think and feel independently will help youths cultivate healthy minds capable of discovering truth, according to the pedagogy Bronson promoted in his Temple School. *Rose in Bloom*, however, may be more specifically intended for readers on the brink of adulthood. The dedication page states that the sequel is written to help "other roses getting ready to bloom." It is safe to infer that the intended audience is of the same age as Rose. Hence, as a guidebook for young adults, *Rose in Bloom* proposes that readers should respect the morality of the Bible and perform good works under its guidance. Being able to express one's thoughts freely about the Bible does not conflict with honoring the Bible's power of moral edification. Alcott clearly sees the Bible as a useful guidebook for adolescents transitioning to adulthood, which is a consistent motif in Alcott's work.[2]

Across her works, Alcott shows a strong interest in portraying how young women might mature into happy, sensible, and useful adults. Particularly, she pleads eloquently for the importance of female communities in the physical, moral, and spiritual wellbeing of women. Guided by their mother, the four March sisters in *Little Women* (1868–69) learn the meaning of self-denial, patience, and good works, and in *An Old-Fashioned Girl* (1870), Polly Milton finds herself strengthened and renewed by "a little sisterhood of busy, happy, independent girls" (196). *Work: A Story of Experience* (1873) explores more fully the themes of women saving, helping, and inspiring other women. Christie Devon could not have "found religion" (L. Alcott, *Work* 319) without the sincere speeches, sympathy, kindness, and love of other women. "How I Went Out to Service" (1874) calls for women to stand up for one another and oppose patriarchal tyranny. Alcott's writings published in the late 1860s and early 1870s before *Eight Cousins* and *Rose in Bloom* demonstrate her increasing investment in young women's growth, identity, and place in society—ideas that *Eight Cousins* and *Rose in Bloom* continue to explore and emphasize.

"The Passing of a Soul thro Many Lives": Alcott's Human-Centered Theology

Despite their different tones, both *Eight Cousins* and *Rose in Bloom* demonstrate Alcott's unorthodox attitude regarding Christ's humanity. Uncle Alec proudly announces his role as the Good Shepherd to Rose; Rose is encouraged to act like a formidable judge, distinguishing the unworthy from the worthy; Mac's silent comparison of himself, Rose, and Dulcinea with the Divine Family is presented approvingly. Influenced by Unitarianism, Alcott rejects the notions of Trinity and Incarnation (*Selected* 215–16) and sees Christ as "a great reformer [...] not God" (278), a virtuous human

---

who works for social justice. A more orthodox reading would consider the verse "[h]ereafter ye shall see heaven open, and the angels of God ascending and descending upon the Son of man" (John 1.51) as proof of Jesus's divine identity, honored and served by the angels. However, Bronson Alcott interprets the verse as "good thoughts entering in and proceeding from the Spirit of man" (187), indicating that Bible readers are not worshippers of Jesus's unique divinity, but witnesses of a perfect model for reason and morality. Theodore Parker, the Unitarian preacher and Transcendentalist social reformer greatly admired by Alcott, contends that Jesus is not God but "our brother, the son of man, as we are; the Son of God, like ourselves" (356). The significance of Jesus's character lies in its "human excellence," proving that it is "possible for all men" (356) to achieve perfection. Acknowledging Jesus's divinity, for Parker, will annul the hope of perfection he symbolizes for humanity. This possibility of human perfection is pivotal to Parker's belief in social reform and social justice, which in turn inspired Alcott to write about social reform in her novels (Trites 61). Valorizing Christ's humanity rather than his divinity, Alcott's theology diminishes Christ's role as the divine Son of God and Savior and sharply contrasts with what a more conventional Protestant would believe.

Additionally, her attitudes toward salvation and immortality are relevant to her use of biblical references in her fiction. In "Conversations with Children on the Gospels," Bronson Alcott defines redemption as "renewing thoughts" and withdrawing "attention from" one's body (185). While he explicitly associates salvation with the power of the human mind rather than with divine grace, Louisa omits any specific reference to redemption through the intervention of the Savior. Instead, she depicts in detail the daily practice of faith. Clearly, she values not only high, noble thoughts, but also doing good works and leaving behind good influences. One journal entry from December 1860 characterizes how she administers both: "All the philosophy in our house is not in the study; a good deal is in the kitchen, where a fine old lady thinks high thoughts and does kind deeds while she cooks and scrubs" (L. Alcott, *Journals* 101).

To clarify, Alcott acknowledges the existence of God and cherishes a tangible, personal relationship with Him. In sorrow, she finds "refuge in the Almighty Friend" and comments that "[i]f this is experiencing religion I have done it" (*Journals* 92). Her posthumous memoir relates that a younger Alcott "'got religion'" after a run in the woods, where she felt "very near to God" and rejoiced over a "new and vital sense of His presence, tender and sustaining as a father's arms" (L. Alcott, "Recollections" 35). Alcott's version of immortality concerned less with reuniting with God in a spiritual form than in one person's legacy passing on to the next one, resulting in an accumulation and amplification of good lives and good works. To put it in the author's own words: "I think immortality is the passing of a soul thro [*sic*] many lives or experiences, & such as are *truly* lived, used & learned help on to the next, each growing richer higher, happier, carr[y]ing with it only the real memories of what has gone before" (L. Alcott, *Selected* 279). Here, immortality is not in Heaven, but on earth, not with God, but among humans. This image echoes the ideas of reincarnation associated with some of the Eastern religions that influenced Transcendentalism. If this transcending process has a destination, it does not appear to involve reunion with a Christian God. The confidence, transcendence, and beauty infused throughout her depiction of immortality imply a kind of divine quality in humans.[3]

In another letter, Alcott's idea of faith is crystallized into the pursuit of good works, virtue, and following others' good examples. Writing to her young friends the Lukens sisters, Alcott advises, "I think you need not worry about any name for your faith but simply try to be & do good, to love virture [virtue] in others & study the lives of those who are truly worthy of imitation" (*Selected* 277). Here again, Alcott's vision is grounded firmly in how human minds think and what human hands can do. For her, faith should motivate believers to make concrete, pragmatic contributions to "serving family and community," a principle inherited from her mother, Abigail Alcott (Fahy 284). That is why Louisa lauds "practical Christianity" (*Journals* 67) and praises Parker as more Christian than many others, since he "turns his back on no one who needs help" (*Journals* 81). It is also why readers frequently find Alcott's heroes and heroines engaging in domestic duties and philanthropic service. For instance, Uncle Alec helps Rose convert some of her properties into women's shelters, and Rose visits orphanages and adopts Dulcinea. Human endeavor is always at the center of Alcott's conception and practice of faith. Alcott's religious ideas focus more on this life than the next, more on human service than God's grace. Viewed in this light, it is easier to perceive why hard work and true charity are not to be trifled with, and why any biblical teaching concerning these virtues should be revered.

Conclusion

Examining the religious allusions in *Eight Cousins* and *Rose in Bloom* expands our awareness of Alcott's beliefs about the role of the Bible in the maturing process of young people and further delineates that for Alcott, the Bible teaches more about how to live the best human life than to submit to orthodox religious practices in hope of heavenly reward. In Louisa's family and intellectual circle, the Bible was only one of many valued philosophical and literary readings. Nevertheless, it was an important and familiar one. As biographer John Matteson confirms, Bronson often read aloud from the Bible and *The Pilgrim's Progress* "[w]ith his silvery voice" (90). More importantly, Bronson used the Bible as a gauge when cultivating the moral characters of his daughters, a practice Louisa inherited and developed in her fiction. Bearing in mind Alcott's focus on human improvement and service to others, it makes sense that the majority of the allusions in *Eight Cousins* and *Rose in Bloom* come from Proverbs and the Gospels. Whereas Proverbs teaches the value of morality, good conduct, and charity, the Gospels deliver, according to Alcott, the best human example of self-denial, good works, and the love of truth and others. Alcott was well versed in the Bible and continued in her later works to frequently incorporate its phrases and concepts. Nonetheless, additional research on biblical allusions and other linguistic, metaphorical, or rhetorical characteristics in Alcott's works is needed in order to further determine how her religious ideas are reflected in her writings and to illuminate more fully her philosophical beliefs and artistic power.

Notes

1. This essay will be referring to the King James Version of the Bible because it was one of the most common versions in Alcott's era and Alcott's father used it when teaching the Gospels at his Temple School. Louisa May Alcott was likely very familiar with this version.

2. See, for instance, Phillips's argument that in *Little Women*, the cherished copies of the "true guide-book" the sisters receive from Marmee on Christmas morning (Alcott, *Little Women* 19) are New Testaments (Phillips 222–23).

3. This view of immortality remains controversial for some Christian readers. For instance, in an online diatribe against Alcott's ideas of immortality and salvation, Mary Van Nattan-Stephens characterizes Alcott as a "degraded woman" and protests against using Alcott's books "in a Christian home" unless to "prove her wickedness to others."

Works Cited

Alcott, Amos Bronson. "From *Conversations with Children on the Gospels*." 1836–1837. *Transcendentalism: A Reader*. Ed. Joel Myerson. New York: Oxford UP, 2000. 181–95.

Alcott, Louisa May. *Eight Cousins*. 1875. New York: Puffin, 1989.

_____. "How I Went Out to Service." 1874. *Alternative Alcott*. Ed. Elaine Showalter. New Brunswick, Rutgers UP, 1988.

_____. *The Journals of Louisa May Alcott*. Ed. Joel Myerson, Daniel Shealy, and Madeleine B. Stern. Athens: U of Georgia P, 1997.

_____. *Little Women*. 1868–69. Eds. Anne K. Phillips and Gregory Eiselein. New York: Norton, 2004.

_____. "A New Way to Spend Christmas." *Youth's Companion* 49.10 (Mar. 1876): 77–78. *ProQuest*. 26 Aug. 2015.

_____. *An Old Fashioned Girl*. 1870. Boston: Little, Brown, 1997.

_____. "Recollections of My Childhood." 1888. *Alcott in Her Own Time: A Biographical Chronicle of Her Life, Drawn from Recollections, Interviews, and Memoirs by Family, Friends, and Associates*. Ed. Daniel Shealy. Iowa City: U of Iowa P, 2005. 32–39.

_____. *Rose in Bloom*. 1876. New York: Puffin, 1989.

_____. *The Selected Letters of Louisa May Alcott*. Ed. Joel Myerson, Daniel Shealy, and Madeleine B. Stern. Athens: U of Georgia P, 1995.

_____. *Work: A Story of Experience*. 1873. Ed. Joy S. Kasson. New York: Penguin, 1994.

Clark, Beverly Lyon. "Audience." *Keywords for Children's Literature*. Ed. Philip Nel and Lissa Paul. New York: NYU P, 2011. 14–17.

Daniell, David. *The Bible in English: Its History and Influence*. New Haven, CT: Yale UP, 2003.

Doyle, Christine. *Louisa May Alcott and Charlotte Brontë: Transatlantic Translations*. Knoxville: U of Tennessee P, 2000.

Eiselein, Gregory. "'A Religion of Their Own': Louisa May Alcott's New American Religion." *Nineteenth-Century American Women Write Religion: Lived Theologies and Literature*. Ed. Mary McCartin Wearn. Burlington, VT: Ashgate, 2014. 119–34.

Fahy, Christopher. "Religion." *The Louisa May Alcott Encyclopedia*. Ed. Gregory Eiselein and Anne K. Phillips. Westport, CT: Greenwood P, 2001. 184.

Gutjahr, Paul C. *An American Bible: A History of the Good Book in the United States, 1777–1880*. Stanford: Stanford UP, 1999.

Howe, Daniel Walker. "Awakenings of Religion." *What Hath God Wrought: The Transformation of America, 1815–1848*. New York: Oxford UP, 2007. 164–202.

Ingraham, Joseph Holt. *The Prince of the House of David*. 1855. Charlottesville: U of Virginia, 2003. *Early American Fiction Full-Text Database*. 26 Aug. 2015.

Kerber, Linda K. "Can a Woman Be an Individual? The Limits of Puritan Tradition in the Early Republic." *Texas Studies in Literature and Language* 25.1 (1983): 165–78.

The King James Bible. *Oremus Bible Browser*. Ed. Simon Kershaw. Vers. 2.2.7. Feb. 2011. Web. 27 May 2015.

Lenahan, Hayley Miller. "Domestic and Subversive: The Roles of Women in the Children's Novels of Louisa May Alcott." Honors Thesis. Wellesley College, 2012.

Matteson, John. *Eden's Outcasts: The Story of Louisa May Alcott and Her Father*. New York: Norton, 2007.

Parker, Theodore. "A Discourse of the Transient and the Permanent in Christianity." 1841. *Transcendentalism: A Reader*. Ed. Joel Myerson. New York: Oxford UP, 2000. 340–66.

Phillips, Anne K. "The Prophets and the Martyrs: Pilgrims and Missionaries in *Little Women* and *Jack and Jill*." Little Women *and the Feminist Imagination: Criticism, Controversy, Personal Essays*. Ed. Janice M. Alberghene and Beverly Lyon Clark. New York: Garland, 1999. 213–36.

Ronda, Bruce. "'Picking the World to Pieces': *Little Women* and Secularization." *Critical Insights:* Little Women. Ed. Gregory Eiselein and Anne K. Phillips. Ipswich, MA: Salem P, 2015. 54–66.

Smith, Joseph, Jr., trans. *The Book of Mormon*. 1830. Ed. Laurie F. Maffly-Kipp. New York: Penguin, 2008.

Tippin, R. Eric. "'Up the Steep Hill by Trying': The Unorthodox Christianity of *Little Women*." *Critical Insights:* Little Women. Ed. Gregory Eiselein and Anne K. Phillips. Ipswich, MA: Salem P, 2015. 128–42.

Trites, Roberta Seelinger. *Twain, Alcott, and the Birth of the Adolescent Reform Novel*. Iowa City: U of Iowa P, 2007.

Van Nattan-Stephens, Mary. "Louisa May Alcott." *Home Maker's Corner*. Mary Van Nattan-Stephens, n.d. Web. 19 Jul. 2015. <http://www.homemakerscorner.com/alcott.htm>.

American Girls and American Literature: Louisa May Alcott "Talks Back" to Henry James_____

Christine Doyle

> Louisa—m–my dear girl—er—when you hear people—er—
> telling you you're a genius, you mustn't believe them; er—what I
> mean is, it isn't true! (Henry James, qtd. in Hawthorne 340)

This astonishing critical assessment was delivered to Louisa May Alcott (stammers and all), according to Julian Hawthorne, by twenty-five-year old Henry James on the occasion of a Boston dinner party at which Alcott (then thirty-six years old) was being celebrated for the success of *Little Women*. Though the James and Alcott families generally moved in different circles due to the Jameses' immense wealth and the Alcotts' chronic poverty, Henry James, Sr. and Amos Bronson Alcott had been intellectual sparring partners since Ralph Waldo Emerson introduced them in the 1840s. Though a New Yorker, Henry, Sr. had enrolled his younger sons, Robertson (Bob) and Garth Wilkinson (Wilky) in school in Concord, and both participated in Louisa's amateur theatricals while they lived in the area. It was neither unusual for the Alcotts to be guests of the Jameses, nor for both families to mutually socialize with other residents, being accorded similar social, if not financial, status. Despite being a "literary youth," as Alcott had dismissively referred to him in an 1865 journal entry (*Journals* 139), James had made presumptuous comments about Alcott's works prior to this dinner. Though only in his twenties, James had already reviewed books for the *Nation* and other periodicals—according to Alfred Habegger, almost always books written by women (12)—and had begun that work at a time "when the *Nation*'s original liberalism on women's issues was rapidly eroding. James himself joined the assault on women's literary culture in those years. His reviews of American women writers had a tone ranging from condescension to outrage" (9). One of those reviews had critiqued Alcott's earlier novel, *Moods* (1864), which had occasioned Alcott's wry journal comment; in it, he commented that "[t]he two most striking facts with regard to 'Moods' are the author's ignorance of human nature, and her self-confidence in spite of this ignorance" (James, "Moods" 223), but he allowed that "there is no reason why Miss Alcott should not write a very good novel, provided she will be satisfied to describe only that which she has seen" (224). Habegger contends that James's first novel (*Watch and Ward*, which, at the time of the dinner party, was soon to be serialized in the *Atlantic Monthly*) owed a great deal to his reading of *Moods* specifically and to Alcott's fiction generally and also that, in fact, "some of the fictions he himself wrote were designed to set hers—and *her*—straight" (68). He further asserts that Alcott took James's critique under serious consideration and that, when she revised *Moods* in 1882, "She wanted to *repair* the faults spotted by the book's critics—chiefly young Henry James" (Habegger 68). Habegger regards her alterations to her first novel "her final reply to the eighty-year-old youth who had lectured her at dinner" (83)—an assertion, perhaps, that James was claiming unwarranted literary prowess and influence far beyond his years. Regardless of whether or not Habegger's contentions about the revisions are accurate—and I believe that her re-envisioning of the novel resulted from a great deal more than James's review, including what she had learned about writing in the ensuing fifteen years—the revised *Moods* was neither Alcott's last nor her only rejoinder to James. Alcott and James had radically different views of American womanhood—and, indeed, of American literature—and can be seen as being in dialogue with one another on both of those subjects for the last two decades of Alcott's life.

Though James published *Watch and Ward* in 1871, the novella *Daisy Miller* (1878) was his first work to earn international fame. Due to the lack of an American copyright and the immediate appearance of pirated editions, he claimed only to have made $200 from the book (Edel 310), but both James and his title character became instant cultural phenomena. Not only was *Daisy* well-received by critics; it became a bestseller. "Daisy Miller" hats appeared, and etiquette books warned girls not to become "a Daisy

Miller"; William Dean Howells wrote in a letter to fellow writer and editor James Russell Lowell that "[t]he thing went so far that society almost divided itself in Daisy Millerites and anti-Daisy Millerites" (qtd. in Novick 392). Party conversations morphed into discussions about the breakdown of parental controls as a prelude to the breakdown of American society and America's unavoidable demise as a result of her independence from Europe.[1]

In *Daisy Miller*, James certainly laid out a compelling vision of American girlhood: innocent and spirited, but also impetuous and naïve and unable to deal with the sophistication of European society without proper guidance from elders. James' biographer Leon Edel claimed that "James had discovered nothing less than 'the American girl'" and added that the few authors who had previously depicted American girls in Europe, such as Hawthorne and Howells, had not particularly used those characters to contrast America and Europe, and that "Europeans who were reading Louisa May Alcott had a picture of the American girl largely in her domestic surroundings" (310). Scholar Sarah Wadsworth provides a corrective to Edel's argument in contextualizing James's story "at the epicenter of a popular literary mode of the 1870s: the narrative of the American woman abroad" ("Innocence" 108). Wadsworth characterizes *Daisy* as not the invention, but the "*Re*-Invention" (107; emphasis mine) of that character type and even refers to Alcott's fictionalized travel writing, *Shawl-Straps* (1872), to illuminate the character as she existed at the time.[2] A full decade before *Daisy Miller*, however, Alcott had already and famously ensconced a pair of Americans in Europe for whom Daisy and her Winterbourne might well have been meant to serve as correctives: *Little Women*'s Amy and Laurie.

Considering the "type" of the American abroad as Alcott proposed it compared to James' "re-invention" truly makes one wonder about the "Daisy Millerites" in the culture who embraced James's character. While James's Americans are damaged, even destroyed, by their inability to negotiate and integrate Old and New Worlds, Alcott's characters assimilate Old World experiences without losing their distinctly American qualities. Amy learns in London, for example, "that it wasn't the thing for young ladies to ride in [Hansom cabs] alone" (Alcott, *Little Women* 247) after she and her cousin Flo endure a wild ride at the hands of a driver who takes offense at their lack of propriety and decides to teach them a lesson; nevertheless, she drives a pony cart by herself in Nice and greets Laurie enthusiastically, "to the great scandalization of a French mamma, who hastened her daughter's steps, lest she should be demoralized by beholding the free manners of these 'mad English'" (296–7). Laurie notices with approval that while Amy has acquired "elegance" from her travels, "her strong will still held its own, and her native frankness was unspoiled by foreign polish" (299). Amy clearly adapts to European customs, while still maintaining her American independence.

Additionally, Amy realizes her artistic capacities as a result of her travel. Citing writers such as Mme. de Staël and Hawthorne, Wadsworth notes that "the cultural richness of Italy" had often served "as a backdrop against which to explore the intellectual and artistic development of creative women" ("Innocence" 113). For Amy—who, on the first page of *Little Women*, imagined herself an artist at twelve; wished for "a nice box of Faber's drawing pencils" for Christmas (Alcott, *Little Women* 11); and is often referred to as the family's Raphael—gazing upon the wonders of Rome is a necessary rite of passage. Upon encountering the great art of Italy, however, she realizes that while she has some talent, she must reconsider making art her life's work, "because talent isn't genius, and no amount of energy can make it so" (317). Further, though tempted by the charming and wealthy Englishman Fred Vaughn's offer of marriage and the "old money" and class distinction it carries, Amy realizes (as Isabel Archer was to realize later, in James' 1881 novel *The Portrait of a Lady*) that "something more than money and position was needed to satisfy [her]" (332). Her reward for resisting this European temptation is marriage—with love *and* money—to Laurie. She will find fulfillment through philanthropically supporting other artists, while still developing her own talents to the best of her ability.

Laurie, who, thanks to his wealth, has already traveled a great deal in Europe, may seem to prefigure *Daisy Miller*'s Frederick

Winterbourne. Initially in a depression caused by Jo's refusal of his proposal, he "made no effort of any kind, but just let himself drift along as comfortably as possible" (Alcott, *Little Women* 314)— perhaps not unlike the "amiable, and universally liked" James character, who doesn't seem to do much of anything but study and devote himself to a "foreign lady" in Geneva (James, *Daisy Miller* 4). Though Laurie may be a blend of cultures (his deceased father was American and his deceased mother Italian), Alcott attributes his flaws, rather than his virtues, to his European heritage. According to the narrator of *Little Women*, the Italian part of Laurie's nature leads him to superstition, melancholy, sentimentality, and dreaminess, from which he is rescued by his "American common sense" (315). More accurately, he is rescued by Amy's common sense, for it is she who catalyzes a change in his behavior. She ridicules his unworn hands—"Aren't you ashamed of a hand like that? It's as soft and white as a woman's and looks as if it never did anything but wear Jouvin's best gloves, and pick flowers for ladies" (320)—and calls him "faulty, lazy, and miserable" (319). Stung by her criticism, he retreats but then applies himself to his music in earnest; he realizes that his talent isn't genius either and returns to Amy in Vevey with a desire to move on with his life. Rowing across Lake Geneva to the famous castle at Chillon, the two decide to "always pull in the same boat" (336). In learning from Europe but not being bound to it, Amy and Laurie earn the reward of each other and return to America to pursue productive lives.

As early as 1938, Alcott biographer Katharine Anthony briefly suggested that James used "the Vevey episode" of *Little Women* in *Daisy Miller* and that "the mutual influence [between them] was perhaps stronger than anyone realizes" (178; 180). Habegger is more direct in suggesting that in James's early fiction, he attempted to show women writers "how they should have told their story" and writing "corrective narratives" for them (25). His "corrections," however, had a particular agenda; as Wadsworth puts it, in *Daisy Miller*, "correcting" the women meant that James "strips the American girl of her intellectual and artistic aspirations and diminishes her mental accomplishments" ("Innocence" 121). This should come as no surprise, since James already had railed, in his review of Alcott's first novel, against "precocious little girls" ("Miss Alcott" 219), such as *Moods'* Sylvia, demonstrating his impatience with the notion that a mere sixteen-year-old could engage in philosophical discussions with men. Later, reviewing Alcott's *Eight Cousins* (1875), he would complain about Rose Campbell being one of Alcott's "pert and shrill" child characters (James, "Review" 165), not to mention "subjective"(166), by which he seems to mean introspective, since he complains about her being "pensive" and then revealing what she had been thinking. It's hard to determine what offends James more about Alcott's females: the idea that they might actually *have* thoughts, or that they might express them.

Some direct comparisons between the two sets of Americans abroad in *Little Women* and *Daisy Miller* reveal how directly James's view contrasts with Alcott's. Daisy is, in fact, stripped of any observable intellect by James's choice to narrate the story from Winterbourne's limited third-person point of view. We never actually know what, if anything, Daisy is thinking, only what she says and does and what others think of her. She defies protocol as Amy does, but whereas Amy's choices are measured, balanced, and attributed to American independence, Daisy's are inexplicable. For example, after using the prospect of an evening outing to the castle at Chillon—the same excursion during which Amy and Laurie had become engaged—merely to tantalize Winterbourne and to upset her mother, she declines once it is arranged, saying, "that's all I wanted—a little fuss!" (James, *Daisy Miller* 21). Whereas Amy had absorbed culture as a means of enrichment, when Daisy and Winterbourne do finally make their trip to the castle, James emphasizes that "the dusky traditions ... made but a slight impression on her" (22). While Amy adapts her dress style and acquires "foreign polish," Daisy's disparaging comments about how European dress compares unfavorably with the styles of Schenectady further characterize her as an unpolished American, unable to appreciate the virtues of Europe. Not only is Daisy not enriched by the sights she sees, but she can't even grasp the most basic and vital aspects of her European experiences; it is her insistence upon ignoring health warnings and visiting the Colosseum at night that results in her death from malaria. As Wadsworth puts it, in James' text, "the shape of the narrative shifts from the development to the demise of the 'international American girl'" ("Innocence" 122).

Nor is Winterbourne excluded from James's critical gaze.[3] Although he can't help being fascinated by Daisy's fresh viewpoint, and even allows that he has "lived too long in foreign parts" (James, *Daisy Miller* 50) to appreciate and to accept her fully, his dalliance with Daisy ultimately has no more effect on him than Europe's "dusky traditions" have on her. Unlike Laurie, who returns to America with the determination to make something of his life, Winterbourne returns to his original setting (Geneva) and takes up the same habits he originally practiced—with no apparent growth or new awareness. In *Daisy Miller*, James shows no indication that young Americans visiting Europe can appreciate its culture, that Americans living in Europe can continue to appreciate American boldness, that either America or Europe can benefit from contact with the other, or that American girls have intelligence, strength of character or influence—all views that directly contradict Alcott's perspectives in *Little Women*.

For both Alcott and James, the debate concerning American and European values as embodied in their young women, as well as the qualities of those young women, is not only indicative of the personal character; it can also be seen as part of a larger debate indicating what constituted good literature. Richard Brodhead points out in *Cultures of Letters* that for a time there were a number of forums in which writers could publish in mid-nineteenth-century America; writers could be publishing in the so-called "story papers" and also in more literary magazines, which at first were "not sharply differentiated" (78). During and immediately after the Civil War, however, publishing became one of the mechanisms whereby culture in general began to differentiate between social classes, so that the inexpensive story papers would come to be considered decidedly "low," domestic fiction generally "middlebrow," and magazines such as the *Atlantic Monthly* "organ[s] of literary high culture" (Brodhead 79). "High culture," as it turned out, excluded Alcott, who had placed four of her stories in the *Atlantic* between 1856 and 1863, but never published there again. James, on the other hand, became a regular and valued contributor. Wadsworth characterizes James's approach to literature as "revising and masculinizing the narrative...in order to reclaim literature as a gentlemanly pursuit" ("Innocence" 118), and Anne E. Boyd argues that "high literary culture" did, in fact, effectively exclude women, including Alcott, from any claim to literary immortality as the century concluded. In 1884, the *Critic* announced its list of "Our 'Forty Immortals,'" American writers destined to be read long-term, supposedly selected by a readers' poll. No women were included. Significantly, a *Critic* staff writer opined at the time that there was no American woman writer with sufficient "masculinity in her composition" to be worthy of inclusion (qtd. in Boyd 244).

The literary debate between Alcott and James about what literature should be and accomplish both exemplifies and expands upon culture and gender tensions of later nineteenth-century America. Both writers, in fact, championed realism—but realism meant different things to each. James had delineated his view as early as 1865, when he published "The Noble School of Fiction" in the first issue of the *Nation* and expounded further on his theories in essays throughout his career. One of his most influential critical essays, "The Art of Fiction" (1884), articulates what he had been practicing for two decades: James pronounced "the air of reality...to be the supreme virtue" (352) and asserted that fiction should "catch the colour, the relief, the expression, the surface, the substance of the human spectacle" (353). He also observed, however, that a story need not have "adventures" in the usual sense to be of high quality, but should instead focus on details of human *psychology*: "There are few things more exciting to me, in short, than a psychological reason" (359). As Brodhead sums it up, James's aesthetic required that "works are made to be defined by their inward properties of formal arrangement, not their larger social connection, and so are made to take value through their deliberated composition or 'art,' not their service to extraliterary goods" (158). That is, to James, a work of literature was an artistic endeavor in and of itself, very much internally directed; it might aim to explore the internal workings of the minds of its characters in realistic ways (i.e., as though they were real people), but needn't propose ideas—morals—to its readers in reference to themselves or to the larger society.

Alcott, too, believed in realism—or at least "truth"—as a literary principle, though her philosophy is articulated in her journals and fiction rather than in critical essays. As early as 1850, reflecting upon her reading tastes, she wrote, "I fancy 'lurid' things, if true and strong also" (Alcott, *Journals* 63). Reading proofs for *Little Women* in 1868, she wrote, "It reads better than I expected. Not a bit sensational, but simple and true ... and if it succeeds that will be the reason of it" (166). Alcott, however, subscribed to the notion that nineteenth-century domestic fiction was a forum for "moral suasion" upon readers and that it could—and should—be a site of "right character formation and value transmission" (Brodhead 72)— those "extraliterary goods." Further, Alcott was adamantly—and morally—opposed to James's interest in probing the psychology of his characters. Though James and others objected to what they termed the "sentimentalism" of many (mostly women) writers, Alcott's (and other women's) notion of "right character formation" was not merely succumbing to a life directed entirely by sentiment, but one that included both emotion and reason (Baym 18–20). In Alcott's novel *A Modern Mephistopheles* (1877), for example, Gladys criticizes the villain Helwyze by referencing Hawthorne's notion of the "unpardonable sin," or as she puts it, "the want of love and reverence for the human soul, which makes a man pry into its mysterious depths, not with a hope or purpose of making it better, but from a cold, philosophical curiosity" (241). In this novel, and throughout her writing, Alcott objects to authorial prying with no notion of making a better human being as a result. The problem is not in using one's intellect; the problem is separating it from the heart.

In "A Country Christmas" (1881), Alcott declared what biographer Madeleine Stern termed "her own literary credo" (288). While she affirms her general beliefs about literature, she also very specifically takes James to task, not only on his views of

American women, but on his theories of writing as well. "A Country Christmas" addresses theories about literature and characterization through a plot in which two cosmopolites spend a holiday in rural Vermont at the invitation of their friend, Sophie Vaughan, who is also from "the city" but has been visiting her relatives on their farm. There seems to be no doubt that the young man of the couple is a stand-in for Henry James. He is a well-known novelist with two first names (Leonard Randal) whose most recent work is appearing in an unnamed magazine as the story takes place (*The Portrait of a Lady* was being serialized in the *Atlantic Monthly* in 1881). The fictional Randal's writing is said to be "of the aesthetic sort, microscopic studies of character and careful pictures of modern life" (Alcott, "Country Christmas" 108). The writer himself is "a true gentlemen in spite of his airs and elegance" (98) and "an accomplished *raconteur*" (119), which perfectly describes James and his work. Daniel Fogel notes that after the publication of *Daisy Miller*, James was "sought after as a guest…for his famous acerbic wit and his considerable personal charm," and dined out some 140 times in England during the succeeding winter (1). These details seem particularly important in that it is the eponymous character and the style of James's first international "hit" that seem to be the particular targets of Alcott's tale.

When Sophie's friend Emily arrives in Vermont with Randal for the holiday, further references reinforce the connection with James. Sophie had proposed in her invitation that Randal might "take notes for his new books" when he came, so that the next one he wrote would be "fresher and truer than the last, clever as it was" (Alcott, "Country Christmas" 95). Sophie's country cousin Ruth is referred to as a "daisy" four different times in the story in association with Randal's view of her; further, he asks Ruth if he might "make a mental study of you" (107), an interesting turn of phrase since James's *Daisy Miller* was subtitled "A Study." The narrator comments that, soon after Randal becomes a guest in the country home, "his trained fancy began to paint the background on which he hoped to copy this fresh, human daisy" (111). Later, when the girls raid Aunt Plumy's store of "antique costumes" for an "old-fashioned dance" (123), it is Ruth who wears muslin with a satin skirt (what Daisy is wearing when she first appears) and a [Daisy-Miller-esque?] "coquettish" (124) hat.

When Ruth responds to Randal's attention with innocent interest, he tries to take advantage: "he assumed the caressing air with which he beguiled [women] into the little revelations of character he liked to use, as the south wind makes flowers open their hearts to give up their odor, then leaves them to carry it elsewhere" (121–22). Several times in the tale, in fact, Randal's behavior is depicted as analogous to destroying flowers—another telling comment, since Daisy Miller had, in fact, been destroyed. Randal's assumptions are in for a rude awakening, however; he assumes that Ruth has fallen in love with him and that her heart is open to his inspection when she shyly suggests to him that "some sweet woman" (133) might help him to turn his life onto a better path. Though charmed by Randal, and interested in his work, Ruth is never taken in by him the way he assumes she is; on the contrary, she is playing a joke on him by pretending to be so, while actually steering him toward a proper appreciation of the woman with whom he is traveling, Emily. In her comic rearrangement of the Daisy-Winterbourne story, Alcott asserts that American innocence should not be mistaken for stupidity and that European sophistication need not destroy American girlhood. The country girl fools the cosmopolite, who does no better in accommodating himself to an unfamiliar life than did James's American girl in Europe. It should be noted, though, that Alcott doesn't kill him off; instead, she allows him to reform.

In fact, not only Ruth, but all the female characters in "A Country Christmas" reinforce Alcott's positive, empowered vision of American girlhood, and none displays the reckless naïveté of Daisy Miller. Ruth happily stays in the country to marry her minister beau, with whom she may visit Randal in the city—someday. Randal's friend Emily thoroughly enjoys her visit to the country but returns to her life in the city (and, it is implied, will marry the now-chastened Randal). Sophie finds in country life virtues that city society does not offer; at the end of the tale, she writes a farewell letter to the city millionaire who wishes to marry her and remains in the country to marry her cousin Saul. Each of these young women is grounded, independent, and able to thrive in new circumstances. Each chooses the place in the world most conducive to her growth and development—all qualities which elude Daisy Miller and, in fact, all the women in James's story.

Alcott does not confine her celebration of American resourcefulness to the young women in the story, either. On the contrary, other characters, including Ruth's mother, Aunt Plumy, and her brother Saul, further illustrate and celebrate her vision of American literature. Aunt Plumy is a gracious hostess, but when Randal condescendingly asks her what she thinks of his books, she "resent[s] the insinuation that country folk could not appreciate light literature as well as city people" (108) and proposes her own definition of "naturalism," complete with rustic dialect, including a floral allusion:

> I ain't no great of a jedge about anything but nat'ralness of books, and it really does seem as if some of your men and women was dreadful uncomfortable creaters. 'Pears to me it ain't wise to be always pickin' ourselves to pieces and pryin' into things that ought to come gradual by way of experience .... Flowers won't blow worth a cent ef you pull 'em open. (109)

When Randal protests that "I cannot help 'picking folks to pieces' ... that is my gift ... I must keep on in order to make a living" (110), Aunt Plumy doesn't back off:

> So rumsellers say, but it ain't a good trade to foller, and I'd chop wood 'fore I'd earn my livin' harmin' my feller man... I'd...hunt up some homely, happy folks to write about; folks that don't borrer trouble and go lookin' for holes in their neighbors' coats, but take their lives brave and cheerful; and rememberin' we are all human, have pity on the weak, and try to be ... full of mercy, patience and lovin' kindness. ... That sort of a book would do a heap of good. (110)

The suggestion that Randal's approach to writing might not only be less satisfying to a reader but actually harmful addresses not only

Daisy Miller the character but also *Daisy Miller* the book. While James pursued psychological realism, Alcott championed writing realistically about people who are models of good human behavior. Alcott thus aligns herself with those who propose that important literature can have "designs" on its readers; that is, the texts are important "not because they manage to escape the limitations of their time and space, but because they offer powerful examples of the way a culture thinks about itself, articulating and proposing solutions for the problems that shape a particular historical moment" (Tompkins xi). In "A Country Christmas," Alcott positions as an alternative storyteller to Randal Sophie's cousin Saul, who recounts a moving episode of everyday heroism from his Civil War experiences,[4] and in contrast with James' cold psychology, Alcott offers readers, in Aunt Plumy's words, a "warmin' and strengthenin'" tale ("Country Christmas" 110).

By all indications, Henry James himself did not "reform" his approach to writing after Alcott's story appeared, if indeed he ever read it. *The Portrait of a Lady* was followed by three decades of aesthetically artful writing, celebrated and approved by Victorian and modern arbiters of taste. Neither did Alcott give up her crusade, or stop voicing her concerns about literature—or about James. There are many scenes in her writing in which characters discuss the relative worth of various books and writers. In one of her very last short stories, "Pansies" (1887), eighteen-year-old Alice comments that "I never read Richardson, but he couldn't be duller than Henry James, with his everlasting stories, full of people who talk a great deal and amount to nothing" (15).[5] Nearly another century would pass before feminist theory and the rediscovery of her sensational "thrillers" would direct critical attention to Alcott's work and make her, for many scholars, an even more interesting writer than James. Regardless of who may have "won" this argument, the more important point is that, even as arbiters of literary merit turned away from serious consideration of her work, Alcott never stopped asserting her own theory of fiction or putting it into practice in stories firmly grounded in practical, positive American qualities, particularly those manifested by strong, sensible American girls.

Notes

1. For further details of the societal reaction to *Daisy Miller*, see also Novick, 390–92; Edel, 304–13; and Fogel, 12–19.

2. As the fictionalized *Shawl-Straps* is largely drawn from Alcott's trip to Europe in 1870 with her sister May and Alice Bartlett (ironically, the young woman who was supposedly James's source for *Daisy Miller*), Amy's adventures in Europe in *Little Women* (especially Chapter 31) are drawn from Louisa May Alcott's letters and journals from 1865–66, when she made her first trip to Europe as a companion to Anna Weld. See Sarah Wadsworth's "Innocence Abroad" as well as "Henry James Rides Again" for further discussions of Bartlett's influence on James's tale. Other contemporary critics have traced James's debt to other women writers as well; see Habegger, for example.

3. For that matter, neither is Daisy's little brother Randolph. In the *Eight Cousins* review, James complains about Alcott's little boys being "aggressive and knowing" and decries the "smart satirical tone" with which they address their elders, concluding that the novel provides children with "both poor entertainment and poor instruction" (105–6). The obnoxious Randolph seems to epitomize just how unappealing James finds such children, even in fiction.

4. Saul's heroism during the Civil War, and Randal's not having served, also appears to be a dig at James, who did not participate in the war, even though he turned eighteen on the day Lincoln issued his first call for troops and even though two of his brothers served as soldiers. Louisa Alcott surely knew this; she had helped to make an afghan for Wilky James when he came home wounded after participating in the Battle at Fort Wagner in 1863 (Alcott, *Journals* 121 [November 1863]).

5. I am grateful to Elizabeth Keyser for suggesting this reference.

Works Cited

Alcott, Louisa May. "A Country Christmas." *Proverb Stories*. Boston: Roberts Brothers, 1882.

_____. *The Journals of Louisa May Alcott*. Ed. Joel Myerson, Daniel Shealy, and Madeleine B. Stern. Boston: Little, Brown, 1989.

_____. *Little Women*. 1868–9. Ed. Anne K. Phillips and Gregory Eiselein. New York: Norton, 2004.

_____. *A Modern Mephistopheles; and, Taming a Tartar*. New York: Praeger, 1987.

_____. "Pansies." *St. Nicholas* 15.1 (November 1887): 12–19.

Anthony, Katharine. *Louisa May Alcott*. New York: Alfred A. Knopf, 1938.

Baym, Nina. *Woman's Fiction: A Guide to Novels by and About Women in America, 1820–1870*. Ithaca: Cornell UP, 1978.

Boyd, Anne E. *Writing for Immortality*. Baltimore: Johns Hopkins UP, 2004.

Brodhead, Richard H. *Cultures of Letters: Scenes of Reading and Writing in Nineteenth-Century America*. Chicago: U of Chicago P, 1993.

Edel, Leon. *Henry James: The Conquest of London 1870–1883*. London: Butler and Tanner, 1962.

Fogel, Daniel Mark. *"Daisy Miller": A Dark Comedy of Manners*. Boston: Twayne, 1990.

Habegger, Alfred. *Henry James and the "Woman Business."* Cambridge: Cambridge UP, 1989.

Hawthorne, Julian. "The Woman Who Wrote *Little Women*." *Louisa May Alcott: An Intimate Anthology*. New York: Doubleday, 1997. 332–41.

James, Henry. "The Art of Fiction." *Tales of Henry James*. Ed. Christof Wegelin. Norton Critical Edition. New York: Norton, 1984. 345–62.

_____. *Daisy Miller: A Study*. 1878. *Tales of Henry James*. Ed. Christof Wegelin. Norton Critical Edition. New York: Norton, 1984. 3–50.

_____. "Miss Alcott's *Moods*." *North American Review* 101 (Jul. 1865): 276–81. Rpt. in *Moods*. By Louisa May Alcott. Ed. Sarah Elbert. New Brunswick: Rutgers UP, 1991. 219–24.

_____. "Review of *Eight Cousins; or The Aunt-Hill*." 1875. *Nation* 21 (14 Oct. 1875): 250–51. Rpt. in *Critical Essays on Louisa May Alcott*. Ed. Madeleine B. Stern. Boston: G. K. Hall, 1984. 165–66.

Novick, Sheldon. *Henry James: The Young Master*. New York: Random House, 1996.

Stern, Madeleine B. *Louisa May Alcott*. 1950. New York: Random House, 1996.

Tompkins, Jane. *Sensational Designs: The Cultural Work of American Fiction, 1790–1860*. New York: Oxford UP, 1985.

Wadsworth, Sarah. "Henry James Rides Again." *The Henry James Review* 31.3 (Fall 2010): 218–231.

_____. "Innocence Abroad: Henry James and the Re-Invention of the American Woman Abroad." *The Henry James Review* 22.2 (2001): 107–127.

Louisa May Alcott, Patti Smith, and Punk Aesthetics_____

Gregory Eiselein

Alcott's Famous Fans

Long is the list of leaders, artists, and writers who have appreciatively and even adoringly acknowledged Alcott's influence on their own works and lives. It includes presidents, first ladies, and Supreme Court justices such as Sandra Day O'Connor, Ruth Bader Ginsberg, and Hillary Clinton. In his *Autobiography*, Theodore Roosevelt tells of how he "worshiped" (269) Alcott's novels, while Laura Bush identified *Little Women* as one of five books that "represented best the values of American society" ("Laura"). Alcott devotees include important feminist icons, like Simone de Beauvoir and Gloria Steinem, and distinguished writers, such as Gertrude Stein, Ann Petry, Ursula LeGuin, Cynthia Ozick, and more. J. K. Rowling, for example, has confessed that she, too, is an ardent fan of *Little Women*: "My favorite literary heroine is Jo March. It is hard to overstate what she meant to a small, plain girl called Jo, who had a hot temper and a burning ambition to be a writer" (Rowling). And the list goes on.

So, why was anyone surprised to learn that the legendary rock star Patti Smith also loved the legendary coming-of-age novel *Little Women*? Smith is the poet, songwriter, singer, and artist whose influential early 70s performances and debut album, *Horses* (1975), helped ignite and then shape the revolution in music and culture known as punk. Although the genre later became associated with mostly male acts, such as The Ramones, The Sex Pistols, and The Clash, Smith's early work preceded and influenced theirs, and she is widely regarded as "Punk rock's poet laureate" (Huey) and "the poet queen of the early New York City punk rock scene" (Cogan 209). When the superb historian and Alcott scholar Barbara Sicherman was told about Alcott's connection to the godmother of punk, she said: "Patti Smith. I am surprised. But I shouldn't be. Jo March has been inspiring girls since she first appeared on the literary landscape nearly a century and a half ago" (qtd. in Mahalek). Even Smith herself, in her National Book Award-winning memoir *Just Kids* (2010), seems to acknowledge the incongruity when talking about Alcott's influence on her development as a writer. While the connection might strike some as odd or surprising, an examination of the connections between Louisa May Alcott and Patti Smith, and their singular masterpieces (*Little Women* and *Horses*, respectively), reveals interesting biographical parallels and important aesthetic similarities. These links shed light, moreover, on underappreciated aspects of Alcott's place within U.S. literary history and culture more generally.

Content: Gender and Biographical and Thematic Connections

In the opening chapter of *Just Kids*, Smith narrates her struggle with gender conformity. She shares, for instance, a conflict that began with her love of "long walks in the outlying woods" (10) and playing soldier with her siblings. One hot summer day, her mother insists that Patti put on a shirt, despite the heat, because "You're about to become a young lady." Smith recalls her fierce objections to her mother's insistence: "I protested vehemently and announced that I was never going to become anything but myself, that I was of the clan of Peter Pan and we did not grow up" (10). Smith loses the argument, but more significantly, she comes to resent the pressure to conform to the ubiquitous feminine role models of the 1950s.

Alcott's work became one of the ways Smith learned to cope with these gendered social pressures and her own indignation about them. In *Just Kids*, Smith explains, in the following words, the significance of *Little Women* to her as she was growing up:

> I drew comfort from my books. Oddly enough, it was Louisa May Alcott who provided me with a positive view of my female destiny. Jo, the tomboy of the four March sisters in *Little Women* writes to help support her family, struggling to make ends meet during the Civil War. She fills page after page with her rebellious scrawl, later publishing in the literary pages of the local newspaper. She gave me

the courage of a new goal, and soon I was crafting little stories and spinning long yarns for my brother and sister. From that time on, I cherished the idea that one day I would write a book. (10–11)

Jo March modeled an alternative for Smith, who admired Jo's rebelliousness and saw in her a "positive view of my female destiny."

In these passages, Smith intertwines not only gender rebellion, but also a desire to be a writer. For Louisa Alcott, Jo March, and Patti Smith, becoming a writer is an expression of refusal to conform to social clichés about femininity. We see this nonconformity in the passages from *Just Kids*, but also in Smith's selection of literary idols, such as Arthur Rimbaud, Allen Ginsberg, and Alcott, who were each socially, sexually, and artistically nonconformist (see Thompson 17–19 and 49). We see it in her music, in the *Horses* album, for example, where she seeks, in her words, "The right to create, without apology, from a stance beyond gender or social definition" (Smith, *Patti Smith Complete* 7). And we see it in her image or self-presentation as an artist. The photographer Kate Simon, for example, captures a nonchalant and very cool Smith in front of a urinal in a men's room at Hofstra University (Smith, *Patti Smith Complete* 48). She's wearing a t-shirt and unzipped blue jeans, and she's holding a cigarette in her left hand and the urinal's manual flush handle in her right. Her expression communicates both punk indifference and, perhaps post-performance, artistic exhaustion.[1] Or, to mention another example, Robert Mapplethorpe's photographs of Smith for the *Horses* album presents Smith in a white men's dress shirt with the cuffs removed, slim black pants, a dark ribbon that looks a like a skinny tie, and a black suit jacket "flung...over [her] shoulder, Frank Sinatra style" (Smith, *Just Kids* 251).[2] In these and numerous other photographs, Smith's look is masculine, intentionally so. As she says of the *Horses* photo shoot, "I had my look in mind. He had his light in mind. That is all" (*Just Kids* 250). She was indeed sometimes mistaken for a young man, as when the gay poet Allen Ginsberg tried to pick her up, thinking she was "a cute boy" (qtd. in McNeil and McCain 113). Moreover, many of her poetic and musical colleagues seem to have loved the fact that, to quote poet Ed Friedman, "she could be one of the guys" (qtd. in McNeil and McCain 113).[3]

Jo March's gender rebellion and masculine identifications are no less pronounced. One of the reasons she so enjoys writing her dramatic pieces, like "The Witch's Curse," is that she gets to "[play] male parts to her heart's content" (Alcott, *Little Women* 23). The "boyish" Jo whistles, uses slang, and laments being born female (12). When Meg reminds her to "leave off boyish tricks" and act more like "a young lady," Jo responds vehemently:

> I ain't!... I hate to think I've got to grow up and be Miss March, and wear long gowns, and look as prim as a China-aster. It's bad enough to be a girl, any way, when I like boy's games, and work, and manners. I can't get over my disappointment in not being a boy, and it's worse than ever now, for I'm dying to go and fight with papa. (Alcott, *Little Women* 12–13)

Though disappointed about not being a boy, she performs masculinity throughout *Little Women*, where she is described as being a "tomboy" (Alcott, *Little Women* 13) and having a "gentlemanly demeanor" (31). She channels much of this masculine independence into her desire to be a writer: "I think I shall write books, and get rich and famous; that would suit me, so that is *my* favorite dream" (118).

Alcott's own merging of writing and gender trouble comes in her creation of tomboy protagonists, like Jo, Nan (who is introduced in *Little Men*), and Josie (who appears in *Jo's Boys*). Though perhaps more famous as the creator of tomboys, Alcott also uses her literary art to disrupt conventional understandings of sex and gender and to condemn patriarchal domination. In "Behind a Mask" (1866), she uses the actress protagonist Jean Muir to reveal how "femininity" is a performance: Jean self-consciously uses her acting skills to perform various forms of female identity, designed to appeal to various members of the Coventry family, into which she hopes to marry. In *Work*, Alcott outspokenly critiques the cruel and arbitrary treatment of women workers, when, for example, the protagonist Christie Devon objects to the way her boss barks commands and expects her to perform humiliating personal tasks: "It isn't the work; it's the degradation; and I won't submit to it" (21).

In short, Alcott's influence seems clearly visible in these key aspects of Smith's work: her gender nonconformity, her resistance to authority and dominant cultural expectations, and her audacious pursuit of life as a writer and artist.

Their shared gender rebellion and insistence on becoming writers may also be linked to other important similarities. For instance, both had romantic attachments to non-heterosexual male artists. Smith's relationship with gay photographer Robert Mapplethorpe is the primary subject of her *Just Kids* memoir, and she describes their relationship with real romantic beauty:

> Wordlessly we absorbed the thoughts of one another and just as dawn broke fell asleep in each other's arms. (42)

> One cannot imagine the mutual happiness we felt when we sat and drew together. We would get lost for hours. His ability to concentrate for long periods infected me, and I learned by his example, working side by side. (57)

Wrapped up in each other and in each other's work, Smith and Mapplethorpe are lovers and friends, artists and fans, who each seem to desire and to identify with the other.

Alcott's connection with Transcendentalist writer Henry David Thoreau may be more difficult to delineate. Thoreau's sexuality is not a clear-cut subject, but a widely accepted view— held by his biographer Walter Harding, among others—is that Thoreau seems to have been romantically attracted to men (much less so or perhaps not at all to women), though there is no sign that he ever had a physical, sexual relationship with a man or woman (Harding 39–40). Around women, he could seem "cold" or embarrassed and annoyed (Harding 23–24). Hence, Thoreau might seem at first to some an unlikely object for Alcott's affection. Yet, as a few biographers have noted, Alcott developed what has been seen as an adolescent crush on Thoreau. According to Harriet Reisen, "In Thoreau, Louisa found an outlet for her romantic imagination"

(126), while Madeleine Stern explains that Alcott "sensed … a magic about Mr. Thoreau. She had never seen eyes that were bluer" (21). Tracey Cummings offers additional perspective on Alcott's attachment to Thoreau: "As a young woman who was struggling with the restrictive nature of gender expectations, Alcott most likely took note of Thoreau's disinterest in allowing such expectations to shape his life" (13). In short, "Alcott admired Thoreau's 'queer' unmarried state" (Cummings 14). Whatever the precise nature of Thoreau's sexual orientation or Alcott's feelings about him, she wrote about him often, most notably in *Moods*, *Work*, *Little Men*, *Jo's Boys*, and "Thoreau's Flute," but also perhaps in *Eight Cousins* and *Rose in Bloom*. Her Thoreauvian characters are not typically handsome, and they often seem frosty and unapproachable. Perhaps the best example of a Thoreauvian persona in Alcott's work is Adam Warwick from *Moods* who is "Violently virtuous" and described in terms of his inner power rather than his external beauty:

> He is a masterful soul, bent on living out his beliefs and aspirations at any cost. Much given to denunciation of wrong-doing everywhere, and eager to execute justice upon all offenders high or low. Yet he possesses great nobility of character, great audacity of mind, and leads a life of the sternest integrity. (37)

Despite their unlovely appearances and distant demeanors, Thoreauvian figures in Alcott's fiction are romantic leads and objects of the heroines' fascinations and not-quite sublimated sexual desires. In *Moods*, for example, Sylvia is smitten: "to her imaginative and enthusiastic nature, there was something irresistibly attractive in the strong, solitary, self-reliant man" (37–38). Earlier, even before she is captivated by his complex inner world, Sylvia is also drawn to his outward, "heroic" appearance and thinks he is "the manliest man that [she] had ever seen" (36).

While it is beyond the scope of this essay to propose a theory that explains why gender rebels like Smith and Alcott are drawn to queer artists, it may be important to note that the common, Freudian dichotomy that separates identification and desire finds itself blurred and undone in the work and lives of Smith and Alcott. Their love and desire for these queer men seems connected to their identification with and emulation of each as intense artists and singular individuals who refused to conform to the heteronormative conventions of their eras.

While attitudes toward gender may be the thematic connection that links the two authors most closely, Smith and Alcott share several other striking similarities. Both claim Germantown, Pennsylvania, as a hometown: Smith lived there as a child, while Alcott was born there. Both wanted to be writers *as well as* performers: Smith a rock star, Alcott an actress. Both grew up working class/working poor, and their earliest jobs shaped their insubordinate attitudes toward capitalism and work. We see this in Smith's 1974 poem "Piss Factory" ("I got this job in a piss factory inspecting pipe... It's so hot in here hot like sahara You could faint in the heat" [*Early Work* 38]) but also in the opening chapters of Alcott's *Work*, as Christie moves from one miserable job to another.

Their religious upbringings may also have developed in each writer a sense of outsider status. Both were raised in what we might call a New American religion. Smith's mother was a devoted Jehovah's Witness, while Alcott was raised in a Unitarian/Transcendentalist family. Neither quite accepted (or fully rejected) their parents' beliefs. Still, the experience seems to have opened up each writer to a curiosity about religion and spiritual worlds, an inclination to see truth not in one belief system but in a whole range of faiths, and a willingness to reject traditional or orthodox beliefs.[4] Take, for example, their complex views of Jesus Christ. Smith begins *Horses* with a rebellious and startling declaration of spiritual independence: "Jesus died for somebody's sins but not mine /...My sins my own/ They belong to me, me" ("Gloria," track 1). Despite her seemingly outright rejection of Christ on this first album, Smith's third album, *Easter*, almost devoutly explores Christian themes of love, prayer, eternity, death and resurrection, and the merging of the human with the divine, and it does so with explicit Christian imagery: "The nail, the grail" ("Till Victory," track 1). Alcott's own view on the subject also separates her from orthodox Christianity. She thinks of Christ as "a great reformer" but "not God" (Alcott, *Selected Letters*

278), a view echoed by Demi's simple description of "Christ, the Good Man" in *Little Men* (47). In other words, their ambivalent relationships to their non-mainstream family religions may have cultivated in each writer an iconoclastic attitude toward received ideas and a willingness to explore and embrace the unconventional.

Form and Process: Aesthetic Connections

Exploring the connections between Smith and Alcott's religious upbringings, lives, and careers provides an important foundation for tracing how *Little Women* strengthened Smith's artistic ambitions and her resolve to resist rigid gender expectations and general cultural conformity. Alcott's work also helped shape Smith's development of a punk aesthetic. Several features of Smith's aesthetic mirror Alcott's own artistic principles and suggest another set of correspondences between this nineteenth-century Transcendentalist and twentieth-century punk.

Both, for example, merge philosophy and high art with popular forms and common language. Alcott wrote a rather philosophical Transcendentalist novel (*Moods*), published literary fiction in distinguished venues ("Love and Self-Love" in *The Atlantic Monthly*, for example), and interacted with many of the nation's greatest authors (Emerson, Thoreau, Fuller, Hawthorne, and many more). But she also published dozens of anonymous and pseudonymous thrillers in the tabloid press—popular stories filled with ghosts, exotic places and adventures, murder and revenge, sex and violence. These sensational stories were not her only efforts in popular forms, however. She also reveled in the popular and folk forms of fantasy and fairy tales, particularly at the beginning (*Flower Fables* [1855]) and end (*Lulu's Library* [1886]) of her publishing career. Perhaps more importantly, Alcott blended these low and high genres in various works throughout her career. *Little Women*, for example, is both a popular girls' story and an epic quest. It alludes as readily to "Twinkle, Twinkle, Little Star" and newspaper fiction of the sort that Jo publishes in the "Weekly Volcano" (Alcott, *Little Women* 273) as to Cervantes, Goethe, Hegel, Schopenhauer, and Shakespeare. Moreover, on the sentence level, Alcott enjoys blending these different levels of language and culture, as when Laurie erupts with "the indecorous exclamation, 'Jupiter Ammon!'" (200)—an interjection that is both a kind of low, minced oath (or euphemistic swearing, like "gosh" or "darn") and an indirect revelation of Laurie's elite classical education in the reference to the Latinized form of the supreme Egyptian deity Amun (see *Little Women*, 200fn5).

Smith, too, blends swearing with highbrow religious references, as in the prose poem/performance piece "Babelogue," which combines profanity and nasty images of rock shows with religious references to ancient Greek polytheism, Islam, and the kind of sacred purity that comes from personal and artistic integrity: "one who has not sold her soul to god or man nor any other" (*Early Work* 117). Like Alcott, Smith's body of work also makes use of multiple popular forms. In *Horses*, for example, she borrows from 1960s rhythm and blues. For example, "Land," the album's hallucinatory, climactic song, erupts into several verses from Chris Kenner's "Land of 1000 Dances" (1962), a song made famous by Wilson Pickett's cover version from 1966. She uses three-chord rock music, as in her rendition of the garage rock classic "Gloria" (1964), in which she blends parts of her own early poem "Oath" (Smith, *Early Work* 7) with Van Morrison's very famous first hit song. Musically, Smith borrows from popular American forms of the 1960s to pave the way for what would become the arty blend of highbrow culture and lowbrow culture that is punk music and the punk aesthetic. Smith's muses were never just popular music, however. Perhaps preeminent among her influences is the French symbolist poet Arthur Rimbaud, whose *Illuminations* she shoplifted when she was sixteen (Smith, *Just Kids* 23). She describes Rimbaud as her "compatriot, kin, and even secret love," attesting that his work "held the keys to a mystical language" that she "devoured" and that shaped her own style and aesthetic (23). Moreover, throughout her development as poet and then rock star, Smith was inspired by the New York avant-garde of the 1960s and 1970s—living with Mapplethorpe, collaborating with the playwright Sam Shepherd, hanging out with artists like Andy Warhol and Robert Rauschenberg, and learning from writers like Gregory Corso and William Burroughs, among many others (see Shaw 48–68). Like Alcott's mid-nineteenth-century Concord, Smith's New York City of the 60s and 70s was a cauldron of creativity and intensity that shaped the writer, teaching her a fierce artistic independence that set her apart from the very popular or mainstream culture from which she would liberally borrow for her own purposes.

A second and related aesthetic connection is their shared use of an intense and unabashed amateur energy. It doesn't seem as if the self-consciously literary Smith, whose lyrics are sometimes hallucinatory and intentionally disturbing, ought to be described as an "amateur." Likewise, the term doesn't seem to describe well a writer who grew up in Concord during the height of Transcendentalism, borrowed books from Emerson, and experimented with writing Transcendentalist novels of ideas. Still, one of the most remarkable things about their greatest works (*Horses* and *Little Women*) is the combination of energy and sincerity that characterizes each. Alcott passionately describes how funny and heartbreaking it was to grow up with her sisters, and in the process, a more proper literary language seems to fall away. One of the great achievements of *Little Women* is its ability to render the seeming trivialities of childhood with compelling emotional intensity—the real danger Meg encounters at the Moffats' party (71–84), the white hot anger Jo feels over Amy's burning of her book (62–71), the joy in producing homemade newspapers (86–89) and theatricals (22–26), or the despair in losing a sister to marriage: "It can never be the same again. I've lost my dearest friend" (184). The novel was, in Alcott's words, "very hastily written to order" (*Selected Letters* 118). But having no clear idea how to write a girls' story except to share her own and her sisters' "queer plays and experiences" (Alcott, *Journal* 166), the novel has an innocent, almost artless vitality: "The characters were drawn from life, which gives them whatever merit they possess" (*Selected Letters* 118).

Likewise, like most good punks, Smith cares less about hitting each note just right and more about expressing herself openly, honestly, without inhibitions. In an article from *Crawdaddy*, Smith described the improvisatory nature of recording *Horses*:

I'll sit down with them [band members] and say "Play some simple chords," and I'll start daydreaming and talking over the music, spilling poetry, and they'll keep me going by play a certain way or changing the chord structure ... and it just grows from there. [...] I control the band only to the point where they get enough freedom to control me. [...] We're all squeezing this piece of coal and I can see the shoots of light starting to come out, the beginnings of a diamond. (qtd. in Shapiro 283)

Later, Smith would say of *Horses*: "The album was spewed from my womb. It's a naked record" (qtd. in Shaw 97). Like Alcott's sisters, Smith's band would provide the content and context that the artist would shape with a hurried, uninhibited, and passionate manner into a kind of artless art.

This intensely energetic, yet not always proper or self-consciously controlled approach to creative composition lends itself to moments of vivid, sometimes shocking images or scenes. As Alcott noted in an interview late in her career, "I think my natural ambition is for the lurid style. I indulge in gorgeous fancies and wish that I dared inscribe them upon my pages and set them before the public" (qtd. in Pickett 42). We see this lurid style in Alcott's thrillers, in the depiction of Sibyl's imprisonment in "A Whisper in the Dark" (51–57), for example, but also in her children's fiction, as in *Little Women* when Jo's writings are burnt, first by Amy (64) and then by Jo herself (280). Smith's own lurid style is apparent throughout her work. For instance, in "Land," Johnny's murder or suicide transpires in terms that are sexual and transcendent: "He picked up the blade and he pressed it against his smooth throat / And let it deep in / Dip in to the sea, to the sea of possibilities / It started hardening in my hand / And I felt the arrows of desire" (*Horses* "Land," track 7). The song's strange combination of lethal violence with sexual fulfillment and religious transcendence is shocking and sordid, but also beautiful as it unfolds alongside galloping horses, ecstatic dancing, and the waves of the sea.

If a tendency toward a "lurid style" might be one result of their liberated artistic energy, this energy itself might be the product of a similar creative process. Both Alcott and Smith see the process of artistic creation in terms that seem drawn from romanticism, but it might actually be best described in terms of what Hungarian psychologist Mihály Csíkszentmihályi calls "flow"—that mental state full of intense concentration and control where one loses one's sense of self and time in an activity that is challenging and rewarding or joyful. For example, Alcott seems to chronicle flow when she describes Jo's creative process in *Little Women*:

> Every few weeks she [Jo] would shut herself up in her room, put on her scribbling suit, and "fall into a vortex," as she expressed it, writing away at her novel with all her heart and soul ... when the writing fit came on, she gave herself up to it with entire abandon, and led a blissful life, unconscious of want, care, or bad weather. (211)

Smith's creative method seems quite similar. One rock magazine from the 1970s described her process this way: "The aura was of controlled insanity as holes in one track intersected perfectly with phrases of another—Patti ran on pure nerve, and after 7 hours emerged with a chilling and affecting piece of true art" (qtd. in Shaw 131). In an attempt to write their own experiences and truths and in their refusal to conform to social norms—in other words, in their attempts to be true to their self—both writers end up losing their self-conscious sense of self, at least temporarily, in the activity of literary creation.

Just Kids and *Little Women*: Youth and Outlaw American Cultures

I am not arguing that Smith learned artistic flow, the lurid style, the possibilities of amateur energy, or the blending of low and high art from Alcott alone. Indeed, as Smith makes clear, Rimbaud was a greater muse or "archangel" (*Just Kids* 23) than Alcott. Still, it does seem clear from *Just Kids* and from Smith's work in general that Alcott was one of the writers who encouraged Smith at an early point in her self development. Alcott served as a role model for Smith, teaching her how to imagine herself as a nonconformist, as a woman who embraced her masculinity, as a writer and artist. Alcott gave her "the courage of a new goal" (*Just Kids* 11) and justified her experimentation with imagination, words, stories, and the expression of what the Existentialists might call an authentic self or the Transcendentalists might understand as self-reliance: "Nothing is at last sacred but the integrity of your own mind" (Emerson 261).

While it may surprise some to realize that Jo inspired the godmother of punk, the defiance and dissent Smith sees in Alcott are at the foundation of her artistic practice. Tracing this influence reminds us that Alcott had a substantial impact on not only wholesome and not-so-wholesome children's writings (such as the Little House series, *Harriet the Spy*, or Beverly Cleary's Ramona Quimby series) but also on the experimental, modernist, and so-called "outlaw" traditions in American literature, such as beat, punk, and queer.[5] A more comprehensive understanding of the connection to Smith and these outlaw traditions and the various other ways Alcott has influenced American writing will help us better appreciate how complex, suggestive, and multi-dimensional her writing really is.

Yet an examination of the Alcott-Smith connection also reminds us that some artists within these traditions, from Transcendentalism to punk and beyond, have seen in youth the particular moment or model for rebellion. Alcott focuses her great novel on her adolescence and early adult years, while Smith captures the moment when she and Mapplethorpe were "just kids" (47). Although some have insisted that children's and adolescent literature must necessarily be conventional and instructive,[6] Alcott and Smith chose instead to imagine youth and youth culture (whether it be girls' novels or rock music) as the opportunity for creativity, rebellion, and a self-discovery that would allow one to transcend the artificial limits imposed by stifling social norms, received artistic conventions, and unbearable gender roles.

Notes

1. This photograph can also be seen online at the archival website known as *Dangerous Minds*: <http://dangerousminds.net/comments/the_patti_smith_group_cover_the_velvet_undergrounds_pale_blue_eyes_in_1976>.

2. Mapplethorpe's photograph of Smith appears on the cover of the *Horses* album and in Smith's *Just Kids* (251).

3. See also the Bob Gruen photograph of Smith as one of the guys in McNeil and McCain, following page 300.

4. For more on Alcott's religion, see Eiselein but also Tippin. For more about Smith's religious upbringing, see Thompson 9 and 85.

5. I borrow the term "outlaw" as a literary descriptor from Alan Kaufman.

6. See, for instance, Perry Nodelman, who has explained that "children's literature is primarily a didactic literature" (157).

Works Cited

Alcott, Louisa May. *Little Men: Life at Plumfield with Jo's Boys*. 1871. New York: Signet, 1986.

_____. *Little Women; or, Meg, Jo, Beth and Amy*. 1868–69. Ed. Anne K. Phillips and Gregory Eiselein. New York: Norton, 2004.

_____. *Moods*. 1864. Ed. Sarah Elbert. New Brunswick: Rutgers UP, 1991.

_____. *The Selected Letters of Louisa May Alcott*. Ed. Joel Myerson, Daniel Shealy, and Madeleine B. Stern. Boston: Little, Brown, 1987.

_____. "A Whisper in the Dark." 1863. *Louisa May Alcott Unmasked: Collected Thrillers*. Ed. Madeleine Stern. Boston: Northeastern UP, 1995. 32–58.

_____. *Work: A Story of Experience*. 1873. Ed. Joy S. Kasson. New York: Penguin, 1994.

Cogan, Brian. *Encyclopedia of Punk Music and Culture*. Westport, CT: Greenwood P, 2006.

Csíkszentmihályi, Mihály. *Flow: The Psychology of Optimal Experience*. New York: Harper, 1990.

Cummings, Tracey A. *"For such as he there is no death": Louisa May Alcott's Rewritings of Thoreau*. Diss. Lehigh University, 2005. *MLA International Bibliography*. 20 May 2013. Web. 8 Dec. 2015.

Eiselein, Gregory. "'A Religion of Their Own': Louisa May Alcott's New American Religion." *Nineteenth-Century American Women Write Religion: Lived Theologies and Literature*. Ed. Mary McCartin Wearn. Burlington, VT: Ashgate, 2014. 119–34.

Emerson, Ralph Waldo. "Self-Reliance." 1841. *Essays and Poems*. Ed. Joel Porte, Harold Bloom, and Paul Kane. New York: Library of America, 1996. 257–82.

Gruen, Bob. Photograph of David Johansen, Lenny Kaye, Dee Dee Ramone, Patti Smith, Jay Dee Daugherty, Tom Verlaine, and John Cale. 1976. *Please Kill Me: The Uncensored Oral History of Punk*. 1996. By Legs McNeil and Gillian McCain. New York: Grove, 2006. 300–301.

Harding, Walter. "Thoreau's Sexuality." *Journal of Homosexuality* 21 (1991): 23–45.

Huey, Steve. "Patti Smith: Biography." *AllMusic*. All Media Network, 2015. Web. 11 Aug. 2015.

Kaufman, Alan, ed. *The Outlaw Bible of American Poetry*. New York: Thunder's Mouth P, 1999.

"Laura Bush Visits Moscow." Narr. Soledad O'Brien. *Wolf Blitzer Reports*. CNN. 30 Sept. 2003. Television.

Mahalek, Gina. "Louisa May Alcott and the Godmother of Punk." *UNC Press Blog*. 9 March 2010. U of North Carolina P, 2010. Web. 19 May 2013.

Mapplethorpe, Robert. Photograph of Patti Smith. *Just Kids*. By Patti Smith. New York: Ecco, 2010. 251.

McNeil, Legs, and Gillian McCain. *Please Kill Me: The Uncensored Oral History of Punk*. 1996. New York: Grove, 2006.

Nodelman, Perry. *The Hidden Adult: Defining Children's Literature*. Baltimore, MD: Johns Hopkins UP, 2008.

Pickett, LaSalle Corbell. "[Louisa Alcott's 'Natural Ambition' for the 'Lurid Style' Disclosed in Conversation.]" *Critical Essays of Louisa May Alcott*. Ed. Madeleine B. Stern. Boston: Hall, 1984. 42.

Reisen, Harriet. *Louisa May Alcott: The Woman Behind* Little Women. New York: Henry Holt, 2009.

Roosevelt, Theodore. *The Rough Riders and An Autobiography*. 1899, 1913. Ed. Louis Auchincloss. New York: Library of America, 2004.

Rowling, J. K. "J. K. Rowling: By the Book." *New York Times*. The New York Times Company, 11 Oct. 2012. Web. 8 Dec. 2015.

Shapiro, Susan. "Patti Smith: Somewhere, Over the Rimbaud." *Crawdaddy* (Dec. 1975). Rpt. in *Rock She Wrote*. Eds. Evelyn McDonnell and Ann Powers. London: Plexus, 1995. 279–83.

Shaw, Philip. *Horses*. New York: Continuum, 2008.

Simon, Kate. "Men's room, Hofstra University" [photograph of Patti Smith]. 1976. *Patti Smith Complete: Lyrics, Notes and Reflections.* By Patti Smith. New York: Anchor, 1999. 48.

Smith, Patti. *Easter.* Arista, 1978. CD.

_____. *Horses.* Arista, 1975. CD.

_____. *Just Kids.* New York: Ecco, 2010.

_____. *Patti Smith Complete: Lyrics, Notes and Reflections.* New York: Anchor, 1999.

_____. *Early Work, 1970–1979*. New York: Norton, 1994. 38–40.

Stern, Madeleine B. *Louisa May Alcott: A Biography.* Rev. ed. Boston: Northeastern UP, 1999.

Tippin, R. Eric. "'Up the Steep Hill by Trying': The Unorthodox Christianity of *Little Women.*" *Critical Insights:* Little Women. Eds. Gregory Eiselein and Anne K. Phillips. Ipswich, MA: Salem P, 2015. 128–42.

Thompson, David. *Dancing Barefoot: The Patti Smith Story.* Chicago: Chicago Review P, 2011.

RESOURCES

Chronology of Louisa May Alcott's Life_____

1830	Abigail May and Amos Bronson Alcott marry in Boston.
1831	Anna Bronson Alcott, Abigail and Bronson's first daughter, is born.
1832	Louisa May Alcott, second daughter of Abigail and Bronson Alcott, is born in Germantown, Pennsylvania, on November 29.
1835	Third daughter, Elizabeth Sewall Alcott, is born. Bronson meets Ralph Waldo Emerson.
1840	Alcotts move to Concord. Fourth daughter, Abigail May Alcott, is born.
1843	Alcotts move to a utopian community known as Fruitlands. Louisa starts a journal and begins writing poems.
1844	Alcotts leave Fruitlands in January. By year's end, they return to Concord.
1845	With financial help from Emerson, Abigail purchases a house in Concord. Bronson names it "Hillside."
1846	Louisa gets her own room at Hillside, and she reads and writes often. Alcott girls produce their own dramatic performances in the barn.
1847	Encouraged by Emerson, Louisa begins reading Goethe, Carlyle, and Shakespeare.
1849	Alcott sisters begin to produce a family newspaper called *The Olive Leaf*.

1851	Louisa attends an antislavery protest. She works as a governess for the Lovering family and then as a servant for James Richardson. She publishes first poem, "Sunlight," under the pseudonym Flora Fairfield.
1852	Louisa and Anna start a school in their home. Louisa publishes first short story, "The Rival Painters."
1854	Publisher James T. Fields rejects story by Louisa, based on her experience as a servant in Richardson house, and advises her to give up writing. Louisa publishes first book, *Flower Fables*, a collection of fairy tales dedicated to Ellen Emerson.
1857	Alcotts purchase residence in Concord, rename it "Orchard House," and move in.
1858	Elizabeth dies. Anna and John Bridge Pratt announce engagement.
1860	Anna marries John Bridge Pratt.
1862	To support the Union's Civil War efforts, Louisa becomes a nurse and relocates to Washington, D.C., to start work at the Union Hotel Hospital.
1863	While working as a nurse, Louisa contracts typhoid and becomes seriously ill. She returns to Concord. Her account of these nursing experiences is published serially and then in book form as *Hospital Sketches*.
1864	Louisa publishes her "Transcendentalist" novel, *Moods*.
1865	Louisa travels to Europe as a companion to an invalid, Anna Weld.

1866	Returning from Europe, Louisa writes and publishes numerous "thriller" stories, including "Behind a Mask."
1867	Editor Thomas Niles of Roberts Brothers invites Louisa to write a girls' book, and she accepts the offer.
1868	Louisa begins work on *Little Women*. Early versions of certain scenes appear in "Merry's Monthly Chat" in the children's magazine she edited, *Merry's Museum*. The first part of *Little Women* is published in October.
1869	The second part of *Little Women* is published in April.
1870	*An Old-Fashioned Girl* is published by Roberts Brothers. With her sister May, Louisa departs on a second trip to Europe, which becomes the basis for her travel narrative *Shawl-Straps* (1872). Anna's husband, John Bridge Pratt, dies.
1871	*Little Men* is published. Louisa returns to the United States, while May stays in Europe to study and paint.
1873	Alcott's novel *Work* is published.
1874	May returns from London. Louisa divides time between Orchard House; Conway, New Hampshire (over the summer); and Boston.
1875	*Eight Cousins* is published. Louisa makes two different trips to New York City and one to the Woman's Congress in Syracuse.
1876	May returns to Europe. A sequel to *Eight Cousins*, titled *Rose in Bloom*, is published.

1877	Louisa writes and anonymously publishes a thriller, *A Modern Mephistopheles*, for Roberts Brothers' No Name Series.
1878	May marries Swiss businessman Ernest Nieriker in London. *Under the Lilacs* is published.
1879	Bronson opens the Concord School of Philosophy. Louisa registers to vote and becomes the first woman in Concord to do so. May and Ernest's daughter, Louise Marie "Lulu" Nieriker, is born in Paris in November. May dies the following month.
1880	Lulu arrives in the United States to live with Louisa. *Jack and Jill* is published.
1881	Louisa meets Walt Whitman. She works on plans for a suffrage organization.
1882	The second, revised edition of *Moods* appears. Louisa organizes a temperance society in Concord. Bronson suffers a stroke.
1884	Lulu starts kindergarten. Louisa tries to work again on *Jo's Boys* but is too ill to work on it steadily.
1886	Dr. Rhoda Ashley Lawrence, a homeopathic physician, cares for the increasingly ill Louisa. *Jo's Boys* is published.
1888	Bronson dies on March 4. Louisa dies two days later, on March 6. Both are buried in Concord's Sleepy Hollow Cemetery on March 8.

Works by Louisa May Alcott

Selected Books

Hospital Sketches (1863)

Moods (1864. Rev. ed. 1882)

Little Women, or Meg, Jo, Beth, and Amy (1868–69)

An Old-Fashioned Girl (1870)

Little Men: Life at Plumfield with Jo's Boys (1871)

Work: A Story of Experience (1873)

Eight Cousins; or, The Aunt-Hill (1875)

Rose in Bloom: A Sequel to "Eight Cousins" (1876)

A Modern Mephistopheles (1877)

Under the Lilacs (1878)

Jack and Jill: A Village Story (1880)

Jo's Boys, and How They Turned Out: A Sequel to "Little Men" (1886)

A Long Fatal Love Chase (1995)

The Inheritance (1997)

Selected Collections

Flower Fables (1854)

On Picket Duty, and Other Tales (1864)

Morning-Glories, and Other Stories (1868)

My Boys: Aunt Jo's Scrap-Bag (1872)

Shawl-Straps: Aunt Jo's Scrap-Bag (1872)

Cupid and Chow-Chow: Aunt Jo's Scrap-Bag (1874)

Silver Pitchers: And Independence, A Centennial Love Story (1876)

My Girls: Aunt Jo's Scrap-Bag (1878)

Jimmy's Cruise in the Pinafore: Aunt Jo's Scrap-Bag (1879)

An Old-Fashioned Thanksgiving: Aunt Jo's Scrap-Bag (1882)

Proverb Stories (1882, later retitled *Kitty's Class Day*)

Spinning-Wheel Stories (1884)

Lulu's Library (1885–89)

Comic Tragedies Written by "Jo" and "Meg" and Acted by the "Little Women" (1893)

Louisa May Alcott: Selected Fiction (1990)

Louisa May Alcott's Fairy Tales and Fantasy Stories (1992)

Louisa May Alcott Unmasked: Collected Thrillers (1995)

Louisa May Alcott on Race, Sex, and Slavery (1997)

The Poetry of Louisa May Alcott (1997)

The Early Stories of Louisa May Alcott, 1852–1860 (2000)

The Poems of Louisa May Alcott (2000)

The Sketches of Louisa May Alcott (2001)

Selected Letters, Journals and Memoirs

Louisa May Alcott: Her Life, Letters and Journals (1889)

Transcendental Wild Oats and Excerpts from the Fruitlands Diary (1975)

The Selected Letters of Louisa May Alcott (1995)

The Journals of Louisa May Alcott (1997)

Alcott in Her Own Time: A Biographical Chronicle of Her Life, Drawn from Recollections, Interviews, and Memoirs by Family, Friends, and Associates (2005)

Bibliography

Alberghene, Janice M., and Beverly Lyon Clark, eds. Little Women *and the Feminist Imagination: Criticism, Controversy, Personal Essays*. New York: Garland, 1999.

Alexander, Lynn M. "Unsexed by Labor: Middle-Class Women and the Need to Work." *American Transcendental Quarterly* 22 (2008): 593–608.

Boyd, Anne E. *Writing for Immortality: Women and the Emergence of High Literary Culture in America*. Baltimore: Johns Hopkins UP, 2004.

Brodhead, Richard H. "Starting Out in the 1860s: Alcott, Authorship, and the Postbellum Literary Field." *Cultures of Letters: Scenes of Reading and Writing in Nineteenth- Century America*. Chicago: U of Chicago P, 1993. 69–106.

Clark, Beverly Lyon. *The Afterlife of* Little Women. Baltimore: Johns Hopkins UP, 2014.

_____, ed. *Louisa May Alcott: The Contemporary Reviews*. Cambridge: Cambridge UP, 2004.

Derrickson, Teresa. "Race and the Gothic Monster: The Xenophobic Impulse of Louisa May Alcott's 'Taming a Tartar.'" *American Transcendental Quarterly* 15.1 (2001): 43–58.

Doyle, Christine. *Louisa May Alcott and Charlotte Bronte: Transatlantic Translations*. Knoxville: U of Tennessee P, 2000.

_____. "Singing Mignon's Song: German Literature and Culture in the March Trilogy." *Children's Literature* 31 (2003): 50–70.

Eiselein, Gregory. "'A Religion of Their Own': Louisa May Alcott's New American Religion." *Nineteenth-Century American Women Write Religion: Lived Theologies and Literature*. Ed. Mary McCartin Wearn. Farnham, UK: Ashgate, 2013. 119–134.

_____. "Modernity and Louisa May Alcott's *Jo's Boys*." *Children's Literature* 34 (2006): 83–108.

_____. "Contradiction in Louisa May Alcott's *Little Men*." *New England Quarterly* 78 (2005): 3-25.

Elbert, Sarah. *A Hunger for Home: Louisa May Alcott's Place in American Culture*. New Brunswick: Rutgers UP, 1987.

Entel, Rebecca. "Writing 'En Masse': Louisa May Alcott's Civil War Experience and *The Commonwealth*." *American Periodicals: A Journal of History, Criticism, and Bibliography* 24.1 (2014): 45–60.

Francis, Richard. *Fruitlands: The Alcott Family and Their Search for Utopia*. New Haven: Yale UP, 2010.

Gaul, Theresa Strouth. "Trance-Formations: Mesmerism and 'A Woman's Power' in Louisa May Alcott's *Behind a Mask*." *Women's Studies: An Interdisciplinary Journal* 32.7 (2003): 835–851.

Keyser, Elizabeth Lennox. *Whispers in the Dark: The Fiction of Louisa May Alcott*. Knoxville: U of Tennessee P, 1993.

Klimasmith, Betsy. "Slave, Master, Mistress, Slave: Genre and Interracial Desire in Louisa May Alcott's Fiction." *American Transcendental Quarterly* 11.2 (1997): 115–135.

Laffrado, Laura. *Uncommon Women: Gender and Representation in Nineteenth-Century U.S. Women's Writing*. Columbus: Ohio State UP, 2009.

Matteson, John. *Eden's Outcasts: The Story of Louisa May Alcott and Her Father*. New York: Norton, 2007.

_____. "An Idea of Order at Concord: Soul and Society in the Mind of Louisa May Alcott." *A Companion to American Fiction, 1865–1914*. Eds. Robert Paul Lamb and G. R. Thompson. Malden, MA: Blackwell, 2005. 451–467.

Maibor, Carolyn. "Upstairs, Downstairs, and In-Between: Louisa May Alcott, on Domestic Service." *New England Quarterly* 79.1 (Mar. 2006): 65–91.

Patterson, Mark. "Racial Sacrifice and Citizenship: The Construction of Masculinity in Louisa May Alcott's 'The Brothers.'" *Studies in American Fiction* 25.2 (Autumn 1997): 147–166.

Petrulionis, Sandra Harbert. "By the Light of Her Mother's Lamp: Woman's Work versus Man's Philosophy in Louisa May Alcott's 'Transcendental Wild Oats.'" *Studies in the American Renaissance* (1995): 69–81.

Phillips, Anne K., and Gregory Eiselein, eds. *Little Women: Authoritative Text, Backgrounds and Contexts, Criticism*. By Louisa M. Alcott. New York: Norton, 2004.

Porter, Caroline. "Reverse Cross-Dressing: Gender Roles, Disguise, and the Essential in Louisa May Alcott's Fiction." *the quint: an interdisciplinary quarterly from the north* 5.2 (March 2013): 90–113.

Ransdell, Ann Daghistany. "Black Ghostliness and Historical Allegory in Alcott's 'The Abbott's Ghost, or Maurice Treherne's Temptation.'" *Women's Studies: An Interdisciplinary Journal* 36.8 (2007): 573–596.

Reynolds, Larry J. "Violent Virtue and Alcott's *Moods*." *Righteous Violence: Revolution, Slavery, and the American Renaissance*. Athens: U of Georgia P, 2011. 132–155.

Schewe, Elizabeth. "Domestic Conspiracy: Class Conflict and Performance in Louisa May Alcott's 'Behind a Mask.'" *American Transcendental Quarterly* 22 (Dec. 2008): 577–592.

Schultz, Lydia A. "'Work with a Purpose': Alcott's *An Old-Fashioned Girl* and the American Work Ethic." *College Literature* 29.4 (Fall 2002): 26–46.

Shealy, Daniel, ed. *Little Women: An Annotated Edition*. Cambridge, MA: Belknap-Harvard UP, 2013.

_____. "Louisa May Alcott." *Prospects for the Study of American Literature II*. Ed. Richard Kopely& Barbara Cantalupo. New York: AMS, 2009. 97–118.

Sherman, Sarah Way. *Sacramental Shopping: Louisa May Alcott, Edith Wharton, and the Spirit of Modern Consumerism*. Durham: U of New Hampshire P, 2013.

Singley, Carol J. *Adopting America: Childhood, Kinship, and National Identity in Literature*. New York: Oxford UP, 2011.

Smith, Gail K. "Who Was That Masked Woman? Gender and Form in Louisa May Alcott's Confidence Stories." *American Women Short Story Writers: A Collection of Critical Essays*. New York: Garland, 1995. 45–59.

Stern, Madeleine B., ed. *Critical Essays on Louisa May Alcott*. Boston, MA: G.K. Hall, 1984.

Trites, Roberta Seelinger. *Twain, Alcott, and the Birth of the Adolescent Reform Novel*. Iowa City: U of Iowa P, 2007.

Vidrine, Jessicca Daigle. "Notions on Marriage: Bisexual Desires and Spinsterhood as Intellectual and Artistic Genius in Louisa May Alcott's 'Happy Women' and *Diana and Persis*." *Women's Studies: An Interdisciplinary Journal* 39.2 (2010): 136–154.

Walls, Laura Dassow. "The Cosmopolitical Project of Louisa May Alcott." *ESQ: A Journal of the American Renaissance* 57.1–2 (2011): 107–132.

Young, Elizabeth. "A Wound of One's Own: Louisa May Alcott's Civil War Fiction." *American Quarterly* 48.3 (Sept. 1996): 439–474.

About the Editors

Anne K. Phillips is an associate professor of English at Kansas State University. With Gregory Eiselein, she has edited *The Louisa May Alcott Encyclopedia* (2001), the Norton Critical Edition of *Little Women* (2004), and *Critical Insights:* Little Women (2015). With Christine Doyle, she has edited a special issue of *Children's Literature* on Louisa May Alcott (2006). She has also published essays on Alcott's works in Little Women *and the Feminist Imagination, Children's Literature, The Lion and The Unicorn,* the *American Journal of Play, American History Through Literature, 1820–1870,* and, with Eiselein, Salem Press' *Critical Insights: Coming of Age* volume. She currently serves as president-elect of The Louisa May Alcott Society.

Gregory Eiselein is Donnelly Professor of English and University Distinguished Teaching Scholar at Kansas State University. He is the author of *Literature and Humanitarian Reform in the Civil War Era* (1996) and several articles on Louisa May Alcott. He is coeditor of *Critical Insights:* Little Women, the Norton Critical Edition of *Little Women* (2004), and *The Louisa May Alcott Encyclopedia* (2001). He has also edited *Adah Isaacs Menken:* Infelicia *and Other Writings* (2002), and *Emma Lazarus: Selected Poems and Other Writings* (2002).

Contributors

Katherine Adams is associate professor of English and the Kimmerling Chair in Women's Literature at Tulane University. Her research and teaching focus on nineteenth-century U.S. literature and culture, women's writing, African American literature, and gender and race theory. She is the author of *Owning Up: Privacy, Property, and Belonging in U.S. Women's Life Writing* (Oxford, 2009) and editor of *U.S. Women Writing Race*, a special issue of *Tulsa Studies in Women's Literature*. Her work has been published in numerous edited collections and in journals such as *ESQ, NEQ, Arizona Quarterly, Hypatia, Legacy*, and *NWSA Journal*. She is currently at work on a book about how regional, national, and global economies shaped conceptions of racial blackness in the period following emancipation, and she is coediting a special issue of *Legacy*: "Recovering Alice Dunbar-Nelson for the 21st Century," which will appear in 2016.

Christine Doyle is professor of English at Central Connecticut State University, where she teaches children's literature, nineteenth-century American literature, and storytelling. She is the author of *Louisa May Alcott and Charlotte Brontë: Transatlantic Translations* (2000) and several essays on Alcott's connections to other writers. She has presented her research at Children's Literature Association conferences, the American Literature Association, Kansas State University, and the Concord School of Philosophy.

Monika Elbert is professor of English and Distinguished University Scholar at Montclair State University. Former editor of the *Nathaniel Hawthorne Review*, she has published widely on Hawthorne and on other nineteenth-century American authors. Recent or forthcoming books include several coedited collections: *Transnational Gothic: Literary and Social Exchanges in the Long Nineteenth Century*; *Romantic Education in Nineteenth-Century American Literature: National and Transatlantic Contexts*; *Haunting Realities: Naturalist Gothic and American Realism*; and the edited volume, *Hawthorne in Context*. Recent essays focus on Alcott, Fuller, Emerson, and Goethe; Alcott, Susan Cooper, and Eleanor Porter; and Alcott, Harriet Spofford, and Mary Peabody Mann.

Christopher Fahy is a senior lecturer at Boston University's College of General Studies. On alternate years, he teaches two semester courses on Western literature and art for freshmen and two semester courses on the history of ethics for sophomores. He has published scholarly work on Louisa May Alcott and Margaret Fuller, Henry James's "Altar of the Dead," and the movie *Affliction*. He has contributed frequently to the poetry journals, *Windhover*, *The Penwood Review*, and *Poem* among others.

Amy Harris-Aber holds a master of arts in English from Kansas State University. She is currently a doctoral student at Middle Tennessee State University's department of English. Her areas of concentration are rhetoric and folklore.

A. Waller Hastings is associate professor of English at West Liberty University in West Virginia, where he teaches young adult literature, among many other subjects. He has previously published on Disney animation, George MacDonald's fairy tales, and science fiction, and while he has taught *Little Women* on numerous occasions, this is his first published study of Alcott's work.

Marilyn Bloss Koester is a Ph.D. candidate in English at the University of Memphis. She received her BA in Art History from Southern Methodist University and her MLA in English from the University of St. Thomas. Her research explores the relationships between art, aesthetics, and children's literature of the nineteenth century. She is the 2013 recipient of the Children's Literature Association's Ph.D. Essay Award. Her current project examines crises of materiality during the development of a distinct children's literature genre in America. She teaches writing and literature at the University of Memphis and Memphis College of Art.

Katie Kornacki teaches English and American studies at the University of Connecticut. She holds a Ph.D. in English from the University of Connecticut and an M.A. in American and New England studies from the University of Southern Maine. The essay included in this volume draws on her larger book-length project, *Margaret Fuller's Conversations: Self and Other in Nineteenth-Century Literary and Intellectual Culture*. In addition to her research and teaching, Katie also works at the Harriet Beecher Stowe Center in Hartford, Connecticut, as an interpreter and museum educator.

Mo Li is a graduate student in nineteenth-century American literature at Middle Tennessee State University. She is fascinated by how religion and science intersect with the literary imagination. Currently, she is working on her dissertation on *Eureka*, Edgar Allan Poe's understudied and frequently misunderstood scientific and poetic treatise.

John Matteson is Distinguished Professor of English at John Jay College in the City University of New York. A graduate of Princeton University, he holds a J.D. from Harvard and a Ph.D. from Columbia. Professor Matteson's first book, *Eden's Outcasts: The Story of Louisa May Alcott and Her Father,* was awarded the 2008 Pulitzer Prize for Biography. His second book, *The Lives of Margaret Fuller*, received the Ann M. Sperber Prize in 2012 and was shortlisted for the Plutarch Prize and the PEN/ Jacqueline Bograd Weld Award. Professor Matteson is the editor of *The Annotated Little Women,* published by W. W. Norton & Company in 2015, and is now at work on a book on the Battle of Fredericksburg.

Kristen B. Proehl is an assistant professor of English at SUNY Brockport, where she teaches courses in children's and young adult literature. She has contributed essays on the March family trilogy to two different essay collections: *Romantic Education in Nineteenth-Century American Literature* and *Sentimentalism in Nineteenth-Century America.* She has also recently published an article in *Jeunesse* on Sentimentalism, family, and queer childhood in Carson McCullers's *The Member of the Wedding.* She is currently revising her book manuscript, *Battling Girlhood: Sympathy, Social Justice and the Tomboy Figure in American Literature.*

Antoinette M. Tadolini holds a Master of Arts degree with an emphasis on children's literature from Kansas State University. Her academic interests focus on Louisa May Alcott and Laura Ingalls Wilder. A retired lawyer, she is an active volunteer for an immigrant assistance program and gets silly reading to preschool kids for a library-sponsored early literacy program.

Amy M. Thomas is an associate professor of English at Montana State University, Bozeman. Her publications include "The Hidden Agenda of *The Hidden Hand*: Periodical Publication and the Literary Marketplace in Late-Nineteenth-Century America," coauthored with Alison M. Scott, in *E.D.E.N. Southworth: Recovering a Nineteenth-Century Popular Novelist* (Tennessee, 2012).

Emily Waples is a doctoral candidate in the department of English at the University of Michigan, Ann Arbor. Her work has appeared in the journals *Tulsa Studies in Women's Literature*, *Configurations*, and *Gothic Studies*.

Index

genius vii, 81, 82, 83, 84, 85, 86, 87, 88, 89, 90, 92, 93, 94, 164, 205, 208, 209
Gérôme, Jean-Léon 164
Gilman, Charlotte Perkins 45
Ginsberg, Allen 223
Ginsberg, Ruth Bader 221
Ginzberg, Lori 103
girlhood 67, 160, 207, 215
Gothic viii, 128, 140, 141, 142, 245, 251, 254
Graham, Julie 170
Grangerford, Emmeline 66
Granger, Hermione 37
Greene, Elizabeth B. 6
Gruen, Bob 234

Habegger, Alfred 205
Harbert, Elizabeth Boynton 152
Harding, Nan 11, 54
Harding, Walter 225
Hart, John Seely 6
Hawkins, Jim 36
Hawthorne, Julian 205
Hawthorne, Nathanial 20
Helwyze, Jasper 90, 138
Higginson, Thomas Wentworth 6
Horwell, Veronica 124
Hosmer, Harriet 164, 174
Howard, June 105
Howells, William Dean 207
Hughes, Thomas 176
Hummels, the 70, 71, 74, 86
humor 12, 34, 36, 45, 66, 119, 121

independence 7, 56, 63, 100, 143, 162, 165, 171, 190, 207, 208, 210, 224, 227, 230
Ingraham, Joseph Holt 193

James, Henry ix, 165, 205, 206, 214, 217, 218, 219, 220, 252
James, Henry, Sr. 205
James, Wilky 218
Jefferson, Thomas 52
Jeffrey, Rebecca 160, 172
Joan of Arc 58

Kaufman, Alan 234
Kemble, Fanny 132
Kenner, Chris 229
Kerber, Linda K. 189
Keyser, Elizabeth Lennox 18, 49, 175
King, Kate 165
Kolodny, Annette 156
Ku Klux Klan 68, 72

Ladies' Art Association, The 170
Lahey, Sarah T. 22
Lane, Charles 19
Larcom, Lucy 6
Lawrence, D. H. 180, 188
LeGuin, Ursula 221
Leibovitz, Annie 37
Lenahan, Hayley Miller 191
Lennox, Mary 37
Lerman, Leo 4
letter-writing 124, 125
Levin, Harry 93
Limon, John 115
Linkon, Sherry Lee 156
Lowell, James Russell 207

MacLeod, Anne Scott 44
Mapplethorpe, Robert 223, 225
March, Amy 3, 75
March, Beth 161